Praise for *Boldly Sustainable*

"Without hesitation, I can say that *Boldly Sustainable* is the most comprehensive and well documented work written on this subject that I have seen to date. It's a very pleasant read and contains the right balance of rationale and useful information to move forward. This book should be assigned reading for every college and university president. It provides clear direction for a new kind of leadership at the highest ranks of the academy."

Nan Jenks-Jay
Dean of Environmental Affairs
Middlebury College

"*Boldly Sustainable* offers a strong and urgent challenge to higher education institutions to rethink what they teach, how they teach, how they conduct themselves, and how they relate to the larger community to ensure that they are contributing to a more healthy, just, and sustainable society. It also provides an up-to-date and hopeful picture of the explosive interest in, and the kinds of innovation for, sustainability in every aspect of higher education that are occurring on hundreds of campuses around the country. The important examples and stories cover a wide range of commitments, programs, and actions that are raising the sustainability bar on college campuses. In its easily accessible style, *Boldly Sustainable* gives the reader a good sense of the contribution that higher education can make in leading society on a more sustainable path and opens up the possibility of rapid progress that can be made by collaboration among senior administrators, faculty, operation staff, and students."

Anthony Cortese, Sc.D.
President, Second Nature

"Today's college students are inheriting the greatest environmental challenge in history. Will they be prepared to address it? In *Boldly Sustainable*, Peter Bardaglio and Andrea Putman provide plenty of encouragement by describing how college campuses across the country are finding innovative ways to practice environmental stewardship. Expertly written and well researched, this book shows how sustainability is a boon not only to campus life but to a college's bottom line as well."

Charles Kutscher, Ph.D., P.E.
Principal Engineer/Group Manager, Thermal Systems
National Renewable Energy Laboratory
Past Chair, American Solar Energy Society

"This is an excellent piece of work that is comprehensive, in-depth, very readable, and well documented. It brings together in one place much of the great work going on in the higher education community to create a more sustainable future. It goes well beyond providing a needed perspective on the state of the movement to making a strong case for why and how colleges and universities must be bolder in demonstrating leadership toward sustainability. *Boldly Sustainable* provided me with a number of new ideas about how to advance the sustainability agenda at Middlebury."

Jack Byrne
Director, Sustainability Integration Office
Middlebury College

"*Boldly Sustainable* is a wonderful overview of where higher education is today in its efforts to contribute to a more sustainable future. It is a well-written, thoughtful contribution that should enable readers to consider the various ways that colleges and universities can become more sustainable."

Geoffrey Chase, Ph.D.
Dean, Division of Undergraduate Studies, San Diego State University
and Chair, Association for the Advancement of
Sustainability in Higher Education Board of Directors

BOLDLY SUSTAINABLE

Hope and Opportunity for Higher Education in the Age of Climate Change

Peter Bardaglio

Andrea Putman

Library of Congress Cataloging-in-Publication Data

Bardaglio, Peter Winthrop.
  Boldly sustainable : hope and opportunity for higher education in the age of climate change / by Peter Bardaglio, Andrea Putman.
    p. cm.
  ISBN 978-1-56972-046-2
  1. Universities and colleges--Environmental aspects--United States. 2. Education, Higher--Economic aspects--United States. 3. Campus planning--Environmental aspects--United States. 4. Sustainable development--Study and teaching (Higher)--United States. I. Putman, Andrea, 1961- II. Title.
  LB2324.B36 2009
  378'.01--dc22

2008052981

NACUBO saved the following resources by using Rolland Enviro 100 paper (FSC certified 100% post-consumer fiber, certified EcoLogo, processed chlorine free, FSC recycled, and manufactured using biogas energy) and New Leaf Reincarnation Matte (designated Ancient Forest Friendly and manufactured with electricity that is offset with Green-e®certified renewable energy certificates, 100% recycled fiber and 50% post-consumer waste, and processed chlorine free: 79 fully grown trees, 45,443 gallons of water, 4,938 pounds of solid waste, 9,171 pounds of air emissions, 30 pounds of suspended particles in the air, 10,832 cubic feet of natural gas, and more than 2 million BTUs of energy. Calculations based on research by Environmental Defense and other members of the Paper Task Force.

Photographs in this book were provided as a courtesy by College of the Atlantic, Emory University, Ithaca College, Beth Clark Joseph, National Renewable Energy Laboratory Photographic Information Exchange, Northland College, Oberlin College, and the University of Hawaii at Manoa, College of Tropical Agriculture and Human Resources. An earlier version of some material in chapter 4 appeared in "'A Moment of Grace': Integrating Sustainabiliy into the Undergraduate Curriculum," *Planning for Higher Education*, vol. 36, no. 1 (October–December 2007): 16-22.

Design by Colburnhouse

National Association of College and University Business Officers
Washington, DC
www.nacubo.org

Printed in the United States of America

ABOUT OUR SPONSORS

Department of Energy's Office of Energy Efficiency and Renewable Energy (EERE)

www.eere.energy.gov

The Department of Energy's Office of Energy Efficiency and Renewable Energy (EERE) works to strengthen the United States' energy security, environmental quality, and economic vitality in public-private partnerships. It supports this goal through enhancing energy efficiency and productivity; bringing clean, reliable, and affordable energy technologies to the marketplace; and making a difference in the everyday lives of Americans by enhancing their energy choices and their quality of life.

Bank of America

www.bankofamerica.com

Bank of America is committed to protecting our environment. This pledge is evidenced in our $20 billion, 10-year initiative to address climate change by championing sustainable business practices through lending, investing, products and services, and operations. Bank of America offers a growing array of products and services to help our clients move toward paperless business solutions. We also finance and advise on a range of energy projects, including distributed generation, renewable technologies and demand-side management.

Johnson Controls, Inc.

www.johnsoncontrols.com

Johnson Controls creates environments for learning and living. For more than 100 years, Johnson Controls has been creating comfortable, safe, sustainable campus environments. Preserve your legacy and prepare for the future through our lifecycle program management, building control systems, and facility management services—all which deliver guaranteed, lower, more predictable costs.

more sponsors...

more sponsors...

Park Foundation

www.parkfoundation.org

The Park Foundation was established in 1966 by the late Roy Hampton Park, Sr.—founder, chairman, and chief executive officer of Park Communications, Inc. The Foundation is dedicated to the aid and support of education, public broadcasting, the environment, and other selected areas of interest to the Park family.

Sodexo Education

www.sodexousa.com

Sodexo, Inc. is a leading integrated food and facilities management services company in North America, employing 120,000 people. Sodexo serves more than ten million customers daily in corporations, health care, long-term care centers, schools, college campuses, government, and remote sites. Sodexo also funds the Sodexo Foundation (www.helpstophunger.org), an independent charitable organization that has granted more than $9.2 million to fight hunger in America.

Andrea dedicates this book with love to her sons and
future college students, Ryan Luke and Justin Patrick Szczerbinski.

Peter dedicates this book with love to his children
Sarah, Jesse, and Anne, and to his grandchildren Parker, Cole, and Lily.

CONTENTS

ACKNOWLEDGMENTS

Writing a book, like any healthy ecosystem, generates its own web of interconnections and interdependencies. We have been fortunate to have the help and support of many outstanding people and organizations, and it is hard to imagine completing this project without their assistance. We are especially indebted to our reviewers, Jeffrey Baker, Charles Kutscher of the National Renewable Energy Laboratory, Nan Jenks-Jay and Jack Byrne of Middlebury College, Anthony Cortese of Second Nature, and Geoffrey Chase of San Diego State University, for their careful reading of the manuscript and thoughtful guidance. We have not always followed their advice but the book is undoubtedly stronger and better because of their input.

Many individuals gave generously of their time and expertise as we carried out the research for this book. Among them are Marian Brown, Ithaca College; Patrice Casey, MaineGeneral Health; Christy Cook, Emory University-Sodexo Campus Services; Leslie Cook, U.S. Environmental Protection Agency; Larry Eisenberg, Los Angeles Community College District; Susan Engelkemeyer, Ithaca College; Melissa Gallagher-Rogers, U.S. Green Building Council; Donna Gold, College of the Atlantic; Richard Johnson, Rice University; William Johnson, Haley & Aldrich; Richard Justis, Johnson Controls; Jeri King, University of Iowa; Derek Larson, The College of St. Benedict/St. John's University; Brian Levite, National Renewable Energy Lab; Bill Massey, Sasaki Associates; Dave Newport, University of Colorado, Boulder; Billy Parish, Energy Action Coalition; Frank Powell, Furman University; Lowell Rasmussen, University of Minnesota, Morris; Robert Sauchelli, U.S. Environmental Protection Agency; James Simpson, Johnson Controls; Eric Singer, Goucher College; Daniel Sze, U.S. Department of Energy; Arlin Wasserman, Sodexo; and Christopher Wells, Macalester College. We owe a special thanks to Wendell Brase from the University of California, Irvine, who contributed the section on smart laboratories in Chapter 7, and to our friends and colleagues at Second Nature, who encouraged us throughout the process of writing this book.

We would also like to thank the staff at NACUBO, including Bill Dillon, Matt Hamill, Donna Klinger, and Michele Madia for their enthusiastic support of this project and professional assistance in bringing it to completion. Karen Colburn and Ellen Hirzy applied their editing and production skills to the manuscript with an admirable commitment to clarity and excellence, and for that we are grateful. We are particularly indebted to our sponsors—the U.S. Department of Energy, Bank of America, Johnson Controls, Inc., the Park Foundation, and Sodexo Education—for their generous support that made possible the research and writing of this book.

There are few ecosystems more complex, dynamic, and essential than families. We are both extraordinarily lucky to have had the unstinting love, patience, and support of our respective spouses, Wrexie Bardaglio and Tom Szczerbinski. They have been partners in this enterprise, listening, asking questions, and sharing their insights as the book evolved, and we want to thank them for believing in us and in our work. We also thank our parents and siblings for the sustenance of their steadfast caring.

Sustainability is about the future and it is for that reason we dedicate this book to our children and grandchildren. We hope that in some small way this book contributes to the possibility that they and their children and grandchildren may live in harmony with all of life on this planet.

FOREWORD
ANTHONY D. CORTESE

Because of exponential population growth, modern technology, and economic globalization, humans have become the dominant force in shaping the well-being of the earth and its inhabitants. No part of the earth is unaffected by humans, and the degree of our impact is huge. All living systems are in an accelerated, long-term decline. Biological species are disappearing 1,000 times faster than normal. Fifty percent of all species will be gone by the end of this century, an extinction rate not seen since the dinosaurs disappeared 65 million years ago.

At the same time, we are not meeting many basic health and social needs: 2.7 billion people are without sanitation and earn less than $2 a day; more than a billion have no access to clean drinking water; and shortages are widespread and getting worse. One billion people are malnourished; in the last year there have been food riots on three continents because the price of food staples has more than doubled. And, of course, there are numerous international conflicts over resources such as oil, arable land, and water.

Human-induced global warming will accelerate these negative trends. A relatively stable climate has helped make possible much of human progress in the last 10,000 years. The location of human endeavors like cities, agriculture, ports and other transportation, and businesses has been based in large part on the predictability of the climate. Now all bets are off. Climate destabilization is taking place faster than the most conservative scientists predict, posing a fundamental threat to civilization.

As these events take place, 25 percent of the world's population is consuming 70 to 80 percent of the world's resources. With about 4 percent of the world's population, the United States produces 22 percent of global greenhouse gas emissions. Scientists have determined that we are already overshooting our biological capacity to support humans by 25 percent. If everyone consumed resources and produced pollution and waste at the same level as the United States, we would need three planets to support the population. The 2.5 billion people in China and India are now big players on the world stage as they seek a better quality of life for their citizens. By 2050 the world will have 9 billion people and a 500 percent increase in gross world product. On a planet whose capacity to sustain life is at risk, how will society assure that all current and future humans are healthy, that communities are strong, thriving, and secure, and that there is economic opportunity for everyone?

The cultural operating instructions of modern society are relatively straightforward: If we just work a little harder and smarter, all these challenges will work themselves out. But as Albert Einstein said, "We can't solve today's problems at the same level of thinking at which they were created." We currently view societal issues as separate, competing, and hierarchical when they are really systemic and interdependent. Twenty-first-century challenges must be addressed in a systemic, integrated, and holistic fashion. We need a deliberate strategy to make a rapid transition to a low-carbon, less auto-dependent economy based on cradle-to-cradle principles. We must undertake a transition that is bigger than the Manhattan Project, Marshall Plan, Apollo Project, and attempt to eradicate cancer combined. In short, it is the greatest human design challenge in history.

A Journey of Hope and Possibility

Imagine a society in which everyone has fair and equitable access to the earth's resources and a decent quality of life. Imagine scientists, engineers, and business people designing systems and activities that sustain the natural environment and enhance human health and well-being. Imagine designing technology in ways inspired by nature and driven by renewable energy. Imagine eliminating the concept of waste by turning every waste product into a raw material or nutrient for another species or activity, or returning it to nature. Imagine using natural resources only at the rate that they can self-regenerate, an idea embodied in sustainable forestry, fishing, and agriculture. In this future society, we could live off nature's interest, not its capital, for generations to come.

Our ecological, health, and social footprint is largely invisible to most of us. The average American does not know that we consume the equivalent of our body weight in solid materials daily, turning more than 94 percent into waste before we ever see the product or the service. Imagine making visible the impacts of so much waste. Wal-Mart now requires its 64,000 suppliers to report and minimize their greenhouse gas footprint. Manufacturers in nearly every major industry have similar supply chain environmental footprint requirements.

Current signals involving economic and ecological costs and benefits are incomplete and inaccurate, creating a false sense of security and inflicting untold damage. Imagine that we have timely and accurate signals: microeconomic signals for price that reflect the true social and environmental cost to society, macroeconomic indicators that reflect the true well-being of society and the earth, and ecological signals that we receive in time to prevent or remedy damage to humans or the environment.

Now, imagine that all current and future generations have the opportunity to pursue meaningful work and realize their full potential. Imagine that we have dramatically reduced resource consumption, pollution, and waste so that everyone—including those in the developing world and poorer communities within the United States—are healthy and enjoy a decent quality of life. Imagine that communities are strong and vibrant because they celebrate cultural diversity, encourage collaboration and participation in governance, and emphasize quality of life over consumption of stuff. Imagine a future in which we have increased the education and the social and economic status of women worldwide, resulting in stabilization of the population at a level that is within the earth's carrying capacity. Think of what it could be like if globalization was humanized to support democracy, human rights, and economic opportunity for everyone.

Can We Do This?

Absolutely, because we must. For example, a clean-energy economy that focuses on energy efficiency will stabilize and lower energy costs, reduce chronic air pollution, and strengthen the economy by shifting

---

More than 600 colleges and universities in 50 states have committed to becoming climate neutral campuses and are partnering with over 900 city mayors who have committed to also reduce greenhouse gas emissions.

---

expenditures for energy to investment in innovation. Such an economy will improve national and international security by easing reliance on fuels from unstable and sometimes hostile parts of the world. It could provide 3.3 million net new jobs by 2020 and add $1.4 trillion in gross domestic product. A clean, green economy will help restore U.S. economic leadership based on new technology and ensure our ability to compete in the world. It will also help countries like China and India make a more rapid transition to an environmentally sustainable economy and reduce global pollution.

Smart leaders in U.S. business, government, and academia see solutions to climate disruption as the greatest foreseeable boon to the economy. DuPont, for example, has reduced heat-trapping emissions by 72 percent since 1990 and saved $2 billion. The renewable energy industry has been growing at the rate of 30 to 40 percent a year.

Hundreds of higher education institutions have connected education and research to strategies aimed at improving their communities and reducing their environmental footprints through programs promoting energy and water conservation, renewable energy, waste minimization and recycling, high-performance buildings, alternative transportation, local and organic food growing, and green purchasing, saving both the environment and money. More than 600 colleges and universities in 50 states have committed to becoming climate-neutral campuses and are partnering with over 900 mayors who have also committed to reducing greenhouse gas emissions.

The Design Revolution Has Begun

To succeed, design principles must be based on a human consciousness that moves us from consumerism, individualism, and domination of nature to one that emphasizes quality of life and connectedness with people who live in distant places, as well as with future generations. This consciousness must move us to a deep reverence for the natural world, complemented by an understanding of our place in the web of life and our dependence on its bounty. These principles must be become the basis for society's economic and governmental framework.

In *Boldly Sustainable: Hope and Opportunity for Higher Education in the Age of Climate Change*, Peter Bardaglio and Andrea Putman explore how these new ways of thinking, learning, and behaving can transform our higher education system to help society move toward a more sustainable future. They make clear that sustainability in higher education, as in all areas of our society and our economy, must become a core strategy that fosters innovation and creative problem solving.

Higher education leadership can help ensure the development of the technologies, economic tools, and strategies necessary to meet the challenge of climate change and sustainable development. Besides the intellectual and social capital that higher education can leverage, it is a $317 billion economic engine that employs millions of people and spends billions of dollars on fuel, energy, products, services, and infrastructure.

Frank Rhodes, former president of Cornell University, suggests that the concept of sustainability offers "a new foundation for the liberal arts and sciences." It provides a new focus, sense of urgency, and curricular coherence at a time of drift, fragmentation, and insularity in higher education—what he calls "a new kind of global map." It can be a vital source of hope and opportunity for facilitating institutional renewal and revitalizing higher education's sense of mission.

We are in the process of breaking away from an old paradigm which, like escaping the pull of gravity, will require a great deal of energy, commitment, and perseverance. We can do it if we set our minds to it. When President John F. Kennedy set a goal for humans to reach the moon in a decade, our country—even scientists and engineers—had no way of knowing if it could be done. But because it was a shared goal, and because we put our minds, hearts, and backs to it, we achieved it in 9 years and unleashed a scientific and technical revolution that led to innovations—from the Internet to materials science to breakthroughs in medicine—that dramatically improved the quality of our lives.

We need that kind of leadership now from our leaders, especially those in higher education. Standing on the sidelines is not an acceptable option. As Bardaglio and Putman put it, we must commit to becoming "boldly sustainable" so that "future generations will be able to build on our achievements rather than dig out from under our failures." This is the great task of our time.

ABOUT THE AUTHORS

Peter W. Bardaglio is a senior fellow at Second Nature, a non-profit committed to the promotion of sustainability in higher education. He is currently coordinating the Tompkins County Climate Protection Initiative, a regional effort involving education, business, government, and community leaders in the Ithaca area.

Bardaglio served as the provost and vice president of academic affairs from 2002 to 2007 at Ithaca College. A professor of history at Goucher College from 1983 to 2002, he was interim vice president and academic dean there from 2000 to 2002. He received several teaching awards at Goucher, including the Outstanding Faculty Award in 1994 and Outstanding Educator of the Year from the Maryland Association of Higher Education in 1998.

A Jessie Ball duPont Fellow at the National Humanities Center in 1999-2000, Bardaglio has also taught at the University of Maryland at College Park and University of Exeter in the United Kingdom. He is the recipient of grants from the National Endowment for the Humanities and the American Historical Association, and was awarded the 1996 James Rawley Prize from the Organization of American Historians for the best book published on the history of race relations in the United States. His numerous publications, conference papers, and invited lectures cover a wide range of topics, including campus sustainability, race and gender in the 19th-century American South, family public policy, new approaches to liberal education, and changing professional identity among faculty in the 21st century.

Bardaglio serves on the Senior Council of the Association for the Advancement of Sustainability in Higher Education, the editorial board of *Sustainability: The Journal of Record*, and as a Higher Education Sustainability Fellow with the Society for College and University Planning. He is also vice chair of the board of trustees for the New Roots Charter High School in Ithaca, NY, a member of the Cayuga Medical Center board of directors, and a member of the History Center in Tompkins County board of trustees.

He received his Ph.D. and M.A. in History at Stanford University and his B.A. in History and English at Brown University.

Andrea Putman is Director of Sustainability Financing for Second Nature, where she co-manages the partnership between the Clinton Climate Initiative and the American College and University Presidents Climate Commitment (ACUPCC). She serves on the Association for the Advancement of Sustainability in Higher Education Advisory Committee. She is also the co-author of *The Business Case for Renewable Energy: A Guide for Colleges and Universities* published by NACUBO, APPA, and The Society for College and University Planning.

Prior to joining Second Nature, Ms. Putman was an associate with the Cadmus Group where she supported the U.S. Environmental Protection Agency's Energy Star program and the Southeast Rebuild Collaborative for higher education. She was president of Green Innovations, a woman-owned small business that provided communications, marketing, and analysis for renewable energy initiatives. She helped establish and develop the Higher Education Committee for the American Council on Renewable Energy; sold wind power for Community Energy, and developed a wind power marketing program for Washington Gas Energy Services.

As senior associate with ICF Consulting working in support of Energy Star, Ms. Putman recruited financial partners representing 95 million square feet of corporate real estate and provided support to develop their energy management programs. Ms. Putman was an energy analyst for Pepco Energy Services and director of marketing for Energy Efficiency Services. Earlier in her career, Ms. Putman worked in the publishing field.

Ms. Putman earned a Bachelor of Arts in Political Science from State University of New York at Binghamton and did graduate work in Environmental Education at New York University. She was a certified Energy Manager and is a LEED Accredited Professional.

"Another world is not only possible, she is on her way. On a quiet day, I can hear her breathing."

—Arundhati Roy, "Come September,"
in *The Algebra of Infinite Justice,* 2002

INTRODUCTION

A huge and rapid cultural shift is in progress. Climate change has entered the mainstream of public dialogue, from town meetings in rural America to board meetings of the largest multinational corporations, from international conferences of the world's leaders to gatherings of thousands of college students on Capitol Hill. Aside from a few outliers, the scientific community has reached agreement on the main contours of global warming and its causes and consequences. The challenge is how to convey what we know to the public at large and act on this knowledge so that future generations will be able to build on our achievements rather than dig out from under our failures.[1]

The sustainability bar in the higher education sector rises virtually every day. A few years ago, any institution that didn't provide easily available bins for recycling of paper, cans, and bottles might have been criticized for its lack of commitment. Now, the purchase or production of renewable energy, the number of green buildings on campus, the use of local and organic foods, and support for the American College and University Presidents Climate Commitment (ACUPCC) have become the new metrics for measuring an institution's seriousness about sustainability.

Taking their cue from the 1987 report of the United Nations World Commission on Environment and Development (the Brundtland Report), most people define sustainability as meeting the vital needs of the present without undercutting future generations' ability to meet their own needs by living within the carrying capacity of the supporting ecosystems. But sustainability involves much more than simply minimizing the negative impact of human activity on the biosphere. It seeks to enhance the quality of life, promoting effective environmental stewardship, an equitable distribution of resources and power, and a healthy economy. It acknowledges the interdependence of society, the economy, and the environment, and it encourages long-term strategic thinking rooted in a whole-systems approach. Consequently, sustainability is less an outcome than a dynamic, evolving process that, in William McDonough's words, is "both restorative and regenerative."[2]

Not since the Industrial Revolution of the late 18th and early 19th centuries has such a profound paradigm shift taken place. What Andres Edwards calls the "Sustainability Revolution" has sparked a transformation of "consciousness and awareness affecting all facets of society." Here and there, amid the SUVs, big-box stores, and sprawl of exurbia, signs of this revolution are increasingly evident: wind turbines, solar panel installations, green buildings, and the local food movement.[3]

Designing a sustainable world is not simply a technocratic exercise. It is as much a cultural and ethical project as a scientific and engineering endeavor. It requires imagination, versatility, and creativity, a willingness to live our lives differently. Only if we come to comprehend that, as the ecologist and theologian Thomas Berry observes, "the universe is a communion of subjects, not a collection of objects," will we achieve a level of awareness sufficient to produce viable solutions.[4] We must understand that we are woven inextricably into the fabric of life and do not stand apart from it, exercising dominion over the world around us. The "environment" is not something that exists separate from human beings but rather is what makes human life possible.

Joseph Conrad's *Heart of Darkness* provides a cautionary tale about what happens if we do not acknowledge that the world is "a communion of subjects" rather than "a collection of objects," if we do not strive toward sustainability. In this story, a British trading company sends Marlow to Africa to look into a disturbing rumor about one of its employees, Kurtz. Marlow arrives at the Central Station on the Congo River to take command of a steamer, which he intends to pilot upriver to Kurtz's trading post in the interior.

While Marlow is undertaking the necessary repairs to get the boat ready for his journey, a band of men who call themselves the Eldorado Exploring Expedition drifts through. Driven by greed and ambition, these men view the world as a collection of objects. As Marlow puts it, "to tear treasure out of the bowels of the land was their desire, with no more moral purpose at the back of it than there is in burglars breaking into a safe." These are men, writes Conrad, who soon disappear "into the patient wilderness, that closed upon [them] as the sea closes over a diver" and are never heard of again.[5]

How do we want to be remembered: as leaders who understood the need to address upstream the pressing issues of our age and acted with courage and foresight, or as people whose primary goals were short-term advantage and gain and who cared for little else besides self-advancement?

The present moment is unlike any other in terms of what is at stake. As Berry writes, it is a moment that calls on us to transform our exploitation of the earth into a relationship that is "mutually beneficial."[6] And, as luck would have it, the moment is brief. Unless we act now to preserve and enhance the life, beauty, and diversity of the planet for future generations, we will become, in Berry's words, "impoverished in all that makes us human."[7]

The question is no longer why we should address climate destabilization, and in some cases, it is not even how. The question has become how fast and effectively we can move forward. In short, to what extent are we willing to be *boldly sustainable*?

With the acceleration of scientific reports indicating that climate change is taking place faster than any of the computer models predicted, college and university leaders also face the question of how to generate hope and opportunity on our campuses.[8] How do we carve out a path toward carbon neutrality? How do we design and implement the business case for doing so?

Other questions quickly arise: How do we strengthen and create value for our institutions while dealing with these immense challenges? How do we give our students the vision, tools, and education to get good jobs in the new carbon-constrained economy? How do we nurture and fortify our students for the challenges ahead?

To do so, colleges and universities must be prepared to engage in a radical rethinking of our cultural values. No longer can decisions about resource allocation be made in a linear fashion without regard to downstream impacts; rather, decisions require a "life cycle" approach

Although colleges and universities may be inherently conservative, they must respond to the dramatically altered circumstances or run the risk of becoming irrelevant....[13] "Boldly sustainable" is not just a battle cry. It is a powerful strategy for higher education to achieve renewal, reformation, and relevance in the 21st century.

where all externalities are taken into account before a commitment to one path or another is made. How do we create a learning environment where the consequences of potential choices are examined holistically over the long run? How do we teach students to be community leaders so that sustainable living practices are transferred to their families and communities?

The growing global crisis in sustainability led the United Nations to declare 2005–2014 the Decade of Education for Sustainable Development. This initiative seeks to raise awareness about the need to create a more sustainable future and to understand how individual and collective choices about the allocation of resources affect the lives of people around the world. The challenge of sustainability has far-reaching implications for those who are committed to educating the citizens, professionals, and leaders of tomorrow. Even as we acknowledge the demands of this challenge, we should recognize the opportunities that it affords. As Frank H. T. Rhodes, president emeritus of Cornell University, contends, the concept of sustainability offers "a new foundation for the liberal arts and sciences." It provides a new focus, sense of urgency, and curricular coherence at a time of drift, fragmentation, and insularity—what Rhodes calls "a new kind of global map." At the same time, though, "the broad range of questions that sustainability raises have no single set of answers." Ambiguity, imprecision, and complexity characterize its landscape. Experimentation, discovery, and exploration rather than dogma and indoctrination are the essential tools.[9]

Given global threats such as the growing disruption of the climate, staggering levels of poverty in the developing world, and the looming peak oil crisis, it is remarkable how insular much of the higher education establishment is. Amid the day-to-day tasks of measuring learning outcomes, recruiting students, cultivating donors, balancing the budget, applying for grants, and keeping controversy to a minimum, surprisingly little time or energy is spent on how to address the truly serious problems that promise to upend the lives of the next generations.

"One could make the case that our universities are actually mired in the Stone Age," notes Michael Crow, president of Arizona State University. "Our universities remain highly static, resistant to change, unwilling to evolve in pace with real time." Just as our prehistoric ancestors went about busting up rocks, we view the world as something to break down and take apart rather than to understand holistically and live in harmony with. In Crow's words, we seek to "heat it, beat it, melt it, smash it, burn it and blow it up."[10]

It is time for a new set of priorities that move us from "the Stone Age to the Sustainability Age."[11] How can it make sense for universities and colleges to keep doing what they do when complacency has contributed in large part to the current predicament? In light of how we got where we are, shouldn't higher education leaders rethink the way that teaching, research, and learning take place and how they operate their facilities? More people, both inside and outside academia, are asking these questions. Now, more than ever, we need to keep in mind Eric Hoffer's acerbic observation that "in times of change, learners inherit the earth, while the learned find themselves beautifully equipped to deal with a world that no longer exists."[12]

Although colleges and universities may be inherently conservative, they must respond to the dramatically altered circumstances or run the risk of becoming irrelevant. Sustainability, as Peter Senge puts it, is "the necessary revolution."[13] The high stakes involved in meeting the challenges of sustainability and climate change mean that effective leadership, strategic thinking, and implementation in higher education are more imperative than ever. They demand a shift from maintaining the status quo to bringing about transformation. "Boldly sustainable" is not just a battle cry. It is a powerful strategy for higher education to achieve renewal, reformation, and relevance in the 21st century. It is an opportunity for colleges and universities to avoid the fate of collapsing under the weight of their own self-absorption, isolation, and obtuseness, to avoid becoming the intellectual equivalent of Easter Island.

What will it take to escape this fate? Higher education must develop a more entrepreneurial culture. Just as Adam Smith called for the end of economic mercantilism at the end of the eighteenth century, so, too, we need to find ways during the Sustainability Age to liberate the innovative spirit of learning and teaching on our campuses. Academic entrepreneurship, in its narrowest sense, involves the creation of new business ventures by university and college faculty, administrators, and students. In its broadest sense, however, academic entrepreneurship seeks to establish connections across disciplines, between student and academic affairs, and between campus and community. It draws on the energy of hope and opportunity that animates entrepreneurial activity in the business world to provide the richest possible learning experiences.

Institutions that adopt this approach will achieve a critical competitive advantage in a market environment where the pool of students is shrinking significantly and where hiring the best possible staff and faculty are crucial to each institution's future. In the face of intensifying competition, higher education leaders are searching for ways to distinguish themselves from the pack, bolster their value proposition, and raise their institutional profiles. This book will examine how colleges and universities can leverage their commitment to sustainability not only to save money and have a positive impact on the environment, but also to carve out a distinctive niche in the marketplace.

In the current economic turmoil, the question naturally arises, "how can I afford to worry about sustainability given the huge financial pressures facing my institution?" The honest answer to that question is, "you can't afford not to." Sustainability can be a key driver when it comes to meeting organizational goals, as Kevin Moss points out, "not just when times are tough, but actually because they are tough." Adopting sustainability as a core strategy will allow institutions to manage their supply chains and business processes more effectively, increase their brand equity, and spur innovation. The latter point is especially important. "I think frugality drives innovation, just like other constraints do," asserts Jeff Bezos, CEO and founder of Amazon.com. "One of the only ways to get out of a tight box is to invent your way out."[14]

Beyond examining how sustainability can enhance organizational effectiveness, we will explore such vital issues as fostering creative leadership, developing a signature curriculum, enriching the learning environment, and integrating campus operations and sustainability pedagogy. We will also consider how a commitment to sustainability can strengthen student, faculty, and alumni support, improve recruitment and retention, encourage corporate-university partnerships, and promote regional economic development. To illustrate the potential for change, this study will share the innovative solutions adopted by colleges and universities across the country.

The experiences of these institutions demonstrate that building a culture of sustainability is a question of political will and can be accomplished if the leadership is committed for the long haul. Tailoring the process to take into account a college or university's distinctive mission, history, location, and culture will go a long way toward ensuring the success of the effort. Every campus has its own unique path into the sustainability conversation. Thus, administrators and planners have a special responsibility to determine what direction makes the most sense in light of their college or university's particular circumstances. Creating a culture of sustainability on campus should be seen as a way to clarify and focus institutional identity, not as a way to replace it.

Geared to both newcomers and experienced practitioners, this book offers higher education leaders a strategy for breaking through the static and capturing the attention of a world overwhelmed with a barrage of information. Showing how sustainability is not only the right thing to do but also the smart thing, we will provide transformational concepts, strategies, and tools that produce a sharper vision, an energized mission, and a firmer footing in the marketplace.

The primary thesis of this book is that adopting an approach that models collaborative learning, inclusivity, and mutual respect allows academic institutions to provide the kind of leadership that results in more sustainable communities. As Thomas Friedman observes, we are moving "from a primarily vertical (command-and-control) value-creation model to an increasingly horizontal (connect-and-collaborate) creation model."[15] In higher education, undertaking this shift means abandoning the ivory tower with its well-entrenched silos and becoming a "community greenhouse" where academics work across departments in teams, "addressing 'real-world problems' and discovering crossbreed shoots of knowledge to share with each other, their students, and the rest of the community."[16]

It also means investing intellectual and political capital in the development of innovative models of shared governance more appropriate to 21st-century communities of learners than the current shopworn, threadbare arrangements. Committing to a revitalized, more democratic process—one that involves all stakeholders in campus decision making and informs them fully of the inherent tradeoffs—may cut against the grain of traditional practices, but it is crucial to the success of the sustainability effort. In the end, we need to transform our relations with each other as much as we need to create a more positive relationship with our natural environment. We may well find out that the success of one depends on the success of the other.

Notes

1. Bryan Walsh, "What the Public Doesn't Get About Climate Change," *Time*, October 28, 2008. www.time.com/time/health/article/0,8599,1853871,00.html?xid=feed-cnn-topics (accessed November 1, 2008).

2. Nancy Roth, "A Building Like a Tree," *Talking Leaves* 11, no. 1 (Spring/Summer 2001). www.talkingleaves.org/node/89 (accessed November 1, 2008).

3. Andres R. Edwards, *The Sustainability Revolution: Portrait of a Paradigm Shift* (Gabriola Island, BC, Canada: New Society Publishers, 2005), p. 2.

4. Colin Beavan, "Moving Beyond Sustainability to Environmental Effectiveness," WorldChanging, October 28, 2008. www.worldchanging.com/archives/008905.html (accessed November 1, 2008); Rich Heffern, "Thomas Berry," *National Catholic Reporter Online*, August 10, 2001. www.natcath.com/NCR_Online/archives/081001/081001a.htm (accessed August 8, 2008).

5. Joseph Conrad, *Heart of Darkness and the Secret Sharer* (New York: New American Library, 1950), pp. 99, 102.

6. Thomas Berry, *The Great Work: Our Way into the Future* (New York: Bell Tower Books, 2007), pp. 3, 196, 198.

7. Ibid., pp. 201, 200.

8. Carbon emissions increased 2.9 percent from 2006 to 2007, according to the Global Carbon Project, in the far upper range of what the Intergovernmental Panel on Climate Change projected. If this rate remains unchanged, it could lead to a global temperature rise of more than 11 degrees Fahrenheit by the end of the century. See Juliet Eilperin, "Carbon Is Building Up in Atmosphere Faster Than Predicted," *Washington Post*, September 26, 2008. www.washingtonpost.com/wp-dyn/content/article/2008/09/25/AR2008092503989_pf.html (accessed November 1, 2008).

9. Frank H. T. Rhodes, "Sustainability: The Ultimate Liberal Art," *Chronicle of Higher Education* (October 20, 2006), p. B24.

10. Michael Crow, "American Research Universities During the Long Twilight of the Stone Age," elaboration on remarks delivered at the Rocky Mountain Sustainability Summit, University of Colorado, Boulder, February 21, 2007, pp. 1–2. http://president.asu.edu/files/2007_0212StoneAge.pdf (accessed August 8, 2008); and Tom Robinson, "The Prophet in the Desert," *Greentree Gazette* (September 2008), p. 18.

11. "Moving from the Stone Age to the Sustainability Age," Green-MagBlog, February 22, 2007. http://greenmagonline.blogspot.com/2007/02/moving-from-stone-age-to-sustainability.html (accessed August 8, 2007).

12. Quoted in Roland Barth, *Learning by Heart* (San Francisco: Jossey-Bass, 2004), p. 28.

13. G. Wayne Clough, Jean-Lou Chameau, and Carol Carmichael, "Sustainability and the University," *The Presidency* 9, no. 1 (Winter 2006): 37; Peter Senge et. al., *The Necessary Revolution: How Individuals and Organizations Are Working Together to Create a Sustainable World* (New York: Doubleday, 2008).

14. Kevin Moss, "Business Solutions in a Tough—But Still Green—Economy," GreenBiz.com, October 27 2008. www.greenbiz.com/blog/2008/10/27/business-solutions-tough-but-green-economy (accessed November 8, 2008); Peter Burrows, "Bezos on Innovation," *BusinessWeek*, April 17, 2008. www.businessweek.com/magazine/content/08_17/b4081064880218.htm (accessed November 8, 2008).

15. Thomas L. Friedman, *The World Is Flat: A Brief History of the Twenty-First Century*, rev. ed. (New York: Farrar, Straus and Giroux, 2006), p. 201.

16. Carolinda Douglass, "The Academy as a Community Greenhouse," *Inside Higher Ed*, September 4, 2007. www.insidehighered.com/views/2007/09/04/douglass (accessed August 10, 2008).

"This distant image of our tiny world... underscores our responsibility to deal more kindly with one another, and to preserve and cherish the pale blue dot, the only home we've ever known."

—Carl Sagan, *Pale Blue Dot*, 1994

THE BIG PICTURE

A n increased commitment to environmental stewardship unites Americans like few other issues. A GfK Roper Green Gauge study released in August 2007 found that an overwhelming majority of those polled were "seriously concerned about the environment" (87 percent) and believed that the federal government should strengthen its enforcement of environmental regulations (73 percent).[1] Among Republicans, Democrats, "tree huggers," military leaders, people of faith, cost-conscious conservatives, heartland farmers, Wall Street tycoons, local, state, and federal politicians, pension fund managers, movie stars, insurance executives, the higher education community, and ordinary people in communities throughout the United States, the sense of urgency is growing.

For the first time since issuing its initial report in 1990, the Intergovernmental Panel on Climate Change (IPCC) declared in 2007 that the evidence for humanity's role in setting off global warming was "unequivocal."[2] The panel cited the increase in extreme weather events, polar ice melting, species extinction, and loss of biodiversity as signs that climate change was already under way. "The world is already at or above the worst-case scenarios in terms of emissions," observed panel member Gernot Klepper. "We are moving past the most pessimistic estimates of the IPCC, and by some estimates we are above that red line." According to scientists at Mauna Loa Observatory in Hawaii, carbon dioxide levels are now at 387 parts per million (ppm), the highest for at least the last 650,000 years and an increase of almost 40 percent since the Industrial Revolution.[3]

New scientific research from U.S., Canadian, and German scientists suggests that to avoid the more dangerous impacts of climate change, atmospheric concentrations of carbon dioxide must be kept significantly lower than 450–550 ppm, the upper level of what the IPCC said could be safely tolerated. Published in separate journals, this research suggests that carbon emissions need to be reduced to near zero by midcentury to avert a dangerous rise in temperature that could alter precipitation patterns and dry up sources of water worldwide. James Hansen, head of the NASA Goddard Institute for Space Studies and one of the world's foremost climate scientists, contends that CO2 levels need to be reduced to 350 ppm if "humanity wishes to preserve a planet similar to that on which civilization developed."[4]

After years of denial, major American institutions are now acknowledging the reality of climate change. In response to what Thomas Friedman calls "global weirding," large insurance companies are increasingly reluctant to insure coastal communities.[5] U.S. intelligence agencies have warned that threats to national security will intensify and accelerate due to growing conflicts over dwindling resources and food supply caused by climate disruption. According to Thomas Fingar, head of the National Intelligence Council, "no country will be immune to the effects of climate change," and "the spillover—from potentially increased migration and water-related disputes—could have a harmful global impact." A joint study of the Center for Strategic and International Studies and the Center for a New American Security went even further in 2008, asserting that "the collapse and chaos associated with extreme climate change futures would destabilize virtually every aspect of modern life."[6]

Developments that would have astounded many of us just a short time ago are increasingly common. Perhaps most telling is the scrapping of plans to build new coal-fired power plants. Existing coal-fired plants produce about one-third of U.S. carbon dioxide emissions. In early 2007, about 150 plants were on the boards in the United States, but rising public opposition has had a profound impact. California, which imports 20 percent of its electricity, banned the signing of new contracts to import electricity produced with coal. Several other states, among them Florida,

Texas, Minnesota, Washington, and Kansas, turned down licenses for coal-fired power plants or otherwise prevented their construction.

The future of coal received another serious blow in July 2007 when Citigroup downgraded coal company stocks and urged their clients to switch to other energy stocks.[7] "This is not a social or moral issue only," noted Edward Kerschner, chief investment strategist at Citigroup. "It's an investment issue. Whether or not you believe in climate change is not germane to how you invest your money." Anticipating that the federal government will cap carbon emissions from coal plants in the next few years, Citigroup, JPMorgan Chase, and Morgan Stanley established new guidelines in February 2008 for investing in energy projects and outlined principles requiring companies to demonstrate that the plants can be viable under more stringent environmental standards. These actions will make it more difficult going forward to finance new coal plants in the United States. The fact that carbon pricing is imminent, a development that will increase the cost of coal-generated electricity, reinforces the reluctance to make new investments in this area.[8]

Demand for energy is expected to increase markedly over the next 25 years, complicating efforts to stabilize the climate. Global demand is forecast to grow by 57 percent, and U.S. demand is expected to increase by 31 percent.[9] Oil reached an all-time high of $140 per barrel in June 2008, and coal prices in the eastern United States reached a record of $98 a ton in May 2008. Gas prices surpassed $4 per gallon in June 2008, and with the damage inflicted by Hurricane Ike on Texas oil rigs and refineries in early September they went as high as $5 a gallon in some parts of the country. Although energy prices have fallen way off these highs as a result of the financial meltdown that began in September 2008, they are still a source of widespread anxiety among the American public, who had become used to oil prices well below $40 a barrel for most of the previous two decades.[10]

Higher energy prices are strengthening the case for improved efficiency, increased renewable energy, more efficient transportation, and expanded public transportation. At the same time, they have generated increased calls for the revival of offshore drilling, opening of the Arctic National Wildlife Refuge, and the construction of new nuclear reactors. All three of these issues attracted much attention in the 2008 presidential campaign and will continue to be hotly debated in the Obama administration.[11]

There has been no new offshore drilling since 1982 because of the federal moratorium, and no new nuclear reactors have been ordered since the 1970s. Several reactors came on line during the 1980s and 1990s, and the Tennessee Valley Authority refurbished the Browns Ferry 1 reactor in Decatur, Alabama, which restarted in May 2007 after a 22-year shutdown. As of May 2008, there are 104 reactors and 9 license applications filed with the Nuclear Regulatory Commission. The Nuclear Energy Institute expects that there will be 30 new reactors over the next 15 to 20 years, although some observers question whether these plants will actually be completed due to their high costs.[12]

Despite these immense and complex challenges, there is good news: We have the necessary technology at hand to reduce carbon emissions radically and meet our energy needs. *Tackling Climate Change in the U.S.*, a 2007 report based on a series of studies by scientists and other experts, examines the potential of current energy efficiency and renewable energy technologies to mitigate climate change. As editor Charles Kutscher notes, this analysis strongly suggests that existing technologies could "provide most, if not all, of the U.S. carbon emissions reductions that will be needed to help limit the atmospheric concentrations of carbon dioxide to 450–500 ppm."[13]

The report, published by the American Solar Energy Society, emphasizes the importance of achieving efficiencies in the energy consumption of buildings, industry, and transportation and reviews the state of renewable technologies such as concentrating solar power, photovoltaic, wind, biomass, biofuels, and geothermal. It estimates the impact of aggressive deployment of efficiency and renewable energy and proposes how the large-scale implementation of existing technologies can reduce carbon emissions to levels recommended by the IPCC. Under the resulting scenario, efficiency improvements would provide approximately 57 percent of the carbon displacement and renewable energy about 43 percent. The biggest challenge, according to the report, is not the development of new technologies but the massive and rapid implementation of existing technologies. Political will and leadership, it makes clear, are the essential variables in determining whether we succeed or fail.[14]

The Policy Climate: Beyond Kyoto

In response to the accumulating evidence of climate change, a number of important policy initiatives at the international, federal, state, and local levels have been launched over the last 30 years seeking to curb greenhouse gas emissions. These climate protection efforts are one of the most influential factors shaping the sustainability conversation in higher education. Consequently, an overview of the changing policy environment since the First World Climate Conference was held in Geneva, Switzerland, in February 1979 will be helpful before proceeding to a detailed analysis of the issues facing colleges and universities.

The years since that conference can be divided into three distinct periods highlighting the evolving nature of the policy debates. In the first era, 1979 to 1996, climate change emerged as a serious topic of discussion, and debates began about the role of human activity in contributing to this phenomenon. For the next eight years, 1997 to 2005, a solid consensus formed in the scientific and policy communities that human-made greenhouse gases had the potential to alter the earth's climate system profoundly in the near term, and these changes would have a disproportionate impact on developing nations. The central theme of the third era, which we have now entered, is that significant climate changes are already under way, and thus adaptation, not just mitigation, needs to be part of the response.[15]

1979 to 1996

The First World Climate Conference, convened by the World Meteorological Organization (WMO), an agency of the United Nations, identified climate change as an urgent international problem and issued a declaration calling on governments to take steps to protect the climate. The WMO joined with the UN Environment Program (UNEP) and the International Council of Scientific Unions (ICSU) to establish the World Climate Program. Several intergovernmental conferences on climate change followed, culminating in 1988 with the Toronto Conference on the Changing Atmosphere.

As a result of the Toronto conference, the UN created the Intergovernmental Panel on Climate Change (IPCC) to assess the scale and timing of changes, estimate their consequences, and draw up response strategies. In 1990, the IPCC issued its first assessment report on the state of the global climate, which had a noticeable impact on policy makers and public opinion, thus broadening awareness of the issue beyond the scientific community. The Second World Climate Conference met in Geneva several months later and, unlike the 1979 conference, included government leaders as well as scientists.[16]

Serious international negotiations got underway with the 1992 Rio de Janeiro Earth Summit, leading to the establishment of the United Nations Framework Convention on Climate Change (UNFCCC). This nonbinding agreement signed by 186 countries, including the United

States, sought to prevent "dangerous anthropogenic interference with the Earth's climate system" by reducing greenhouse gas emissions. Signatory countries acknowledged climate change as a major issue and agreed to take measures that would bring emissions down to 1990 levels by 2000. The agreement, however, was not enforceable.

Unfortunately, the years following Rio saw little substantive action, and global emissions of greenhouse gases increased dramatically. In 1995 the IPCC published its second assessment report, which highlighted the continuing rise in emissions despite the pledges made at the Earth Summit. Clearly, a more rigorous approach was needed.[17]

1997 to 2005

The Kyoto Protocol of the UNFCCC in 1997 marked a move toward mandatory targets for reducing emissions. It committed signatory countries to an overall reduction of 5.2 percent below 1990 levels by 2012, but it placed the burden of responsibility on industrialized nations for meeting this target. Under the terms of the Kyoto Protocol, developing countries were not subject to emission reduction targets. Those who supported this approach emphasized the extent to which developed nations had generated the great majority of emissions so far and their ability to afford the costs of curbing emissions. Developing nations, in contrast, needed to focus on economic growth before they could take on these costs.

This position became a source of heated debate when the United States insisted that all countries should have emissions targets. The Bush administration refused to budge on this point and announced in 2001 that the United States would not participate in the Kyoto Protocol. That same year the IPCC published its third assessment report, which made it clear that the threat of global climate change over the next 10 to 20 years was unavoidable and that its impact would be most serious in the poorer countries of the world.

In contrast to the U.S. stance, Russia ratified the Kyoto Protocol in 2004, allowing it to become binding on the other members. In February 2005, almost exactly 26 years after the First World Climate Conference, it entered into force. Implementation of the Kyoto Protocol set in motion an emissions trading system among industrialized nations. The details of how the system should work were not spelled out in the original language, however, and they became the subject of intense negotiations.[18]

2006 to Today

Two reports set the current era in motion: the release in October 2006 of the Stern Review, commissioned by the British government and led by the former chief economist of the World Bank, Nicholas Stern, and the IPCC's fourth assessment report in February 2007. Together these documents painted a startling picture of human-induced climate change already in progress. Pointing to events such as glacial ice melt in Greenland, droughts in Africa, heat waves in Europe, and floods in Asia, these reports argued that the cost of adopting low-carbon technologies paled in comparison to the damage that would be inflicted by the destabilization of the planet's climate system. The message was loud and clear: time was running out, and the costs would only get higher the longer we waited to address the problem in a comprehensive manner.[19]

Although more robust than previous efforts, the Kyoto Protocol has turned out to be ineffective. It has done little to control emissions, and there are no effective mechanisms for enforcement. China and India, whose rapidly increasing emissions have neutralized any gains made elsewhere, are not required to establish targets, and one of the biggest contributors of greenhouse gas emissions, the United States, has adamantly refused to join the treaty. Consequently, the burden of making any progress has fallen on Western Europe, Russia, Canada, Japan, Australia, and New Zealand. Despite the European Union's implementation of a cap-and-trade system in 2005, carbon emissions are still rising in those countries.[20]

In the meantime, a growing political and scientific consensus has called for a 50 percent reduction in global emissions by 2050, with 80 percent reductions in developed countries, in order to avoid "the likelihood of massive and irreversible disruptions of the global ecosystem." More than 200 scientists at the UN Climate Change Conference in December 2007 signed the Bali Climate Declaration, calling for policies to ensure a dramatic decline in global emissions within the next 10 to 15 years. At the Bali conference, 187 countries agreed on a two-year negotiating process, led by the UN, to forge a successor to the first phase of the Kyoto Protocol, which ends in 2012. Those talks are scheduled to conclude in Copenhagen in December 2009.[21]

Whether that goal is achieved remains to be seen. Efforts to build momentum for a new global emissions framework before the close of the Kyoto Protocol's first phase have not been encouraging. Success hinges on persuading China, India, and Brazil, among other developing nations, to embrace targets for their countries and on securing U.S. agreement to show more flexibility on what those targets should be. Given the complex politics involved, there is no reason to be more than cautiously optimistic. Whatever the outcome, 2009 will be decisive for global action on the climate change front.

The G8 Foreign Ministers Meeting in July 2008 made clear that major hurdles still exist. The leaders of the world's eight largest economies agreed at the gathering in Japan to cut global emissions in half by 2050, but they provided little information about how this target would be achieved. "There is no detail in the communiqué; no medium-term targets; no commitment to agreeing on a legally binding successor to the Kyoto Protocol at Copenhagen next year," the *Independent UK* pointed out in a scathing editorial. Calling the announcement "a worthless gust of hot air," the British newspaper noted that there is not "even agreement on the date from which CO2 cuts will be measured."[22]

U.S. Climate Protection Initiatives

After taking office in January 2001, President George W. Bush became an outspoken opponent to required reductions of greenhouse gas emissions. Little headway was made on securing political support for a mandatory cap-and-trade system or carbon tax. The latter would impose a fee for energy use based on the amount of carbon dioxide generated. Although supported by many economists as a more effective solution than a cap-and-trade system, with the recent global economic crisis there is little likelihood that politicians would risk backing the imposition of new taxes. Senator Joseph Lieberman (I-CT) and Senator John Warner (R-VA) mounted the most serious effort to establish a cap-and-trade system during President Bush's second term, seeking to reduce greenhouse gas emissions by 70 percent by 2050. With President Bush threatening to use his veto power and a coalition of corporations and environmental groups splintering after originally supporting the legislation, however, the Lieberman-Warner bill failed in June 2008 to gain the necessary support in the Senate.[23]

Although political stalemate characterized climate policy during President George W. Bush's eight years in office, Congress has moved on the energy policy front. Passed after long debate, the Energy Independence and Security Act of 2007, according to the *New York Times*, "will slowly but fundamentally change the cars Americans drive, the fuel they burn, the way they light their homes and the price they pay for food." The new law establishes higher fuel economy standards for cars and light trucks for the first time in 32 years and requires a fivefold increase from current production levels of ethanol by 2022. The measure also sets new efficiency requirements for household appliances and government buildings and requires phasing out the incandescent light bulb within 10 years.

The bill originally included elimination of subsidies to the oil and gas industry in order to promote the development of wind, solar, geothermal, and other alternative energy sources, as well as a requirement that utilities generate a growing proportion of their electricity from renewable sources, but these proposed tax changes were dropped. Congress extended existing tax credits for clean energy, however, as part of the massive financial bailout plan passed in October 2008. Included in this measure were a one-year extension of a production tax credit for wind, an eight-year extension of the 30 percent tax credit for solar residential and commercial solar installations, and the elimination of the $2,000 cap on this tax credit for solar electric panels installed after 2008.[24]

In the absence of action on climate change policy at the federal level, state and local political leaders have launched a number of initiatives. Responding to the government's refusal to ratify the Kyoto Protocol, the U.S. Conference of Mayors in 2005 organized a coalition of municipalities that committed to a 7 percent reduction from 1990 levels by 2012, which would have been the target for the United States if it had ratified this treaty. As of December 2008, more than 900 mayors have signed the U.S. Mayors' Climate Protection Agreement.[25] Frustrated with the federal response to climate change, cities have enacted energy efficiency measures, planted more trees, generated electricity with methane from landfills, and installed waterless urinals.[26]

The failure to pass federal legislation has also generated significant action at the state level. Republican Governor George Pataki of New York led an effort that culminated in the 2005 Regional Greenhouse Gas Initiative, in which 10 northeastern states established the first mandatory cap-and-trade program in the United States. Another Republican governor, Arnold Schwarzenegger of California, signed an agreement in 2006 with British Prime Minister Tony Blair to cut emissions, laying the groundwork for a transatlantic carbon trading market.[27]

Governor Schwarzenegger also challenged the federal government on the issue of standards for greenhouse gas emissions from automobiles and light trucks. A 2004 California law would have forced automakers to cut emissions by 30 percent, with the cutbacks beginning in the 2009 model year. The U.S. Environmental Protection Agency (EPA), however, refused in 2007 to grant the state the necessary waiver that would have allowed it to exceed federal standards. The governor, in response, filed suit against the EPA in January 2008 and vowed to take the case to the U.S. Supreme Court if necessary, a process that could take years.[28]

Continuing to press the case for climate action, Governor Schwarzenegger joined his counterparts from 17 other states in April 2008 to insist in a declaration on climate policy that federal and state governments work together to implement mandatory approaches to greenhouse gas emission reductions. The election of Barack Obama in November 2008 offered promise that the federal government would enact more aggressive measures on climate change, energy efficiency, and renewable energy. Indeed, President Obama has already announced that he will be seeking support from Congress to establish a cap-and-trade system and provide $15 billion a year to encourage the growth of the renewable energy industry.[29]

In striking contrast to his predecessors' inaction, President Obama issued a stirring call to arms in his inaugural address, underscoring the hope and opportunity created by a more sustainable future. "We will harness the sun and the winds and the soil to fuel our cars and run our factories," he declared. "And we will transform our schools and colleges and universities to meet the demands of a new age."[30]

Carbon Markets and Trading

In the absence of a federal cap-and-trade program or carbon tax, a number of different trading systems have emerged. The Regional Greenhouse Gas Initiative's (RGGI) cap-and-trade program focuses on carbon dioxide emissions from power plants, but it may be extended to include other sources of greenhouse gas emissions. Connecticut, Delaware, Maine, Massachusetts, New Hampshire, New Jersey, New York, Maryland, Rhode Island, and Vermont are participating. In 2009, RGGI will begin capping emissions at current levels, followed by a reduction of emissions of 10 percent by 2019.[31]

In another bipartisan initiative, six governors in 2007 signed the Midwestern Regional Greenhouse Gas Reduction Accord, an agreement to implement emissions reduction targets and a regional cap-and-trade system.[32] Seeking to reduce greenhouse gases by 60 to 80 percent below current emissions levels as recommended by the IPCC, it involves Illinois, Iowa, Kansas, Michigan, Minnesota, Wisconsin, and the Canadian province of Manitoba.[33]

The Western Climate Initiative (WCI), also launched in 2007, includes seven states (Arizona, California, Montana, New Mexico, Oregon, Utah, and Washington) and four Canadian provinces (British Columbia, Manitoba, Ontario, and Quebec). WCI's goal is to develop a regional cap-and-trade program and reduce the region's emissions 15 percent below 2005 levels by 2020 for the six primary greenhouse gases identified by the UN Framework Convention on Climate Change (carbon dioxide, methane, nitrous oxide, hydrofluorocarbons, perfluorocarbons, and sulfur hexafluoride).[34]

The Chicago Climate Exchange (CCX) is a voluntary cap-and-trade system launched in 2003. Members make a legally binding commitment to emission reductions. From 2003 to 2006, members committed to reduce emissions at least 1 percent per year, for a total reduction of 4 percent below their baseline, which was an average of their annual emissions from 1998 to 2001. For the next phase of the agreement, they have committed to achieving emission reductions of 6 percent below baseline. Members who reduce beyond their targets have surplus allowances to sell or bank; those who do not meet the targets must purchase exchange allowances and offsets. A variety of industries, counties, electric power companies, financial instititutions, municipalities, states, offset aggregators, and universities participate in the CCX. U.S. university members include Michigan State University, University of California San Diego, University of Idaho, University of Iowa, University of Minnesota, University of Oklahoma, and Tufts University.[35]

The newest carbon trading market in the United States is the New York Mercantile Exchange's (NYMEX) Green Exchange, which began in March 2008. Trading kicked off in the first quarter with an offering of futures contracts tied to the cost of pollution in European Union.[36] The Green Exchange, according to NYMEX, "will serve as the nexus for trading environmental products designed to combat global climate change, improve air quality, and build environmentally sustainable energy sources." Partners include Morgan Stanley, Credit Suisse, JPMorgan Chase, and Evolution Markets, Inc.[37]

The value of emission credits traded globally jumped from $31 billion in 2006 to $64 billion in 2007. Economists estimate that the domestic emissions cap-and-trade system in the United States will be a $1 trillion market by 2020.[38] The extent to which this system will help reduce carbon emissions remains to be seen. It is also not clear what the impact of a federally mandated cap-and-trade system or carbon tax will be on the American economy. In the midst of these uncertainties, one thing is clear: If a cap-and-trade system or carbon tax is enacted, the long-term costs of energy inefficiency will become markedly higher—a likelihood that should concern all higher education leaders.

Notes

1. "Americans Reach Environmental Turning Point... Companies Need to Catch Up," CSRwire, August 22, 2008. www.csrwire.com/News/9473.html (accessed August 31, 2008).

2. Richard Monastersky, "International Scientific Panel on Climate Change Is 90% Sure that Human Actions Have Warmed the Planet," *Chronicle of Higher Education*, February 2, 2007. http://chronicle.com/daily/2007/02/2007020208n.htm (accessed September 9, 2008).

3. Elisabeth Rosenthal, "U.N. Report Describes Risks of Inaction on Climate Change," *New York Times*, November 17, 2007. www.nytimes.com/2007/11/17/science/earth/17climate.html (accessed September 9, 2008); David Adam, "World CO2 Levels at Record High, Scientists Warn," *Guardian UK*, May 12, 2008. www.guardian.co.uk/environment/2008/may/12/climatechange.carbonemissions (accessed September 9, 2008).

4. Juliet Eilperin, "Carbon Output Must Be Near Zero to Avert Danger, New Studies Say," *Washington Post*, March 10, 2008. www.washingtonpost.com/wp-dyn/content/article/2008/03/09/AR2008030901867.html (accessed September 9, 2008); Ed Pilkington, "Climate Target Is Not Radical Enough—Study," *Guardian UK*, April 7, 2008. www.guardian.co.uk/environment/2008/apr/07/climatechange.carbonemissions (accessed September 9, 2008).

5. Thomas L. Friedman, "The People We Have Been Waiting For," *New York Times*, December 2, 2007. www.nytimes.com/2007/12/02/opinion/02friedman.html (accessed September 8, 2008); Victoria Schlesinger and Meredith Knight, "Insurers Claim Global Warming Makes Some Regions Too Hot to Handle," *Scientific American*, August 1, 2007. www.sciam.com/article.cfm?id=insurers-claim-global-warming-makes-some-uninsurable (accessed September 9, 2008).

6. Kevin Whitelaw, "Climate Change Will Have Destabilizing Consequences, Intelligence Agencies Warn," *U.S. News and World Report*," June 25, 2008. www.usnews.com/articles/news/2008/06/25/climate-change-will-have-destabilizing-consequences-intelligence-agencies-warn.html (accessed September 8, 2008).

7. Lester B. Brown, *Plan B 3.0, Mobilizing to Save Civilization*, rev. ed. (New York: W.W. Norton, 2008), p. 215.

8. Steven Mufson, "Renewable Power Plays," *Washington Post*, August 26, 2007. www.washingtonpost.com/wp-dyn/content/article/2007/08/25/AR2007082500211.html (accessed September 8, 2008); "Investment Banks Line Up Against Coal Plants," *GreenBizJournals*, February 4, 2008. www.greenbizjournal.com/index.php/2008/02/04/investment-banks-line-up-against-coal-plants/ (accessed September 8, 2008); Melanie Warren, "Is America Ready to Quit Coal?" *New York Times*, February 15, 2009. www.nytimes.com/2009/02/15/business/15coal.html (accessed February 15, 2009).

9. "The Energy Picture: Where Are We Now? Where Are We Headed," EnergyStar. www.energystar.gov/index.cfm?c=business.bus_energy_strategy (accessed September 8, 2008).

10. Kenneth Musante, "Oil Hits $140 for the First Time," CNN-Money.com, June 26, 2008. http://money.cnn.com/2008/06/26/markets/oil/index.htm (accessed September 9, 2008); Christopher Martin, "Coal Price in U.S. East Climbs to Record $98 on Rising Exports," Bloomberg.com, May 9, 2008. www.bloomberg.com/apps/news?pid=20601207&sid=av37CGSju_LA&refer=energy (accessed September 9, 2008); Elizabeth Douglass, "Hurricane Ike Being Felt at the Gas Pump," *Los Angeles Times*, September 13, 2008. www.latimes.com/business/la-fi-oil13-2008sep13,1,726465.story (accessed September 13, 2008); "Oil Price History and Analysis," WTRG Economics. http://www.wtrg.com/prices.htm (accessed November 28, 2008).

11. Sheryl Gay Stolberg, "Bush Will Seek to End Offshore Drilling Ban," *New York Times*, June 18, 2008. www.nytimes.com/2008/06/18/washington/18drill.html (accessed September 8, 2008); Jim Marshall and Roscoe Bartlett, "Drilling for Clean Energy," *Washington Post*, September 5, 2008. www.washingtonpost.com/wp-dyn/content/article/2008/09/04/AR2008090402844.html (accessed September 8, 2008).

12. Steve Kerekes, Nuclear Energy Institute, personal communication, May 16, 2008.

13. Charles Kutscher, ed., *Tackling Climate Change in the U.S.: Potential Carbon Emissions Reductions from Energy Efficiency and Renewable Energy by 2030* (Boulder, Colo.: American Solar Energy Society, 2007), p. 5.

14. Ibid., p. 37.

15. The division of these years into three periods draws on but differs from Saleem Huq, "Three Eras of Climate Change and the Emergence of Concern for Global Justice," ClimateEthics.org. http://climateethics.org/?p=26 (accessed August 16, 2008).

16. UNFCCC, *United Nations Framework Convention on Climate Change Handbook* (Berlin: UNFCCC, 2006), pp. 17–19. http://unfccc.int/resource/docs/publications/handbook.pdf (accessed August 16, 2008).

17. Warwick J. McKibbin and Peter Wilcoxen, *Climate Change Policy After Kyoto: Blueprint for a Realistic Approach* (Washington, DC: Brookings Institute Press, 2002), pp. 41–42.

18. Christoph Bohringer and Michael Finus, "The Kyoto Protocol: Success or Failure?" in *Climate-Change Policy*, ed. Dieter Helm (Oxford, Eng.: Oxford University Press, 2005), pp. 266–68; Organisation for Economic Co-operation and Development, *Action Against Climate Change: The Kyoto Protocol and Beyond* (Paris: OECD Publishing, 1999), pp. 8–9, 15–16, 19.

19. Michael McCarthy, "Inaction Spells a World of Floods, Drought, and Economic Disaster," *The Independent*, October 31, 2006. www.independent.co.uk/environment/climate-change/michael-mccarthy-analysis-inaction-spells-a-world-of-floods-drought-and-economic-disaster-422493.html (accessed August 17, 2008); Elisabeth Rosenthal and Andrew C. Revkin, "Panel Issues Bleak Report on Climate Change," *New York Times*, February 2, 2007. www.nytimes.com/2007/02/02/science/earth/02cnd-climate.html (accessed August 17, 2008).

20. Emily Flynn Vencat, "The Carbon Folly," *Newsweek*, March 12, 2007. www.truthout.org/article/the-carbon-folly-policymakers-favorite-global-warming-fix-isnt-working (accessed August 17, 2008); Alan Zarembo, "Kyoto's Failures Haunt New U.N. Talks," *Los Angeles Times*, December 3, 2007. http://articles.latimes.com/2007/dec/03/science/sci-kyoto3 (accessed August 17, 2008).

21. Commission of the European Communities, *Limiting Global Climate Change to 2 Degrees Celsius: The Way Ahead for 2020 and Beyond* (January 10, 2007), p. 3; Paul Eccleston, "Scientists Issue Bali Climate Change Warning," *The Telegraph*, June 12, 2007. www.telegraph.co.uk/earth/main.jhtml?xml=/earth/2007/12/06/eabali106.xml (accessed August 17, 2008); Thomas Fuller and Andrew C. Revkin, "Climate Plan Looks Beyond Bush's Tenure," *New*

York Times, December 16, 2007. www.nytimes.com/2007/12/16/world/16climate.html (accessed August 17, 2008).

22. Sheryl Gay Stolberg, "Richest Nations Pledge to Halve Greenhouse Gas," *New York Times*. July 9, 2008. www.nytimes.com/2008/07/09/science/earth/09climate.html (accessed August 17, 2008); "A Worthless Gust of Hot Air," *The Independent*, July 9, 2008. www.independent.co.uk/opinion/leading-articles/leading-article-a-worthless-gust-of-hot-air-862894.html (accessed August 17, 2008).

23. Marc Gunther, "Chances Dim for Climate-Change Legislation," *Fortune*, May 30, 2008. http://money.cnn.com/2008/05/30/news/economy/gunther_legislation.fortune/ (accessed August 17, 2008); Christopher Kutruff, "Senate Inaction Kills Climate Change Bill," Truthout.org, June 6, 2008. www.truthout.org/article/senate-inaction-kills-climate-change-bill (accessed August 17, 2008).

24. John M. Broder, "Bush Signs Broad Energy Bill," *New York Times*, December 19, 2007. www.nytimes.com/2007/12/19/washington/19cnd-energy.html?hp (accessed August 17, 2008); Martin LaMonica, "Bailout Plan Bails Out Clean-Energy Sector," CNET News, October 3, 2008. http://news.cnet.com/8301-11128_3-10057936-54.html (accessed November 28, 2008).

25. Eli Sanders, "Rebuffing Bush, 132 Mayors Embrace Kyoto Rules," *New York Times*, May 14, 2005. www.nytimes.com/2005/05/14/national/14kyoto.html (accessed August 17, 2008); "List of Participating Mayors," Mayors Climate Protection Center. www.usmayors.org/climateprotection/list.asp (accessed December 2, 2008).

26. Stephanie Simon, "Global Warming, Local Initiatives," *Los Angeles Times*, December 10, 2006. www.truthout.org/article/global-warming-local-initiatives (accessed August 17, 2008); Anthony Faiola and Robin Shulman, "Cities Take Lead on Environment as Debate Drags at Federal Level," *Washington Post*, June 9, 2007. www.washingtonpost.com/wp-dyn/content/article/2007/06/08/AR2007060802779.html (accessed August 17, 2008).

27. "Seven Northeast States Launch Regional Greenhouse Gas Initiative," *Environment News Service*, December 20, 2005. www.ens-newswire.com/ens/dec2005/2005-12-20-05.asp (accessed August 17, 2008); Patrick Wintour, "Blair Signs Climate Pact with Schwarzenegger," *The Guardian*, August 1, 2006. www.guardian.co.uk/environment/2006/aug/01/greenpolitics.usnews (accessed August 17, 2008).

28. "EPA Decides Against Calif. Emissions Standards," Online NewsHour, December 20, 2007. www.pbs.org/newshour/updates/environment/july-dec07/epacalifornia_12-20.html (accessed August 17, 2008).

29. "Eighteen States Sign Declaration on Climate Policy," Pew Center on Global Climate Change, April 18, 2008. www.pewclimate.org/node/5893 (accessed August 17, 2008); Regional Greenhouse Gas Initiative. www.rggi.org/about.htm (accessed September 14, 2008); Geoffrey Lean, "Obama's Green Start," *The Independent*, November 23, 2008. http://www.independent.co.uk/news/world/americas/obamas-green-start-1031239.html (accessed December 2, 2008).

30. "Barack Obama's Inaugural Address," *New York Times*, January 20, 2009. www.nytimes.com/2009/01/20/us/politics/20text-obama.html (accessed February 20, 2009).

31. Regional Greenhouse Gas Initiative. www.rggi.org/about.htm (accessed September 14, 2008); "Regional Greenhouse Gas Initiative," Pew Center on Global Climate Change. www.pewclimate.org/what_s_being_done/in_the_states/rggi/ (accessed September 14, 2008).

32. "Eighteen States Sign Declaration on Climate Policy," Pew Center on Global Climate Change, April 18, 2008. www.pewclimate.org/node/5893 (accessed August 17, 2008); John Rondy, "Midwest Governors Sign Climate Change Accord," *Reuters*, November 15, 2007. www.reuters.com/article/environmentNews/idUSN1528878720071117 (accessed August 17, 2008).

33. "Regional Initiatives," Pew Center on Global Climate Change. www.pewclimate.org/what_s_being_done/in_the_states/regional_initiatives.cfm (accessed October 16, 2008); "Ten Midwestern Leaders Sign Greenhouse Gas Reduction Accord: Also Establish Regional Goals and Initiatives to Achieve Energy Security and Promote Renewable Energy." State of Wisconsin press release, November 15, 2007. www.wisgov.state.wi.us/journal_media_detail.asp?locid=19&prid=3027 (accessed October 16, 2008).

34. "Regional Initiatives," Pew Center on Global Climate Change. www.pewclimate.org/what_s_being_done/in_the_states/regional_initiatives.cfm (accessed October 16, 2008); "The Western Climate Initiative." www.westernclimateinitiative.org/Index.cfm (accessed October 16, 2008).

35. "Emission Reduction Commitment," Chicago Climate Exchange. www.chicagoclimateexchange.com/content.jsf?id=72 (accessed September 14, 2008); "Members of CCX," Chicago Climate Exchange. www.chicagoclimateexchange.com/content.jsf?id=64 (accessed May 15, 2008).

36. Adam Davidson, "Carbon-Trading Exchange Opens in New York," NPR Morning Edition, March 17, 2008. www.npr.org/templates/story/story.php?storyId=88382450 (accessed September 14, 2008).

37. "The Green Exchange Initiative," NYMEX. www.greenfutures.com/overview/ (accessed September 14, 2008); "Partners," NYMEX, www.greenfutures.com/partners/ (accessed September 14, 2008).

38. Shawn McCarthy, "Global Carbon Market Takes Flight," *Toronto Globe and Mail*, May 14, 2008. www.theglobeandmail.com/servlet/story/RTGAM.20080514.wrcarbon14/BNStory/energy/home (accessed September 14, 2008); "U.S. Carbon Trading Market Valued at $1 Trillion," *GreenBizJournal*, February 15, 2008. http://green.bizjournals.com/index.php/2008/02/15/us-carbon-trading-market-valued-at-1-trillion/ (accessed September 14, 2008).

"A ship in harbor is safe, but that is not what ships are built for."
—**John A. Shedd**, *Salt from My Attic*, 1928

2

ADOPTING NEW LEADERSHIP
MODELS FOR SUSTAINABILITY

"There are two types of education," John Adams shrewdly observed. "One should teach us how to make a living, and the other how to live." These well-chosen words capture the central tension in the long-running debate about the purpose of American higher education. The essence of this often-heated discussion comes down to whether a college education should emphasize the liberal arts and sciences or professional studies.

But are these two approaches mutually exclusive, or can we bring them together without losing the ethical grounding that has been the foundation of liberal education? Viewed through the lens of sustainability, it quickly becomes clear that we must. Today's students will not be able to build a more sustainable society if they are not prepared to do both. They must be able to ask the critical questions, grasp the big picture, and commit to an ethos of stewardship (how to live) and to acquire the necessary knowledge, skills, and professional training to make a real difference in the world (how to make a living).

The key to reconciling the conflict can be found in the notion of vocation, commonly viewed as a calling or profession for which one has a sense of special fitness. Vocation demands that each of us asks two fundamental questions: Who am I? How can I best serve others? It creates a space where, as William Sullivan puts it, "liberal and professional education meet."[1]

Careful consideration of what it means to have a vocation gets to the heart of higher education's mission and creates an alternative approach to educating our future leaders. It puts the liberal arts and professional learning in conversation with each other and aims beyond simply acquiring a job and becoming financially secure. Understood more broadly as a process rather than final discovery, a sense of vocation fosters an expanded consciousness of one's potential as a human being and one's place in the larger world. As an ongoing experience of self-realization and a way to link our learning with our interests, values, and ambitions, it also generates a determination to have a positive impact on the world. Vocation connects being with doing, providing the crucial starting point for nurturing the kind of "new professional" that sustainability requires and for achieving success in the new global knowledge economy.[2]

By putting renewed emphasis on learning that leads to vocation rather than on a narrower sense of vocationalism, "liberal arts colleges and universities can help people live productively, responsibly, and well, amidst all the confusions of the present times," observes Ellen Condiffe Lagemann. "By making matters of vocation central to all they do, liberal arts colleges and universities can play a more direct role in improving the world."[3] What more important outcomes could higher education pursue in the 21st century?

In their recent study, *A New Agenda for Higher Education*, William Sullivan and his colleagues at the Carnegie Foundation for the Advancement of Teaching outline how to integrate practices from professional education and the liberal arts, providing an inspiring new vision of educational purpose.[4] Their analysis reflects a growing movement to end the old battles over practical versus liberal education and to reconnect a fragmented academy. To the extent that a commitment to social, economic, and environmental sustainability will help hasten this process, higher education could well be on the verge of a historic reformation.

The urgent need to nurture a healthier economy, society, and biosphere could lead not only to a more holistic and purpose-driven education but also to the development of more collaborative leadership models that foster a stronger sense of campus community and promote positive change. Colleges and universities, unlike families, are "communities of choice." To paraphrase Marshall Goldsmith, faculty, students, and staff are community members because they want to be, not because they have to be. The reality of most campuses, unfortunately, falls well short of the ideal community that we often envision. Among other developments, the bifurcation of colleges and universities into faculty and administrators has led to an excessively technocratic culture of specialization that defeats the spirit of community and undercuts excellence.

The irony is not that our institutions have embraced the corporate worldview, but that they have become wedded to such an outdated version. Higher education governance is stuck on General Motors, to use an analogy from the automobile industry, when it should be looking to Toyota for ways to improve colleges and universities. The most progressive thinking in the private sector, as in the case of Toyota, seeks to flatten the organization, break down silos, disseminate best practices laterally, and encourage cross-functional collaboration. In this kind of an organization, according to Barry Spiker, the goal is to have "each individual inside the organization... feel as if they are a part of the solution versus being part of the problem."[5]

Jon Wergin's concept of leadership in place offers an effective way to move in a new direction. To create a more vibrant and change-oriented community is not magic, but an act of political will that requires a particular kind of leadership. In Wergin's words, "real academic leadership has to come from within—from academic professionals who do not necessarily aspire to formal administrative positions but want instead to exert a positive influence on their campuses." Leadership in place, as he insists, "promotes collaboration and joint exploration of issues."[6]

This concept resonates nicely with Helen and Alexander Astin's notion of transformative leadership. "A leader can be anyone—regardless of formal position—who serves as an effective social change agent," they note. "In this sense, every faculty and staff member, not to mention every student, is a potential leader." Given the range of social, economic, and political issues students will confront upon graduation, colleges and universities have a responsibility to demonstrate this kind of leadership. "If the next generation of citizen leaders is to be engaged and committed to leading for the common good," the Astins say, "then the institutions which nurture them must be engaged in the work of the society and the community, modeling effective leadership and problem-solving skills, demonstrating how to accomplish change for the common good."[7]

We need, then, a more inclusive and fluid approach that stands in stark contrast to the top-down arrangements of power and authority that characterize most colleges and universities. Leading from the center rather than from the top, creating a complex of interactive neural networks that energize individual and collective efforts in alignment with the organization's mission and strategic priorities, is the central dynamic of the new inside-out leadership. Such an approach can generate profound organizational shifts that will create more humane campus communities inspired by "a sense of shared purpose and hope for the future" rather than individual agendas and empire building.[8]

The initial call to green an organization may have to come from the top, but stakeholders must be engaged across the enterprise if the sustainability initiative is going to be successful, especially once the easier tasks have been accomplished. Mitchell Thomashow, president of Unity College, understands the need for stakeholder engagement as well as anyone in higher education. A longtime environmentalist, he sums up his strategy as "frugal sustainability."

Nowhere can the success of this approach be better seen than in Unity's per capita carbon emissions. While a typical four-year college annually produces 8,000–12,000 pounds of carbon dioxide equivalent emissions per student, and a major research university may produce as much as 30,000 pounds, Unity generates only 4,000 pounds. Carefully calculating cost-benefit and payback, Unity has decreased its per capita emissions 28 percent since 2001, and overall emissions by almost 20 percent, despite adding buildings, building additions, and students. This estimate includes student, faculty, and staff travel-to-school emissions, and those produced by the college's vehicle fleet.

How did Unity manage to make such impressive progress despite significant financial constraints? Thomashow emphasizes the importance of "fixing the whole campus" rather than focusing on a single showcase project and encouraging students to become co-creators in the process. In addition, Unity College is driving its programs by incorporating sustainability initiatives into job descriptions and performance evaluations, working with the board of trustees, and implementing extensive curricular changes. By working from the center out, Thomashow has fostered a culture of frugality that stresses common sense, practicality, and whole-systems thinking.[9]

A good example of how inside-out leadership at the middle level of an institution promotes the growth of a sustainability culture can be found at Ithaca College, which received a Campus Sustainability Leadership Award in November 2008 from the Association for the Advancement of Sustainability in Higher Education (AASHE). Networks among faculty and staff, more than leadership provided from the top, have shaped the sustainability initiative and led to its deepening support. Faculty have taken responsibility for efforts such as the innovative collaboration with EcoVillage at Ithaca, the Finger Lakes Curriculum Project, which integrates sustainability into courses across the college, and the Finger Lakes Environmental Film Festival (FLEFF). Staff from campus operations, student affairs, and academic affairs have worked together to involve students in sustainability initiatives that connect learning inside the classroom with learning outside the classroom.

Anyone who doubts the effectiveness of networking across the silos to ensure the success of campus sustainability should meet Marian Brown, special assistant to the provost at Ithaca College. Brown served as head of purchasing at the college for years before taking on a short stint as special assistant to the vice president for finance and administration. Her keen knowledge of institutional culture, many contacts throughout the college, ability to win the trust of faculty and engage students, commitment to sustainability, and organizational savvy have provided the provost's office with a critical ability to identify resource needs and opportunities for early wins, mount high profile events that mobilize support, anticipate where the speed bumps and pot holes are, and document campus progress on the sustainability front.

Brown currently provides staff support for the college's Climate Commitment Committee, which oversees efforts to meet the goals of the American College and University Presidents Climate Commitment. She provides logistical support for FLEFF, the Resource and Environmental Management Program steering committee, the Natural Lands and Sustainable Transportation committees, and the Center for Natural Science Sustainability Group. Off campus, Brown has played key roles in the establishment of Sustainable Tompkins, Ithaca Carshare, the Finger Lakes Environmentally Preferred Procurement, and Tompkins Renewable Energy Educational Alliance. She also represents Ithaca College on the city's steering committee for the local climate action plan. More information about these projects can be found in chapters 4 and 6.

The leadership of individuals such as Thomashow and Brown is crucial to the development of a new culture of sustainability, both inside and outside of higher education. Energy generated by relationships rather than positions or titles, it reaches out rather than down or up and seeks to facilitate co-creation rather than simply secure buy-in. As Thomashow writes in *Ecological Identity*, power should not be used as an "instrument of control," but rather "as a means to expand choices; not as something external to a situation, but as intrinsic to an inclusive decision-making process."[10] This approach to sustainability leadership is built for the

If colleges and universities can demonstrate how to cultivate a sense of collective responsibility for the good of the whole, they will not only bring about a long overdue transformation of higher education but also create the possibility of a more sustainable civilization.

long haul: driven by mission rather than personality, bringing people to the table rather than assigning them to a place in the chain of command, clearing the space for multiple voices and synergistic alliances.

A revitalized sense of mission, more sustainable communities, and leadership styles that address the complex, interconnected problems of our time, both in the academy and in the world at large: these are the hallmarks of what could be a new era in higher education. "Occasionally something different happens," writes Peter Senge, "a collective awakening to new possibilities that changes everything over time—how people see the world, what they value, how society defines progress and organizes itself, and how institutions operate."[11] If colleges and universities can demonstrate how to cultivate a sense of collective responsibility for the good of the whole, they will not only bring about a long overdue transformation of higher education but also create the possibility of a more sustainable civilization.

Stories of Campus Sustainability Leadership

Effective leaders of campus sustainability share a few vital characteristics. They know how to see around corners, adapt quickly to changing circumstances, be decisive, and inspire others. They understand how to use sustainability to guide institutional strategy, how to apply the concepts of the triple bottom line (people, planet, profit), life-cycle analysis, full-cost accounting, and sustainability reporting, and how to make the business case for sustainability. Most important of all, however, effective sustainability leadership takes courage.[12] Setting sail in largely uncharted waters, these leaders are not afraid to get out in front of the conventional wisdom, and they know that uncertain times require creative thinking and decision making. A closer look at some examples from campuses around the country will help illuminate these aspects of effective sustainability leadership.

American College & University Presidents Climate Commitment

Perhaps the most dramatic example of what it means to be boldly sustainable is the American College and University Presidents Climate Commitment (ACUPCC). Launched in October 2006 by 12 forward-looking presidents, this historic agreement now has more than 600 signatories.[13] These college and university presidents and chancellors have committed their institutions to pursue climate neutrality and integrate sustainability into the curriculum. They represent a broad range of institutions, including independent and public, large, medium, and small, community colleges, religious institutions, research universities, and university systems from all 50 states. Collectively, these colleges and universities enroll more than 30 percent of the college students in America. Nonprofits providing support for the ACUPCC include the Association for the Advancement of Sustainability in Higher Education (AASHE), ecoAmerica, and Second Nature.

The ACUPCC is flexible, does not mandate a timeframe, and acknowledges that each institution needs to analyze and determine its best path toward climate neutrality, taking into account its distinctive history, culture, and mission. At the same time, it recognizes the value of collective action in the higher education arena. Three very different institutions—an independent liberal arts college, a public research university, and an urban community college district—offer insight into how ACUPCC signatories are addressing the complex and ambitious challenge of achieving climate neutrality.

College of the Atlantic

David Hales, president of College of the Atlantic (COA), is not one to mince words. An early supporter of ACUPCC, he drew a line in the sand. "If higher education is not relevant to solving the crisis of global warming," he declared, "it is not relevant, period."[14] In December 2007, COA, a small, environmentally focused college in Bar Harbor, Maine, became the first college or university in the nation to achieve climate neutrality.

Leadership from the top was a driving factor in achieving this impressive goal. Hales made clear early on his commitment to meeting the challenge of global climate change, announcing at his inauguration in October 2006 that COA would seek climate neutrality. Founded with an environmental mission, the college already had many programs in place, such as hosting zero- and low-waste graduations, serving local foods in the cafeteria, and using recycled paper everywhere. In 2007

Hales launched the college on an aggressive course of energy savings, improving efficiency in all buildings, promoting alternative transportation, and encouraging flexible work plans that allowed employees to work from home. In addition, the college moved to procure all of its electricity through a low-impact hydroelectric generator in Maine. COA offset the remainder of its carbon output by investing in a project of the Climate Trust of Oregon that optimizes traffic signals, manages traffic flows, and reduces the amount of time cars spend idling at traffic lights in Portland, Oregon.[15]

The new residential facilities for the 320-student college are among the most sustainable housing of any college in the United States. Featuring composting toilets, preheating of hot water via a gray-water recovery system, and maximum use of sunlight, the complex of three duplexes are so well insulated and tight that wood-pellet boilers can meet their minimal heating needs. In recognition of the institutions's outstanding leadership in the sustainability movement, *Grist* named it the Greenest College in the World in 2007. A year later *Forbes* included COA in its list of America's 10 Greenest Colleges and Universities, and it made *Princeton Review*'s Green Honor Roll.[16]

University of Minnesota, Morris

Committed to becoming climate neutral and energy independent by 2010, University of Minnesota, Morris (UMM) is well on its way. In the process, it has gained national recognition for its leadership in innovative clean energy technologies. The University of Minnesota's Biofuels and Bioproducts Innovative Laboratory, established in 2003 to carry out research on biomass conversion and analysis, marked the beginning of this new direction.[17] Then in 2005 UMM installed the first large-scale (1.65 megawatts) wind research turbine at a U.S. public university, locating it at the nearby University of Minnesota West Central Research and Outreach Center (WCROC). The onsite turbine supplies electricity to nearly all of UMM's buildings. The WCROC is now developing a wind-to-hydrogen demonstration system in partnership with the state, Xcel Energy, and other stakeholders. This system seeks to encourage the use of renewable hydrogen in such applications as fuel cells and localized fertilizer production.[18] In addition, an on-campus biomass gasification plant under construction will use local products, including corn stover, corn cobs, and mixed prairie grasses, providing 80 percent of the campus' heating and cooling needs and putting $500,000 back into the local economy. In 2008, UMM received authorization to issue Clean Renewable Energy

Bonds for the installation of two additional wind turbines, one in partnership with the Mille Lacs Band of Ojibwe. The U.S. Department of Energy and U.S. Environmental Protection Agency have inducted UMM into the Green Power Leadership Club for the university's outstanding commitments and achievements in green power.[19]

Los Angeles Community College District

The Los Angeles Community College District (LACCD), the nation's largest community college district, has nine campuses and serves more than 185,000 students. It is undertaking one of the largest public-sector efforts in sustainable building, funded by voter-approved bonds totaling more than $2.2 billion for new construction and modernization projects. The goal is nothing less than getting all nine campuses off the electric grid by the end of 2008. As part of this initiative, LACCD is installing photovoltaic (PV) panels on nearly all of its parking lots and roofs, as well as architectural-scale wind generators, solar thermal tubes, and geothermal heat pumps on each campus. This comprehensive alternative energy plan to generate nearly 40 megawatts is expected to meet all of LACCD's daytime and evening electricity needs. Excess electrical energy generated during the daytime will be stored in state-of-the-art battery systems and be used to generate hydrogen gas for fuel cells to meet the evening electrical demand. LACCD has a sustainable central plant that uses solar heat tubes, thermal storage, and co-generation, among other methods. When completed, more than 40 new buildings will meet or exceed U.S. Green Building Council's Leadership in Energy and Environmental Design (LEED) certification standards.

LACCD's approach to implementing its renewable energy goals has been especially innovative. A private-sector third-party owns, operates, and maintains the renewable energy systems, selling the electricity back to the institution through power purchase agreements (PPAs). By implementing various clean energy technologies, LAACD expects immediate savings of $3 million per year, with the prospect of no energy bill at all. When LACCD buys out the PPAs in a few years, the savings could reach $10 million per year. Furthermore, LACCD has installed energy-efficient equipment in all buildings, using energy performance contracts that pay for themselves through future savings and require no up-front costs.[20]

As these examples illustrate, leaders may commit to achieving climate neutrality without knowing exactly the path their institutions will travel to achieve it. Inevitably, they will need to deal with variations on age-old questions. What does it cost? What is the business case for sustainability?

How do you bring reluctant trustees and other stakeholders on board? Not having all the answers but knowing "what ships are built for," sustainability leaders in higher education have recognized the need to act now on the moral imperative that defines our era.

Higher Education Associations Sustainability Consortium

ACUPCC is collaborating with the Higher Education Associations Sustainability Consortium (HEASC), U.S. Conference of Mayors, Clinton Climate Initiative, and other organizations to facilitate, synergize, and expand its efforts beyond the campus. HEASC consists of 15 higher education associations that have coalesced around the issue of global climate change, recognizing the preeminent role that higher education needs to assume.[21] By providing leadership and disseminating information throughout its membership networks, HEASC has become an important forum for grappling with difficult questions and discussing possible solutions.

HEASC organizations are integrating sustainability into their overall strategic plans and future directions, redesigning their conferences, increasing educational resources, offering sustainability workshops and tracks at conferences, and publishing articles and books. They are collaborating in new and more effective ways to streamline the implementation of processes and projects. For example, APPA has worked with a group of sustainability experts to publish an ACUPCC implementation guide that complements and augments the original guide. The National Association of College and University Business Officers (NACUBO) has convened a sustainability financing advisory council of CFOs who are working to develop innovative financing approaches. The Society for College and University Planning (SCUP) offers annual Campus Sustainability Day Webcasts viewed by thousands of people on hundreds of campuses. In addition, HEASC has launched a National Fellows program to encourage dialogue and leverage efforts among individuals and higher education institutions throughout the country.

The Millennial Generation: Student Leadership in the Sustainability Movement

Building the next generation of leadership is, of course, the key to a sustainable future. Students at many colleges and universities are taking matters into their own hands, becoming the driving force behind campus sustainability initiatives. In the words of *USA Today*, "a youthquake of activism is hitting college campuses as students—armed with cellphones, lots of contacts, and political savvy—tackle global warming."[22] Students across the United States are organizing enthusiastically to create a clean energy future. They are educating themselves, peers, administrators, and members of their communities about the challenges of global warming and ways to mitigate its impact and adapt to the changing climate. They represent a broad spectrum of political ideologies, academic disciplines, and religious beliefs, as *Business Week* notes, ranging from "the 3,000-member Engineers for a Sustainable World to the Evangelical Youth Climate Initiative to Net Impact, a green business school network with 130 chapters."[23]

"Getting the entire world on board to make the kind of dramatic changes we need is completely unprecedented, and with that comes enormous opportunity and a need for innovation not only in technology but the way we see ourselves as global citizens," remarks Jessy Tolkan, a young climate action leader. More pragmatic than cynical, millennial student activists are focused on concrete change. As Cornell University student Carlos Rymer puts it, "Once students feel that they can create change, they are ready to work to make a particular project or campaign a reality."[24]

In addition, millennial students are willing to open their own pocketbooks to bring about change. Students at dozens of institutions have proposed and approved plans to impose annual student fees on themselves to pay for the purchase of alternative energy and reduce their institutions' reliance on fossil fuels.[25]

Billy Parish is an outstanding example of how students have responded to the challenge of climate change. As a Yale University student, he traveled in 2002 to the source of the Ganges River in northern India, where he witnessed the impact of global warming. He spoke with scientists studying the glaciers and realized that this river, the holiest in India and the source of drinking and farming water for 450 million people, was in danger of drying up.

Transformed by this experience, Parish decided that his work to combat climate change should concentrate on changing American attitudes and behaviors, given that the United States is one of the largest sources of greenhouse gases. Returning home, he dropped out of Yale and launched the Energy Action Coalition, a nonprofit dedicated to working with students to mobilize and create a "clean, efficient, just and renewable energy future." Energy Action now includes 48 organizations in the United States and Canada.[26] Students involved with the Campus Climate Challenge, a project of Energy Action, work on an assortment of projects to cool the planet at 1,000 North American colleges and universities.

In November 2007, 6,000 student leaders and activists gathered at the University of Maryland, College Park, and on Capitol Hill for Power Shift 2007, organized by Energy Action to call for a clean energy future. Their ambitious agenda included putting a halt to coal use, reducing the country's energy use by 20 percent over the next eight years, and putting the United States on course to cut greenhouse gas emissions 80 percent by 2050.[27] In a biodiesel bus with solar panels, students drove down K Street toward the U.S. Capitol, joining hundreds of their peers to testify before Congress and lobby their elected representatives. "Global warming, environmental injustices, and social injustices are so closely tied together that you can't separate one from another," says Katelyn McCormick, one of the students who testified at a special congressional hearing chaired by Rep. Ed Markey (D-MA). "I definitely have found my passion and plan to make this part of my life."[28] Power Shift participants and those they inspired continue their work on campuses and in communities across the country.

Focus the Nation

The ongoing commitment to spreading the word about global warming fueled what was among the country's largest teach-ins in January 2008. Called "Focus the Nation," this nationwide undertaking involved about 1,800 colleges and other groups. In an effort to move beyond "preaching to the green choir," it sought to reach out to students who might not be aware of climate change issues and their impact. "We're talking about the possibility of losing one out of every two creatures on the planet," pointed out Eban Goodstein, an economics professor at Lewis and Clark College who came up with the idea for the event. "If you're a smart and aware young person, you hear these things and think, Wow, my future is at stake."

Faculty members from a wide range of disciplines—from chemistry to costume design—agreed to incorporate climate change issues into their classes. "It's about infusing sustainability into the curriculum of higher education, so students can graduate prepared to deal with the world they have been handed," said Lindsey Clark, a recent graduate who helped to organize events at the University of Utah. Eighty faculty members agreed to participate in the teach-in there, and Governor Jon M. Huntsman Jr. and four city mayors took part in a panel discussion.

Elsewhere, Glendale Community College in Arizona and the University of Kentucky served "low carbon" meals all week. Organizers at Fordham University put up a mock wind farm to show people that, in the words of philosophy professor Jude Jones, "solutions are close at hand." Western Carolina University hosted a recycled fashion show, and in a more dramatic gesture, a student at the University of California, San Diego dressed as a polar bear and sat in a mock electric chair to underscore the impact of climate change on the species' habitat.[29]

Clinton Global Initiative University

Another large-scale gathering of young sustainability activists took place in March 2008, when 700 students from 40 states and 15 countries met for three days at Tulane University to explore how to put their communities on a path toward a better future. Sponsored by the Clinton Foundation, the Clinton Global Initiative University (CGI U) featured sessions and panels on global health, human rights and peace, poverty alleviation, and energy and climate change issues. "A lot of people know they want to do something about climate change or global health," observed Robert Harrison, chief executive officer of the Clinton Global Initiative. "We're here to work on refining those commitments and provide a marketplace where people who have ideas and potential solutions to global challenges can come together and commit to action."[30] Participants made personal commitments to follow through when they returned to their campuses and communities.

Among the commitments announced by former President Bill Clinton was a pledge by a Morehouse College student group to raise funds to install one million energy-efficient light bulbs over four years in low-income households in Atlanta. President Scott Cowan of Tulane University committed his institution to creating a network of neighborhood-based health centers throughout New Orleans for residents without health insurance. In October 2008, CGI U announced the first round of Outstanding Commitment awards. Forty-five students and their organizations received awards totaling $150,000. Two university awards went to a partnership between Brown University in Providence, Rhode Island, and Dillard University in New Orleans and to the College of Menominee Nation in Keshena, Wisconsin.[31]

In light of the devastation caused by Hurricane Katrina and the distance that still needs to be traveled before New Orleans fully recovers, it is especially appropriate that the inaugural Clinton Global Initiative University convened in the Crescent City. If nothing else, the epic struggle of New Orleans to get back on its feet highlights the significance of civil society and the need to cultivate effective leadership skills at every level. The role of civil society and its leaders will surely grow in importance as communities around the world confront the multiple crises spawned by peak oil, climate change, and the like. Now more than ever, young people need to learn not just how to make a living but how to live. Colleges and universities must be part of this effort if our children are to be properly prepared for the days ahead. This is no time for ships to stay in the harbor.

Notes

1.   William Sullivan, "Vocation: Where Liberal and Professional Education Meet," paper presented at the Fourth Annual Conversation on the Liberal Arts, Institute for the Liberal Arts at Westmont College, February 2004. www.westmont.edu/institute/pages/2004_program/Papers04/Sullivan.pdf (accessed August 6, 2008).

2.   National Leadership Council for Liberal Education and America's Promise, *College Learning for the New Global Century* (Washington, D.C.: Association of American College and Universities, 2007). www.aacu.org/leap/documents/GlobalCentury_final.pdf (accessed August 11, 2008); Parker J. Palmer, "A New Professional: The Aims of Education Revisited," *Change Magazine* 39, no. 6 (November/December 2007). www.carnegiefoundation.org/change/sub.asp?key=98&subkey=2455 (accessed August 11, 2008).

3.   Ellen Condiffe Lagemann, "The Challenge of Liberal Education: Past, Present, and Future," *Liberal Education* (Spring 2003): 6–13. www.aacu.org/liberaleducation/le-sp03/le-sp03feature.cfm (accessed August 6, 2008).

4.   William M. Sullivan and Matthew S. Rosin, *A New Agenda for Higher Education: Shaping a Life of the Mind for Practice* (San Francisco: Jossey-Bass, 2008).

5.   Gary L. Neilson and Bruce A. Pasternack, "The Cat That Came Back," *Strategy + Business Resilience Report*, August 17, 2005, p. 6. www.strategy-business.com/media/file/resilience-08-17-05.pdf (accessed August 8, 2009); Barry K. Spiker, "The Business of Sustainability—Part 2," Million Ready Minds, June 30, 2008. www.millionreadyminds.org/2008/06/business-of-sustainability-part-2.html (accessed September 14, 2008).

6.   Jon L. Wergin, "Leadership in Place," *The Department Chair* 14, no. 4 (Spring 2004): 2. www.acenet.edu/resources/chairs/docs/Wergin_LeadershipFM.pdf (accessed August 8, 2008).

7. Helen Astin and Alexander Astin, *Leadership Reconsidered: Engaging Higher Education in Social Change* (Battle Creek, MI: W. K. Kellogg Foundation, 2000), pp. viii, 2.

8. Larry A. Braskamp and Jon F. Wergin, "Inside-Out Leadership," *Liberal Education* 94, no. 1 (Winter 2008): 33.

9. Unity College, "Sustainability Progress at Unity College." http://www.unity.edu/EnvResources/Sustainability/ProgressAtUnity.aspx (accessed November 23, 2008); Mitchell Thomashow, personal communication, November 17, 2008.

10. Mitchell Thomashow, *Ecological Identity: Becoming a Reflective Environmentalist* (Cambridge, MA: MIT Press, 1996), p. 105.

11. Peter Senge et. al., *The Necessary Revolution: How Individuals and Organizations Are Working Together to Create a Sustainable World* (New York: Doubleday, 2008), p. 5.

12. Nikola Acutt, "The Qualities of a Sustainable Leader" GreenBiz.com, July 7, 2008. www.greenbiz.com/column/2008/07/07/qualities-a-sustainable-leader (accessed August 9, 2008).

13. See Appendix 1 for the full text of the ACUPCC and its signatories.

14. Quoted in "A Call for Climate Leadership: Progress and Opportunities in Addressing the Defining Challenge of our Times," *American College & University Presidents Climate Commitment*. www.presidentsclimatecommitment.org/pdf/climate_leadership.pdf (accessed August 27, 2008).

15. Juliet Eilperin, "Maine College Makes Green Pledge," *Washington Post*, October 10, 2006. www.washingtonpost.com/wp-dyn/content/article/2006/10/09/AR2006100901096.html (accessed August 27, 2008); College of the Atlantic, "COA Achieves Carbon Neutrality," December 19, 2007. www.coa.edu/html/pressreleases_402.htm (accessed August 27, 2008).

16. "15 Green Colleges and Universities," *Grist*, August 10, 2007, www.grist.org/news/maindish/2007/08/10/colleges (accessed August 27, 2008); Brian Wingfield, "America's Greenest Colleges," *Forbes*, May 2, 2008. www.forbes.com/2008/05/02/college-harvard-uvm-biz-energy-cx_bw_0502greenu.html (accessed October 11, 2008); Kristin Underwood, "Green College Rankings Now Available from the Princeton Review," *TreeHugger*, August 1, 2008. www.treehugger.com/files/2008/08/green-college-rankings-by-princeton-review.php (accessed October 21, 2008).

17. University of Minnesota at Morris, "Biofuels and Bioproducts Innovative Laboratory." www1.umn.edu/iree/bil (accessed August 27, 2008).

18. University of Minnesota at Morris, "Wind Turbine for Researching and Demonstrating Renewable Hydrogen Production to Be Commissioned," April 12, 2005. www.morris.umn.edu/ummnews/View.php?itemID=650 (accessed August 27, 2008).

19. University of Minnesota at Morris, "Green Fact Sheet." www.morris.umn.edu/alumni/universityRelations/GreenCampusFacts.pdf (accessed August 27, 2008).

20. Los Angeles Community College District, "LACCD is Building Green." www.laccdbuildsgreen.org/building_green_laccd_is_building_green.php; "Bond Construction Program." www.laccdbuildsgreen.org/_pdfs/laccd_is_building_green/Prop%20A-AA%20-%20GREEN%20Buildings%20Program%20-%20Fact%20Sheet%20-May%202008.pdf (accessed August 27, 2008); Larry Eisenberg, Los Angeles Community College District, personal communication, June 22, 2008.

21. See Appendix 3 for a complete list of HEASC members.

22. Daniel Horgan, "College Students Seeing Green as the Way to Go," *USA Today*, March 12, 2008. www.usatoday.com/news/education/2008-03-12-focus-the-nation_N.htm (accessed August 27, 2008).

23. Heather Green, "The Greening of America's Campuses," *BusinessWeek*, April 9, 2007. www.businessweek.com/magazine/content/07_15/b4029071.htm (accessed August 27, 2008).

24. Andrew C. Revkin, "Whose Climate Is It, Anyway?" *New York Times*, November 2, 2007. http://dotearth.blogs.nytimes.com/2007/11/02/whose-climate-is-it-anyway (accessed August 27, 2008); Tom Robinson, "Student Empowerment: Carlos Rymer, Cornell University," *Greentree Gazette*, July 2008, p. 26.

25. Green, "Greening of America's Campuses"; Elia Powers, "Cents and Sustainability," *Inside Higher Ed*, May 18, 2008. www.insidehighered.com/news/2007/05/18/fees (accessed September 26, 2008).

26. Daniel Parr, "Billy Parish Keynote Address," *Student Conservation Association*. www.thesca.org/EarthVision_Dailies/EarthVision_Dailies/Billy_Parish_Keynote_Address (accessed August 27, 2008); Energy Action Coalition. http://energyactioncoalition.org (August 27, 2008).

27. Revkin, "Whose Climate Is It, Anyway?"

28. Horgan, "College Students Seeing Green."

29. Beckie Supiano, "Campuses Nationwide Take Creative Approaches to Climate-Change Event," *Chronicle of Higher Education*, February 1, 2008. http://chronicle.com/daily/2008/02/1484n.htm (accessed November 12, 2008); and Julia Silverman, "Hundreds of Profs Hold Green 'Teach-In'," *San Francisco Chronicle*, January 31, 2008. www.sfgate.com/cgi-bin/article.cgi?f=/n/a/2008/01/31/national/a173858S05.DTL (accessed November 13, 2008).

30. Elia Powers, "Calling All Students: Bill Clinton Wants You (in New Orleans)," *Inside Higher Ed*, February 14, 2008. www.insidehighered.com/news/2008/02/14/clinton (accessed August 27, 2008).

31. Clinton Global Initiative University, "President Clinton Announces Student and University 'Commitments to Action' on Pressing Global Issues," March 15, 2008. http://www.clintonglobalinitiative.org/NETCOMMUNITY/Page.aspx?pid=2106&srcid=1878; "Clinton Global Initiative Announces Student and University Winners of CGI U Outstanding Commitment Award", October 9, 2008, www.clintonglobalinitiative.org/NETCOMMUNITY/Page.aspx?pid=2979&srcid=2356.

"Work for something because it is good, not just because it stands a chance to succeed."

—**Vaclav Havel,** *Disturbing the Peace,* 1991

3

GAINING A COMPETITIVE EDGE AND BUILDING VALUE

Colleges and universities that ignore sustainability or treat it as one more thing to stir into the mix, rather than an approach that transforms everything, will find it increasingly difficult to compete. There are compelling reasons why financial analysts and management consultants view sustainability factors as important indicators of organizational quality and effectiveness. "They show that companies tend to be more strategic, nimble, and better equipped to compete in the complex, high-velocity global environment," says Matthew J. Kiernan, CEO of Innovest Strategic Values, an international research and advisory firm.[1] The same argument applies to higher education.

Companies traditionally gain competitive advantage by lowering costs or differentiating products. As markets go global, however, it is becoming more difficult to secure and maintain competitive advantages. In this new landscape, creativity and innovation will be the keys to success and human capital the most significant resource. The challenges of the 21st century, in the words of Daniel Pink, require "a whole new mind." As we move from a postindustrial economy that generates wealth through the production of information to a creativity economy that turns information into knowledge, connecting the dots in new ways rather than just producing the dots will yield the highest rewards. In this new economy, "high concept and high touch" will be the order of the day, and "inventive, empathetic, big-picture capabilities" will become essential.[2]

In higher education, as in the corporate world, sustainability provides a source of hope and opportunity for facilitating institutional renewal and ensuring an organization's future. Growing out of a deepening awareness that the economy, society, and environment are deeply intertwined, sustainability fosters a culture of innovation, resourcefulness, and holistic thinking. It provides a way to bring fresh thinking to bear on old problems and identifies new solutions that can move an organization forward. In a rapidly changing, increasingly complex, and more interconnected world, as Daniel Esty and Andrew Winston maintain, sustainability strategy will "emerge as a critical point of competitive differentiation."[3]

Intangible Assets and Sustainability

Corporations readily recognize the intangible value of their products and services and pour millions of dollars into advertising, public relations, and branding in an effort to craft and communicate messages that increase their value even further. As Baruch Lev explains, an intangible asset "is a source of future benefits" that "lack a physical embodiment." Lev's research indicates that intangible assets such as intellectual property, goodwill, and brand recognition make up roughly three-quarters of the value of publicly held corporations, an assessment in line with other studies.[4]

Increasingly, corporations are also realizing that environmental sustainability and social responsibility are crucial variables in the intangible assets equation. Sometimes this realization occurs in the form of a rude awakening. Sony, for example, lost $85 million in 2001 when illegal cadmium was found in PlayStation cables purchased from outside suppliers. Not only did Sony lose ground in the highly competitive market of video gaming, but its overall corporate reputation suffered serious damage. In response, Sony established a new system for managing its global supply chain to ensure regulatory legal compliance and rebuild its position in the market. Risk management and cost avoidance, however, are not the only reasons why corporations are embracing the principles of sustainability and social responsibility. As Michael Porter and Mark Kramer observe, they can be transformed into a rich "source of opportunity, innovation, and competitive advantage."[5]

The significance of this paradigm shift is hard to overstate. Management guru Jim Collins has underscored the importance of "conscious choice" and a "culture of discipline" in organizations that want to move from "good to great." It is clear that environmental sustainability and corporate social responsibility are conscious choices that must be woven into an organization's culture of discipline if it hopes to make this move to the next level successfully. Doing so will lead to new markets, new ways to meet customer demands, and new sources of brand equity. In the words of Jeffrey Immelt, the CEO of General Electric, "To be a great company, you have to be a good company."[6]

Of course, corporations have not arrived at this understanding without external pressure. They recognize that their success depends on how the public perceives their ethical and environmental practices. With growing effectiveness and alacrity, nonprofits and concerned citizens scrutinize corporations' practices and mobilize to spread the word and demand accountability for perceived or real transgressions. The extent to which external stakeholders now seek to hold companies accountable for social and environmental issues is one of the most remarkable features of contemporary society, a development on par with the emergence in the early 20th century of the progressive reform movement and muckraking journalism. Corporations have come under a microscope and have been left little choice but to engage with a broad range of stakeholders and the larger community to protect their reputations and ability to do business.[7]

Intangible values are inherently difficult to quantify, and no calculation can be absolutely precise. Some approximate numbers, however, can be factored into an analysis. How much does it cost to replace a professor who decides to transfer to a different institution because of its strong and active sustainability commitment? How much does it cost for a college to recruit a top student? What additional tuition income does a college receive from a new sustainability-oriented degree? How much is it worth to have an employee productivity gain of 4 to 6 percent because of the increased comfort of working in a green building?

Questions that are more difficult to quantify abound. What is the importance of an institution's commitment when it applies for research funding? What is the value of a robust sustainability program for an institution's brand? How does this affect fund raising among alumni who are concerned about the consequences of climate change for their children and grandchildren? What is the impact on an institution's value proposition when it maintains the status quo while its competition rolls out their sustainability initiatives? How will these issues grow in importance in the next decade and thereafter? How does the sense of an institution on the move influence the job satisfaction of faculty, administration, and staff? And how does it enhance the students' learning experience? What will be the financial result of being ahead of the regulatory curve? In the era of a strong national desire for energy independence, how does a commitment to clean on-site generation affect school pride? What is the value of strengthening students' job prospects and career paths so that they may prosper and become part of the solution in our warmer future?

Branding and Marketing

A company's brand has become the most significant overall corporate asset. Recent studies indicate that it accounts on average for about one-third of a company's total market value.[8] The increasing importance of branding can also be seen in the higher education sector. For the vast majority of colleges and universities that do not have gold-plated brands and huge endowments like the Ivies, developing an identity that differentiates the institution from its competitors is essential.[9] With limited resources, these colleges and universities must be sure that they invest their branding and marketing dollars wisely. How can sustainability provide a branding strategy that builds value?

Just as sustainability has the potential to stimulate more effective operations and more creative problem solving, it can spark a new way of thinking about branding. Sustainability, to be effective, has to be more than a tagline and a logo. Every decision made in an organization that commits to sustainability becomes a branding decision. Stakeholders must become co-creators rather than passive spectators, and the brand story must be authentic. Most important, in the words of Raphael Bemporad and Mitch Baranowski, sustainable brands "deliver ideas, experiences, and opportunities to address the issues that matter most to us."[10]

What does this new approach to branding mean for higher education? For most institutions, particularly during difficult economic times, the primary challenge is developing an adequate revenue stream while containing costs to the extent possible. Yield, retention, and fund raising become critical metrics in this context. Most colleges and universities outside the first tier have plenty of room for improvement in these three areas. Success in strengthening yield, retention, and fund raising all depend on increasing the value proposition of the institution. This, in turn, depends on telling a persuasive story about why the college or university matters and getting this story out to the target audiences—in this case, students, their parents, alumni, and donors.

Sustainability, to be effective, has to be more than a tagline and a logo. Every decision an organization makes becomes a branding decision. Stakeholders must become co-creators rather than passive spectators, and the brand story must be authentic.

If branding and marketing efforts are successful, students will want to come to the college or university, they will want to stay there, their parents will be satisfied that the experience is worth the tuition, alumni will value their degrees and maintain ties with the institution, and donors will want to give money. If not, then in all likelihood the college or university will endure a bleak future trying to make do in an increasingly competitive world with only the resources it has at hand. Of course, things are never quite so simple, but this admittedly rough summary captures the essence of the dynamic.

The key to success, then, is making the case for distinctiveness—that is, articulating clearly and convincingly how an institution meets a particular demand in the higher education marketplace in a way that few others do. Although hundreds of books and articles have been written on this topic and each year dozens of conference sessions address it, there is no real mystery when it comes to branding in higher education. In almost every case, the three most significant assets that any college or university has to carve out a successful niche in the marketplace are place, academic program mix, and approach to teaching and learning.

Let's assume, for the sake of argument, that the college or university in question has exceptional advantages in each of these three areas. The campus is located in a community that has received wide recognition for its quality of life, perhaps due to its unique natural environment, its cultural vibrancy, or its historical character. The institution offers a distinctive mix of professional and liberal academic programs that sets it apart from traditional liberal arts colleges and offers cutting-edge programs in such increasingly popular areas as communications, environmental sciences, and socially responsible entrepreneurship. And, finally, the faculty has a vigorous commitment to and solid experience with hands-on, collaborative teaching and learning that engage students from the outset and focus them on solving real-world problems, making it possible for the college to claim that it is helping to create a path-breaking "third way" in undergraduate education.

These are all crucial competitive advantages, and any college or university would be happy to have them in its toolbox. To leverage these strengths fully, however, the institution needs to identify the interconnections among the three components of place, academic program mix, and approach to teaching and learning and then package them in a coherent message. Only in this way will a college or university be able to capture the attention of a world overwhelmed with messages about being the best and the biggest and the newest. To break through the static and get its message heard, in other words, it needs to find a way to generate a whole that is more than the sum of these parts.

The trick, of course, is creating new synergies among what are more often than not constant, longstanding components. The value of sustainability, from this perspective, is that it offers one of the most powerful means currently available to weave together in new ways place, academic program mix, and approach to teaching and learning. It accomplishes this by abandoning the notion of education as a commodity, emphasizing relationships, shared values, and common purpose, and focusing on the whole person and allowing stakeholders to make a difference in the world around them.

To pick just one example, Green Mountain College has made "Cow Power" the hallmark of its brand identity. Using a dash of humor, it has taken one of its major weaknesses—its relatively isolated rural setting—and turned it into a distinctive strength. Clearly, far more than the use of methane released from manure to generate electricity is involved here. By staking a claim to being the first campus in the nation to derive its electricity from cows, the college has underscored its location in a progressive, environmentally aware state that values its natural surroundings.[11]

"Cow Power" not only resonates with the college's location in the Green Mountains. It also highlights a commitment to reducing the environmental footprint, offering an innovative interdisciplinary program that blends the liberal arts and professional studies in the service of a more sustainable future, and providing students with a living laboratory that includes a farm, thus connecting learning inside the classroom with learning outside of it.

Leveraging the powerful synergies generated by this strategy, Green Mountain College under the leadership of President John Brennan underwent one of the great turnarounds in higher education. It has produced five consecutive budget surpluses, a 35 percent increase in student enrollment, and several successful online master's degree programs (including an MBA in sustainable business). It has also completed the largest capital campaign in its history. These are impressive results for an institution that was on the brink of financial ruin a few years ago.[12]

A college or university can make its mark if it commits to an authentic and comprehensive sustainability effort that involves curriculum and research, campus operations, and community outreach. But it needs to be bold, or the commitment won't matter. Halfhearted measures won't work. By taking on one of the greatest problems the world currently faces and coming up with pragmatic solutions, the college or university can not only dramatically increase its value proposition. It can also make a positive and enduring contribution to the betterment of all. In short, it can provide an education that matters.

Colleges and universities have a once-in-a-generation opportunity to take advantage of their accumulated intellectual, social, and cultural capital in a way that is grounded in their location, academic program mix, and approach to teaching and learning. By having the vision and courage to do so, they will provide the kind of leadership that will reinvent higher education and help transform the quality of life on our planet in the age of climate change. Of course, the devil is in the details. Each college and university needs to transform itself in an authentic, substantive way that is true to its past at the same time it assures the institution will matter in the future.

What do we mean by "reinvent"? In part, we mean a revitalized sense of civic mission and a renewed commitment to undergraduate teaching and learning. We mean lowering the walls among the various campus silos, rewiring the campus, and turning up the heat by providing a sense of coherence and purpose that has been all too lacking in contemporary higher education. Ernest Boyer's vision of the "New American College"—one that combines liberal and professional learning with a strong emphasis on experiential learning and civic engagement—seems especially appropriate for the age of climate change.[13] This marriage of pragmatism and idealism equips undergraduates with the ability to solve real-world problems and become effective citizens and leaders.

Although closely related, branding is one thing and marketing another. How should one communicate the message of climate protection and sustainability? Arizona State University (ASU) has emerged as one of the strongest and most dynamic voices in the national sustainability movement by pursuing many aspects of the "boldly sustainable" strategy. The ASU example demonstrates, in particular, the importance of presidential leadership and commitment. ASU announced in 2006, with much fanfare, the establishment of the first school of sustainability in the United States, a move featured prominently in the national press and higher education publications.[14] At the same time, ASU billed itself as "The New American

University," proclaiming that it was committed to being "a university that is responsible for the economic, social, and cultural vitality of our region." It defined "The New American University" as

> an institution that measures its academic quality by the education its graduates have received rather than by the academic credentials of its incoming freshman class; one whose researchers, while pursuing their scholarly interests, also consider the public good; one whose students, faculty, and staff transcend the concept of community service to accept responsibility for the economic, social, cultural, and environmental vitality of the communities they serve.[15]

One of the marketing campaign's brochures, called "Building a Sustainable Campus," leaves little doubt about President Crow's strong backing and the audaciousness of his vision. "The ideal of sustainability is much more than an academic concept to be researched and taught," he declares. "It is an all-encompassing philosophy, a way of life that must be emulated to be successfully promoted." Reinforcing the message is this statement:

> [ASU] has embarked on a university-wide sustainability initiative that seeks to blur the line between operations, academics, and research. While we have long sought to develop a 'sustainable campus,' we are reevaluating our accomplishments; building on our strengths, using the campus and surrounding region as a living laboratory; and developing a new, innovative trajectory.[16]

Robert Sevier, a pioneer in higher education marketing, reminds us that when it comes to branding and marketing, making "a promise that matters" is the first step.[17] Making it in a way that gets heard is the second step. To accomplish this, as ASU clearly understands, the institution needs to take a stand and claim the territory, even as it recognizes what still needs to be accomplished.

Having driven the stake in the sand, ensuring that the effort continues to gain momentum and becomes self sustaining is crucial. Unfortunately, too many efforts to convey the message of sustainability drop the ball at this point by raising the specter of apocalyptic consequences if the message is not heeded. Nothing is guaranteed to turn off one's target audience faster than adopting this approach. As recent research shows, efforts to mobilize support for climate protection, energy efficiency, and sustainability must move beyond the traditional doom-and-gloom approach of the environmental movement. For "boldly sustainable" to be an effective marketing strategy, in other words, it must stress hope and opportunity rather than fear and despair.[18]

The reason for this approach is not hard to find. If the problem is unsolvable and our fate is sealed, if there is no hope and no opportunity, then why bother with a college degree? At the heart of education is the belief that it is possible to better one's life and make a positive difference in the world and that acquiring new knowledge and skills provide the critical tools to do so. Thus, one must tell a hopeful story of opportunity, avoiding the compulsion to emphasize what has gone wrong.

Striking the right tone, then, is absolutely necessary. In addition, there needs to be substance at the heart of the marketing effort. If branding is about making a promise that matters and marketing is about communicating this promise effectively, then "living one's promise" (as Sevier puts it) is what distinguishes a credible effort from greenwashing.

Besides being bold, framing the sustainability story in terms of hope and opportunity, and communicating through consistent actions, building consensus among the internal stakeholders is key to a successful branding and marketing campaign. As Joel Makower points out, "They're the first group that needs assurance that any claims you make hold water and the first to become cynical if they find out otherwise." By bringing the various campus constituencies into the process in a way that allows them to be co-creators, a sense of shared purpose and common language can be forged.[19] One advantage of the American College and University Presidents Climate Commitment is that it provides a focus for the campus sustainability conversation and an excellent opportunity for a college or university president to put together a task force to make a recommendation about whether the institution should become a signatory. If it does, then the same or a similar task force will need to develop and implement a plan of action. It is hard to imagine a better process for building consensus on campus.

Finally, persuading the target audiences that sustainability is a core attribute of the college or university's brand identity requires being able to demonstrate bottom-line results. Developing metrics, establishing benchmarks, measuring progress, and sharing this information in regular reports make it clear that the institution is serious about its commitment and building value as a result. A consistent, transparent effort along these lines will build stakeholder trust and loyalty and reap a continuing return on investment for an institution's reputational endowment.

MAKING A CREDIBLE SUSTAINABILITY EFFORT

According to Ann Rappaport and Sarah Hammond Creighton, a credible sustainability effort includes at least eight main characteristics:

(1) A campus master plan that considers sustainability
(2) Funding for the implementation and monitoring of energy efficiency systems
(3) Standards for new construction and extensive retrofitting of old lighting
(4) A campus-wide recycling program
(5) Integration of climate change, energy, and sustainability issues across the curriculum
(6) Development of alternative transportation
(7) Establishment of a baseline of the institution's greenhouse gas emissions
(8) Monitoring for improvements[20]

Any plan that contains these elements, we believe, will have an excellent chance of securing the trust of campus and community stakeholders and engaging them in the process. Leave even one out, however, and you run the risk of being accused of greenwashing. Given the highly skeptical and even cynical nature of the public these days, the risk simply is not worth it.[21] Once a college or university heads down the sustainability road, it had better be ready to demonstrate progress on all of these fronts. Otherwise, the blowback can cause the kind of damage to an institution's reputation that can take months and even years to restore. If you doubt this, ask anyone in the Cornell University administration about the "Redbud Controversy," a dispute over replacing a copse of rather ordinary trees with a parking lot that threw the university into an uproar that took two presidencies to tamp down.[22]

At a time when the rising cost of tuition and demands for accountability have brought higher education under public fire, the importance of such results is obvious.

Recruitment, Retention, and Productivity

Currently, 30 to 40 percent of the workers in the United States are knowledge workers, and these numbers are projected to grow rapidly. There is a tremendous demand, consequently, for creativity, innovation, big picture thinking, powerful storytelling, and real results.[23] As colleges and universities assume a central role in the drive to compete in the new global economy, they are becoming subject to the same external pressures and trends as corporations. What does this shift in the landscape mean for higher education? Two specific issues—recruitment and retention of students, faculty, and staff and productivity—highlight the extent to which human capital development has become essential to a healthy economic future and point to ways in which colleges and universities need to rethink their 21st-century strategic priorities.

It is not surprising that today's college students worry about making ends meet financially and performing well academically. But, according to a recent survey of entering freshmen, their "number one social concern" is not getting a job but rather protecting the environment. "Kids are becoming the green movement's stealth weapon," says the *Wall Street Journal*, "pressuring their parents on everything from light bulbs to composting." When they head off to college, young people are bringing these concerns with them.[24]

The greening of the economy, of course, means that getting a job and becoming an environmentalist are not mutually exclusive priorities. By adopting the "boldly sustainable" strategy outlined here, a college or university has a tremendous opportunity to demonstrate how it prepares students to both meet the challenges of competing in a global knowledge economy and take advantage of its greening. As climate change and peak oil become major economic drivers, jobs will expand significantly in fields related to the environment, energy efficiency, and alternative energy. A recent report issued by the American Solar Energy Society found that renewable energy and energy-efficient industries were responsible for the creation of nearly 8.5 million jobs in 2006, including about 4.8 million indirect jobs such as accountants, computer analysts, and consultants. By 2030, according to the report, the number of direct and indirect jobs related to renewable energy and energy efficiency is expected to reach 40 million.[25]

In response, colleges and universities are offering new programs related to the emerging clean-energy economy to entice prospective students and prepare them for well-paying careers. They are also discovering that going green can boost student recruitment.[26] The sustainability mission statement of the University of Colorado at Colorado Springs says explicitly that it "actively pursues sustainability as a way to address the University's focus on increased student recruitment and retention." At Mills College in California, applications expressing interest in environmental studies and natural sciences jumped in response to the college's touting of its new green, energy-efficient science building. Since Warren Wilson College in North Carolina opened its EcoDorm in 2004, featuring a converted railroad tank car that collects storm water for the building, students have clamored for spots. The School of Business at Ithaca College saw its academic profile improve noticeably and enrollment rise from 589 students in fall 2004 to 704 in fall 2007 as it rolled out plans for and undertook construction of the first LEED Platinum business building in the world.[27]

There is also growing evidence that going green can have a positive impact on the recruitment and retention of staff and faculty. More than two-thirds of the students (70 percent) in a 2003 survey by GlobeScan disagreed that salary is more important than a company's social and environmental reputation when deciding which company to work for.[28] According to a 2007 Ipsos Mori survey, 81 percent of respondents in the United States said that they would prefer working for a company that "has a good reputation for environmental responsibility."[29]

It is not surprising, in light of this data, that greening the campus may have a positive impact on recruitment and retention. Ciannat Howett, director of the Office of Sustainability Initiatives at Emory University, suggests that a serious commitment to sustainability "can enhance recruitment and retention of the best and brightest students, faculty, staff." Alex Wilson agrees, pointing out that attracting "quality students, faculty, and staff can be a challenge for any college or university." "The quality of the space in which prospective students, faculty, and staff will be learning and working in," he says, "including such features as daylighting, views to the outdoors, and indoor air quality, can have a significant impact on drawing the best and keeping them there." Many younger staff and faculty, notes the United Kingdom's Higher Education Environmental Performance Improvement Project, "see good sustainable performance as a key feature of a good employer generally."[30]

This last point is particularly germane. As the Baby Boomers retire, the U.S. labor market is expected to tighten because the new generation of workers is much smaller than the one it is replacing. The Bureau of Labor Statistics is projecting a shortfall of 10 million workers in the United States by 2010.

In such a tight labor market, one observer notes, "employers will have to pull out all stops to continue to attract top talent." An effective way in which employers are seeking to set themselves apart from the pack is to market their companies to employees and prospects as green.[31] "Companies know that having an active sustainability policy acts as a differentiator, a competitive advantage," says Solitaire Townsend, managing director of Futerra, a sustainable development communications firm. "Graduates and new recruits expect a certain amount of sustainability, and if you are a bright individual with several offers of similar money, undoubtedly you will choose the company that is more socially responsible."[32]

Higher education is no exception to the demographic pressures set in motion by generational turnover. In 1987, 24 percent of the nation's faculty were 55 or older; this percentage jumped to more than 31 percent in 1998. In the University of North Carolina system, the percentage of tenured and tenure-track faculty in this same age category doubled over 20 years, from about 18 percent in 1983 to 35 percent in 2003.[33] The coming changing of the guard among faculty poses a profound challenge to higher education in recruiting the best and the brightest of those coming out of graduate programs and in bridging the gap between the belief systems of older and younger professors.

As Cathy Trower and Richard Chait show, new and late-career faculty members operate in very different "assumptive worlds." The older generation places great weight on prestige, career ambition, and competition. Younger faculty tend to emphasize quality of life, flexible work arrangements, and collaboration.[34] Sustainability might be a high priority for newly minted PhDs with their commitment to quality of life. But senior faculty may very well discount sustainability efforts, viewing them as falling outside the core mission of the college or university. How do administrators negotiate this potential generational conflict in a way that moves sustainability forward without alienating senior faculty who wield much of the power in the academic arena? Does a commitment to campus sustainability improve the ability to compete for the best professors, or will it drive some of them elsewhere? Much depends on how administrators frame the issues and engage the stakeholders.

In one crucial area of sustainability, there seems to be real potential for forging a strong consensus on campus: sustainable building design. While poorly designed and operated facilities can create serious health problems, a number of studies show that sustainable buildings can have a positive impact on occupants. A growing body of research and empirical evidence suggests that building occupants experience a higher satisfaction level, better health, and improved personal productivity in high-performance buildings. Lawrence Berkeley National Laboratory found in 2000 that improvements to indoor environments could lead to reductions in health-care costs and work losses from communicable respiratory diseases of 9 percent to 20 percent and from reduced allergies and asthma of 18 percent to 25 percent. According to this study, potential savings from health and productivity gains following the national implementation of indoor environmental quality improvements would range from $17 billion to $48 billion. A 2003 report issued by the Federal Energy Management Program reviewed several case studies that indicated sustainable design resulted in productivity increases of 6 percent to 16 percent. In addition, Carnegie Mellon University's Center for Building Performance program, Building Investment Decision Support (BIDS), analyzed more than 1,500 studies and concluded that better lighting, ventilation, and thermal control noticeably improved the well-being and productivity of occupants.[35]

What about the impact of green buildings on student learning? As with employee health and productivity, few studies have been carried out in higher education specifically. But findings in the K–12 sector provide reason to believe that the positive benefits could be substantial. In fall 2005 Turner Construction released a survey of 665 executives in the building sector. Of those involved with green schools, more than 70 percent reported that these new facilities reduced student absenteeism and improved student performance. A large number of school-specific studies affirm these findings. A Washington State report, for example, estimated a 15 percent reduction in absenteeism and a 5 percent increase in student test scores. The Third Creek Elementary School in Statesville, North Carolina, the country's first LEED Gold K–12 school, produced positive results as well. As Gregory Kats notes, "documented student test scores before and after the move provide compelling evidence that learning and test scores improve in greener, healthier buildings."[36]

Given the many variables and the complexity of their causal relationship, the above results may not be conclusive. Since labor makes up by far the biggest chunk of an organization's operating expenses, however, any small increase in employees' productivity can add up to serious savings. Some of the individual effects might be quite subtle, but the cumulative benefits could be significant. In any event, research on faculty, staff, and student performance, health, and productivity should continue. The initial results are intriguing, but we need to know more about the impact of the "soft" benefits on the bottom line.[37]

Rankings and Awards

Perhaps the clearest indication of sustainability's growing brand value in the higher education market is the proliferation of green campus rankings and other forms of recognition for sustainability efforts. Increasingly, colleges and universities are scrutinized, judged, rated, ranked, and sometimes rewarded on their environmental record and stewardship. Notably, the *Princeton Review* added a section on green campuses for the first time in its 2008 edition, and *Peterson's* is following suit.[38]

Inevitably, controversies arise regarding methodologies and why one university ranks high and another ranks low (or doesn't rank at all).

Skeptics question the worth of such exercises and argue, not unreasonably, that they take valuable time away from the core responsibilities of already overstretched sustainability coordinators, who often are assigned the task of completing these surveys. Regardless, the rankings are likely to only grow in influence. Already they are attracting the attention of major media outlets such as *Forbes* and *USA Today*.[39] *Grist* jumped into the ring in August 2007, recognizing "15 Green Colleges and Universities." *Kiwi* magazine released its first "Green College Report" one month later, and the Sierra Club named its top 10 soon after.[40]

More specialized assessments have also entered the public arena. Perhaps the best known is *Beyond Grey Pinstripes*, a project of the Aspen Institute Center for Business Education, which produces a "biennial survey and alternative ranking of business schools." Its mission is to "spotlight innovative full-time MBA programs that are integrating issues of social and environmental stewardship into curricula and research." Established in 1998, it is now used by tens of thousands of students, academics, and corporations. According to *Time* magazine, universities promote their placement in *Beyond Grey Pinstripes* along with their *U.S. News and World Report* rankings.[41] Another assessment rapidly growing in influence is the *College Sustainability Report Card*, published by the Sustainable Endowments Institute. This project evaluates campus operations and endowment investments and assesses the 200 public and private universities with the largest endowments, ranging from $230 million to nearly $35 billion.[42]

Both the Association for the Advancement of Sustainability in Higher Education (AASHE) and U.S. Environmental Protection Agency (EPA) have established awards that seek to publicize, encourage, and recognize campus leadership in sustainability and alternative energy. AASHE recognizes institutions and students with its four Campus Sustainability Leadership Awards for "greatest overall commitment to sustainability as demonstrated in their governance and administration, curriculum and research, operations, campus culture, and community outreach" and a Student Sustainability Leadership Award for demonstration of exceptional leadership in promoting campus sustainability.[43]

EPA's Green Power Partnership (GPP) seeks to accelerate and increase renewable energy purchases and installations across the nation. Its Web site lists GPP partners that are purchasing varying percentages and amounts of green power. Tracking and comparing the lists over time provides a sense of the impressive increase in green power purchases over the last few years. In January 2006, the University of Pennsylvania was the leader in terms of quantity of green power purchased: 40,000 kWh, representing 10 percent of its consumption. For 2007 and into 2008, New York University led the pack, becoming the largest higher education institution to purchase 100 percent wind power. Then in early 2008, Penn bumped its purchase up again to 46 percent, amounting to 192.7 million kWh, again making it the number one campus purchaser of green power. At the same time, the 100 percent club has grown, from 11 partners that purchased or produced 100 percent green power in March 2007 to 19 as of July 2008.[44]

As much as any indicator, this 72 percent increase over 16 months in the number of higher education institutions making such a dramatic commitment to sustainability reflects the quickly spreading awareness that going green can grant campuses a significant competitive advantage and effectively build value for them. In the words of Leith Sharp, director of the Green Campus Initiative at Harvard University, sustainability "is not just right, it is also the financially viable, business-minded thing to do."[45]

Notes

1.   Quoted in Pete Engardio, "Beyond the Green Corporation," *BusinessWeek*, January 29, 2007. www.businessweek.com/magazine/content/07_05/b4019001.htm (accessed September 2, 2008).

2.   Daniel H. Pink, *A Whole New Mind: Why Right-Brainers Will Rule the Future* (New York: Riverhead Books, 2006), pp. 51, 2.

3.   Daniel C. Esty and Andrew S. Winston, *Green to Gold: How Smart Companies Use Environmental Strategy to Innovate, Create Value, and Build Competitive Advantage* (New Haven: Yale University Press, 2006), pp. 283–84.

4.   Baruch Lev, "Intangible Assets: Concepts and Measurements" in *Encyclopedia of Social Measurements*, vol. 2, K. Kempf-Leonard, ed. (New York: Elsevier, 2004), pp. 300, 299.

5.   Engardio, "Beyond the Green Corporation"; Michael E. Porter and Mark R. Kramer, "Strategy and Society: The Link Between Competitive Advantage and Corporate Social Responsibility," *Harvard Business Review* (December 2006): 80.

6.   Jim Collins, *Good to Great: Why Come Companies Make the Leap and Others Don't* (New York: HarperCollins, 2001), pp. 11, 13; Esty and Winston, Green to Gold, pp. 29, 284.

7.   Collins, *Good to Great*, pp. 9–10; Porter and Kramer, "Strategy and Society," pp. 80-81.

8. The Economist, *Brands and Branding* (New York: Bloomberg Press, 2004), p. 2.

9. Robert M. Moore, "The Rising Tide: 'Branding' and the Academic Marketplace," *Change Magazine* 36, no. 3 (May/June 2004): 59.

10. Raphael Bemporad and Mitch Baranowski, "Branding for Sustainability: Five Principles for Leveraging Brands to Created Shared Value," CSRwire.com, September 17, 2008. http://www.csrwire.com/News/13158.html (accessed November 8, 2008).

11. Audrey Williams June, "College Hopes to Use Cow Manure for Half of Its Energy Needs," *Chronicle of Higher Education* (November 10, 2006), p. A26.

12. "New England Board of High er Education Honors GMC President John F. Brennan." www.greenmtn.edu/news_events/new_releases/nebhe_award_12908.aspx (accessed August 11, 2008).

13. Ernest Boyer, "Creating the New American College," *Chronicle of Higher Education* (March 9, 1994), p. A 48.

14. See, most recently, Stefan Thiel, "The Campus of the Future," *Newsweek*, August 9, 2008. www.newsweek.com/id/151686/page/1 (accessed August 11, 2008).

15. Arizona State University Web site, http://mynew.asu.edu/ (accessed August 11, 2008).

16. "Building A Sustainable Campus," marketing brochure, Arizona State University.

17. Robert A. Sevier, *Building a Brand That Matters: Helping Colleges Capitalize on the Four Essential Elements of a Block-Buster Brand* (Hiawatha, IA: Strategy Publishing, 2002), p. 55

18. Peter Gorrie, "Beyond the Doom and Gloom of Climate Change," The Star.com, October 27, 2007. www.thestar.com/sciencetech/Environment/article/270970 (accessed August 11, 2008).

19. Joel Makower, "The Four Simple Steps to Pitch-Perfect Green Marketing," GreenBiz.com, November 24, 2008. http://www.greenbiz.com/feature/2008/11/24/the-four-simple-steps-pitch-perfect-green-marketing (accessed December 2, 2008).

20. Ann Rappaport and Sarah Hammond Creighton, *Degrees That Matter: Climate Change and the University* (Cambridge, MA: MIT Press, 2007), pp. 305–6.

21. Eric Pfanner, "Cooling Off on Dubious Eco-Friendly Claims," *New York Times*, July 18, 2008. www.nytimes.com/2008/07/18/business/media/18adco.html?ref=business (accessed August 11, 2008).

22. Barbara Whitaker, "At Cornell, a Push to End Stalemate Over a Parking Lot," *New York Times*, July 18, 2005. www.nytimes.com/2005/07/18/nyregion/18cornell.html (accessed August 11, 2008).

23. Thomas H. Davenport, *Thinking for a Living: How to Get Better Performance and Results from Knowledge Workers* (Cambridge, MA: Harvard Business School Press, 2005), pp. 4–6.

24. Key Education Resources, "Environment—More than Jobs—Occupying Minds of Today's College-Bound Students," May 16, 2007. www.prnewswire.com/cgi-bin/stories.pl?ACCT=104&STORY=/www/story/05-16-2007/0004589840&EDATE= (accessed August 31, 2008); Ellen Gamerman, "Inconvenient Youths," *Wall Street Journal*, September 29, 2007. http://online.wsj.com/public/article_print/SB119101716857043113.html (accessed August 31, 2008).

25. John A. Challenger, "Looking for a Job? Go Green Collar," *Office-Politics*, August 10, 2008. www.officepolitics.com/advice/?p=354 (accessed August 31, 2008).

26. See Chapters 4 and 5 for detailed examinations of these developments.

27. University of Colorado at Colorado Springs, "Sustainability Mission." www.uccs.edu/~sustain (accessed September 2, 2008); Tiffany Hsu, "Campus Innovations Point to Green Future," *Los Angeles Times*, July 7, 2008. http://articles.latimes.com/2008/jul/07/local/me-ecocollege7 (accessed August 31, 2008); personal communication with Susan West Engelkemeyer, dean of the School of Business, Ithaca College, September 10, 2008.

28. Mike Pierce and Katherine Madden, "Driving Success: Human Resources and Sustainable Development" (World Business Council for Sustainable Development, HRH The Prince of Wales's Business and the Environment Programme, and University of Cambridge Programme for Industry), p. 5. www.wbcsd.org/web/publications/hr.pdf (accessed September 2, 2008).

29. Tandberg and Ipsos-Mori, "Corporate Environmental Behavior and the Impact on Brand Values," October 2007. www.ivci.com/pdf/corporate-environmental-behaviour-and-the-impact-on-brand-values.pdf (accessed September 2, 2008).

30. Vanessa Strickley, *Sustainable Campus Practices: Green Facilities, Purchasing and Business Practices*, Campus Sustainability White Paper Series (Little Falls, NJ, 2008), p. 9. www.paper-clip.com/Media/GenComProductCatalog/wpsustainable%20practicesfinalEK.pdf (accessed September 4, 2008); Alex Wilson, "Making the Case

for Green Building: Cataloguing the Benefits of Environmentally Responsible Design and Construction," in *The Green Campus: Meeting the Challenge of Environmental Sustainability*, ed. Walter Simpson (Alexandria, VA: APPA, 2008), pp. 139–40; Higher Education Environmental Performance Improvement Project, "Staffing," *Good Campus Self-Assessment Toolkit*. http://81.29.69.220/~uni99/toolkit/categoryInfo.php?catID=37 (accessed September 2, 2008).

31. Ken Dychtwald, Tamara J. Erickson, and Robert Morison, *Workforce Crisis: How to Beat the Coming Shortage of Skills and Talent* (Cambridge, MA: Harvard Business School Press, 2006), p. 9; "Retention Rates Grow with Green Training," *One Greener*, August 25, 2008. www.onegreener.com/index.php?option=com_myblog&show=Retention-rates-increase-with-green-policy.html&Itemid=203 (accessed September 4, 2008).

32. Louisa Peacock, 'Sustainability: Taking a Responsible View to Improve Employer Brand and Staff Retention," *Personnel Today*, November 2007. www.personneltoday.com/articles/2007/11/05/43112/sustainability-taking-a-responsible-view-to-improve-employer-brand-and-staff.html (accessed September 14, 2008).

33. Robert Clark, "Changing Faculty Demographics and the Need for New Policies," in *Recruitment, Retention, and Retirement in Higher Education: Building and Managing the Faculty of the Future*, ed. Robert Clark and Jennifer Ma (Northampton, MA: Edward Elgar Publishing, 2005), p. 2; Piper Fogg, "Advancing in Age," *Chronicle of Higher Education*, June 3, 2005. http://chronicle.com/free/v51/i39/39a00601.htm (accessed September 6, 2008).

34. Cathy A. Trower and Richard P. Chait, "Faculty Diversity: Too Little for Too Long," *Harvard Magazine* 104, no. 4 (March/April 2002). www.harvardmagazine.com/on-line/030218.html (accessed September 4, 2008).

35. *Federal Energy Management Program, The Business Case for Sustainable Design in Federal Facilities* (U.S. Department of Energy, August 2003), pp. 11–12. www1.eere.energy.gov/femp/pdfs/bcsddoc.pdf (accessed September 4, 2008); Gregory Kats, *Greening America's Schools: Costs and Benefits* (October 2006), pp. 10–11. www.cap-e.com/ewebeditpro/items/O59F9819.pdf (accessed September 6, 2008).

36. Kats, *Greening America's Schools*, pp. 11–12.

37. *Green Buildings and the Bottom Line* (Oak Brook, IL: Building Design+Construction, November 2006), p. 5. www.bdcnetwork.

com/contents/pdfs/whitepaper06.pdf (accessed September 8, 2008).

38. Scott Carlson, "Princeton Review Will Issue 'Green' Ratings in Coming College Guide," *Chronicle of Higher Education*, April 22, 2008. http://chronicle.com/daily/2008/04/2582n.htm (accessed September 6, 2008); Tracy Jan, "The Greenest Colleges? Harvard, UNH, and Maine's Atlantic Top List," *Boston Globe*, July 28, 2008. www.boston.com/lifestyle/green/greenblog/2008/07/the_greenest_colleges_harvard.html (accessed September 6, 2008).

39. Brian Wingfield, "America's Greenest Colleges," *Forbes*, May 2, 2008. www.forbes.com/2008/05/02/college-harvard-uvm-biz-energy-cx_bw_0502greenu.html (accessed September 6, 2008); G. Jeffrey MacDonald, "Colleges Graded on Environmental Practices," *USA Today*, January 24, 2007. www.usatoday.com/news/education/2007-01-23-eco-university_x.htm (accessed September 6, 2008).

40. "15 Green Colleges and Universities," *Grist*, August 10, 2007. www.grist.org/news/maindish/2007/08/10/colleges/index.html (accessed September 4, 2008); *The Kiwi 2007 Green College Report* (September/October 2007). www.kiwimagonline.com/green-college-report/pdfs/KiwiGreenReport.pdf (September 4, 2008); Jennifer Hattam, "10 That Get It," *Sierra Club* (November/December 2007). www.sierraclub.org/sierra/200711/coolschools/ten.asp (accessed September 6, 2008).

41. *Beyond Grey Pinstripes*. www.beyondgreypinstripes.org/index.cfm (accessed September 8, 2008); Sonja Steptoe, "Getting Schools to Think and Act Green," *Time*, August 10, 2007. www.time.com/time/specials/2007/article/0,28804,1651473_1651472_1652067,00.html (accessed September 8, 2008).

42. Sustainable Endowments Institute, *College Sustainability Report Card 2008: A Review of Campus and Endowment Policies at Leading Institutions*. www.endowmentinstitute.org/sustainability/CollegeSustainabilityReportCard2008.pdf.

43. "AASHE Awards." www.aashe.org/programs/awards.php (accessed September 8, 2008). See Chapter 7 for a discussion of AASHE's Sustainability Tracking, Assessment, and Rating System (STARS), a voluntary and self-reporting system that provides a framework toward sustainability.

44. Green Power Partnership, "Top 10 College and University Partners," January 10, 2006. www.epa.gov/greenpower/documents/

top10ed_2006.pdf (accessed September 8, 2008); "100% Green Power Purchasers: as of July 8, 2008." www.epa.gov/greenpower/toplists/partner100.htm (accessed September 8, 2008).

45. Leith Sharp, "Campus Power," *Times Higher Education*, April 14, 2006. www.timeshighereducation.co.uk/story.asp?sectioncode=2 6&storycode=202346&featurecode=105 (accessed September 8, 2008).

"It is not education, but education of a certain kind, that will save us."
—David Orr, "What Is Education For?"
in *Earth in Mind: On Education, Environment,
and the Human Prospect*

4

TRANSFORMING TEACHING AND LEARNING

lthough the sustainability movement in higher education has made considerable headway in research, campus operations, and community outreach, it has been much less successful in greening the classroom. In fact, the National Wildlife Federation reported in August 2008 that efforts to integrate sustainability into teaching and learning on college campuses were losing ground. Fewer students, according to the survey results, had taken courses in sustainability by the end of senior year, and fewer institutions were providing support for faculty development programs on sustainability topics.[1]

What accounts for this "failure to preach what they practice"?[2] At the heart of the problem is the extent to which sustainability as a way of thinking cuts against the grain of the dominant paradigm in academe. While sustainability encourages whole-systems thinking that explores interconnections, feedback, and synergies, the tendency in higher education toward specialization leads to an approach that draws boundaries and creates divisions. The prevailing model of education also focuses on the transmission of knowledge and treats the student as a passive consumer.

In contrast, Stephen Sterling observes, the "ecological paradigm" involves an inclusive rather than an exclusive approach recognizing that human and natural systems are "inextricably linked." Underscoring the importance of deep learning—that is, "learning about learning"—and concentrating more on interdependence than divisions, it stresses creation instead of consumption and connects theory and practice.[3]

Transforming teaching and learning involves more than just education *about* sustainability. What Sterling defines as "first-order" learning concentrates on the transmission of knowledge and is easily assimilated within existing educational systems; the only thing that changes is the content. "Second-order" learning—education *for* sustainability—also pays primary attention to content delivery but emphasizes "learning for change." According to Sterling, most of the so-called "greening of the university" activities fall into this category. While there is often some critical and reflective thinking involved, there is an assumed set of shared values about what changes are necessary and what knowledge and skills must be acquired to effect them. Sterling advocates the implementation of a "third-order" learning model: education *as* sustainability. This approach stresses deep learning and is an "essentially creative, reflexive, and participative process" where learning takes the form of continual exploration through practice.[4]

It is no accident that most of us can hardly recall the courses we took, never mind what we learned in them. Most of those we do remember involved the opportunity to shift from biology student to biologist, from history student to historian, from anthropology student to anthropologist—in other words, to become immersed in the experience and engaged in questions to be investigated rather than answers to feed back to the instructor.

If the highly specialized, discipline-centered higher education system constitutes a serious barrier to the successful integration of sustainability into curriculum, then it must be overhauled. We need to develop a learning environment that fosters students' ability to comprehend the big picture, makes the necessary connections among what are framed as isolated problems, and takes effective action to protect humanity's life support system. Unless we change the climate on campus, we are unlikely to stave off the global climate change that threatens our future.

When it comes to undergraduate education, we do our students a serious disservice by treating professional studies and the liberal arts as mutually exclusive. An effective education that fosters sustainability must find a way not just to balance the liberal arts and the professional programs, but also to put them into creative tension and dialogue with each other. It must create an immersive learning environment where faculty and students can meet at the crossroads of the liberal arts and professional programs, connecting in new and exciting ways. As Mary Catherine Bateson urges in *Composing a Life*, to meet the challenges of our time, we need to move away from a zero-sum mentality and embrace the language of mutual interdependence.[5] In short, we need to move from providing an education that focuses on specialization and making distinctions to a new kind of ecological, synergetic education that emphasizes interrelatedness.

Creativity, according to Jerome Bruner, "explores connections that before were unsuspected." Paradoxically, these moments of surprise "have the quality of obviousness about them when they occur" because creativity gives us a new perspective, helping us to see what was there all along.[6] The ecological paradigm of learning encourages such creativity because it looks at questions, issues, and problems as a whole, generating a new angle of vision. It understands that each part of a system is related to every other part, and all systems are connected to one another. As Mary Taylor Huber and Pat Hutchings point out, this kind of integrative learning "does not just happen"; a major commitment is required to construct the new kinds of "institutional scaffolding" necessary to promote it.[7]

Fortunately, several higher education institutions have made this commitment, building an academic culture that supports the exploration of sustainable development from a variety of disciplinary perspectives. The seven examples examined here—Northern Arizona University, Emory University, Arizona State University, Berea College, Green Mountain College, College of the Atlantic, and Ithaca College—employ similar models, but adapt them to suit their unique organizational cultures. They share a desire to instill a deeper understanding of sustainability among faculty and students, and all have put in place extensive "scaffolding" to support the changes in teaching and learning necessary to facilitate deep learning about sustainability.

Northern Arizona University

The earliest and most influential effort to infuse sustainability across the curriculum is the Ponderosa Project at Northern Arizona University. In *Sustainability on Campus*, Geoffrey Chase and Paul Rowland detail the genesis of the Ponderosa Project, which Chase led as a faculty member. In 1992, Northern Arizona joined seven other universities to work with the nonprofit organization Second Nature to explore ways to "green" the curriculum. The institutions came together in a workshop, led by Second Nature staffers, designed to help faculty and administrators become champions of sustainability on their campuses. Workshop participants discussed the role of higher education in the sustainability movement, examined case studies, and considered ways to incorporate such materials into their courses. They promised to implement programs that would expand the number of faculty who included sustainability ideas and thinking in their teaching.[8]

Using the Second Nature model, in 1995 Chase, Rowland, and several colleagues brought together 20 Northern Arizona faculty from various disciplines. With support from the Department of Energy, Ponderosa Project organizers provided $1,000 stipends for these faculty to participate in the two-day workshop and revise their syllabi. The program has continued, using the same format and meeting regularly to continue to "green" the curriculum. An online directory lists 31 departments or units at Northern Arizona that collectively offer 262 undergraduate courses, 116 liberal studies courses, and 97 graduate courses with environmental content.[9]

Central to the Ponderosa Project has been the belief that the entire university, not just a single program, is responsible for sustainability. Project leaders have insisted that the best way to educate students about sustainability is to integrate it into a variety of subjects, rather than isolate it in an environmental studies program. Furthermore, recalling Sterling's "third-order learning," the faculty participants have sought "to focus as much on how they taught as what they taught."[10] They have placed a high priority on encouraging critical thinking, engaging students in active learning, giving them the opportunity to deal with real-world sustainability issues, and establishing a foundation for lifelong learning.

Emory University

Several years after the Ponderosa Project got underway, anthropologist Peggy Barlett and biologist Arri Eisen launched a similar initiative at Emory University, Atlanta, known as the Piedmont Project. In 1999, Barlett convened a group of faculty to discuss sustainability issues facing the Atlanta area. These meetings evolved into the Faculty Green Lunch Group, which became the seedbed for the Piedmont Project. Members met for lunch, listening to presentations by colleagues about their research on the environment, followed by discussion.

Graduates are expected to understand not only the concepts of sustainability and the issues involved, but also the ways different disciplines can address sustainability challenges. In addition, they are expected to learn how to work collaboratively in multidisciplinary teams, understand the ethical issues related to sustainability, and develop the ability to engage in creative problem solving.

After attending a Ponderosa Project faculty training workshop in 2000, Barlett set out to start a similar program at Emory. Under a grant from the University Teaching Fund, about 20 faculty met in 2001 for a two-day workshop to learn about environmental issues and sustainability, design new courses, and revise teaching modules.

Building on the success of the first workshop, Emory continues to offer the program every summer. According to Barlett, the daily walks in the campus woods led by an ecologist are an especially valuable way to engage faculty who were not involved in environmental issues. "Our deeper connection with the *place* where we live and the joy of spending time outdoors," she observes, "not only strengthens environmental knowledge but deepens the connection among group members."[11] Another key aspect of the initiative is its strong multidisciplinary character. As Eisen contends, sustainability "simply cannot be addressed effectively without rich multidisciplinary conversation, investigation, experimentation, and action." The Piedmont Project Web site currently lists nearly 90 different courses at Emory across a variety of disciplines that deal with environmental issues and sustainability.[12]

Arizona State University

Another urban institution, Arizona State University, has established the first degree-granting school of sustainability in the United States as part of a larger effort to shift from specialized academic training to more interdisciplinary, collaborative efforts to address complex, real-world issues. Under the leadership of President Michael Crow, according to *Newsweek*, ASU has embarked on "one of the most radical redesigns in higher learning since the research university took shape in 19th-century Germany." Arizona State's School of Sustainability, which opened in fall 2007, brings together faculty from 35 disciplines with expertise in everything from urban development to desert-water ecology.[13] The school now offers BA, BS, MA, MS, and PhD degrees as well as a professional certificate. Graduates are expected to understand not only the concepts of sustainability and the issues involved, but also the ways different disciplines can address sustainability challenges. In addition, they learn how to work collaboratively in multidisciplinary teams, understand the ethical issues related to sustainability, and develop the ability to engage in creative problem solving.[14]

Student opportunities for research abound at all levels, in part because the school is a division of the Global Institute of Sustainability. A $15 million gift in 2004 from Julie A. Wrigley of the chewing gum family helped to establish funding for the institute. A longtime supporter of conservation, Wrigley donated another $10 million in 2007 to launch the school. The institute carries out research, education, and problem solving on a wide range of issues related to sustainability, with a special focus on urban development. Using Phoenix as a sustainability laboratory, faculty, students, and researchers investigate how rapidly growing cities can, in President Crow's words, "work in concert with the natural systems as opposed to in conflict with the natural systems."[15]

Berea College

In contrast to Northern Arizona, Emory, and Arizona State—all large research universities—Berea College is a small liberal arts institution. Located in eastern Kentucky, Berea has a long history of support for progressive causes such as abolitionism and women's rights. Its mission includes, in the words of President Larry Shinn, "a long-standing commitment [to] "engage in good stewardship of our natural, human and material resources."[16] Pursuing a multipronged approach to campus sustainability, the college wants to bring its physical plant, operations, and curriculum into alignment with this ideal. "Those of us who study the environment but don't incorporate what we know into how we operate as an institution," Shinn insists, "are failing in our educational task."[17]

The main vehicle for Berea's initiative has been the Sustainability and Environmental Studies (SENS) Program. SENS seeks to "infuse the teaching of sustainability concepts throughout the College curriculum while guiding and supporting the efforts of the College to practice sustainability." The college's 1,000 acres of farms and gardens and 8,000 acres of forests, including reservoirs, ponds, and streams, serve as ecological laboratories for SENS classes, internships, and projects. The physical centerpiece of Berea's commitment to environmental stewardship is its cutting-edge $5.5 million complex of 32 townhouse apartments for students who are married or single parents. The use of green design in this project, completed in 2003, has reduced energy and water use by 75 percent. The complex includes the Child Development Lab, which provides childcare for campus children, and the SENS House, a unique living and learning environment for students interested in sustainability that is almost entirely self-reliant in terms of energy, water, and waste treatment.[18]

Berea's ultimate goal, according to a 1998 faculty report, is an education that furnishes "both a knowledge base and a model for sustainable living—economically, socially, ecologically, and spiritually—rather than serving as a ticket to hyper-consumption."[19] The curriculum and programming at Berea reflect this shared ethos, and the institutional call for "plain living" carries over into campus operations. Students earn a portion of their education costs by working 10 to 15 hours a week in one of 130 campus departments, including the college farm operation. The college offers full financial aid to every accepted student, and all fees and other expenses are covered by their participation in the work program as well as by other grants and scholarships.

Green Mountain College and College of the Atlantic

Two other small institutions, Green Mountain College in Poultney, Vermont, and College of the Atlantic in Bar Harbor, Maine, push the envelope in an effort to incorporate sustainability into every aspect of learning. Both colleges belong to the Eco League, a consortium of colleges established in 2002 that are dedicated to sustainability. Other members of Eco League include Alaska Pacific University, Northland College in Wisconsin, and Prescott College in Arizona. Students who attend Eco League institutions can transfer from one to the other with minimal red tape and still pay the tuition of their home institution. In this way, they can study the unique ecosystem in which each college is located.[20]

Seven years before the founding of Eco League (www.ecoleague.org), Green Mountain adopted the environment as a unifying theme for its campus culture and academic curriculum. Out of this commitment grew the concept of the environmental liberal arts, a curricular framework that embraces a broad understanding of the environment that includes "natural, social, and physical communities." Taking the traditional general education core program and converting it into liberal arts courses that focus on the environment, the faculty transformed the teaching of writing, history, literature, mathematics, philosophy, and other disciplines. Furthermore, they linked student learning in these courses with research projects, field work, and service learning activities outside the classroom. This interdisciplinary, hands-on approach has not led to the watering down of liberal arts principles and values, according to President John Brennan. Instead, in his words, it has produced "a tremendous enhancement of students' relationships to their environment and an awakening of their performance as responsible citizens."[21]

Green Mountain has revised its core curriculum while maintaining traditional liberal arts departments and majors. College of the Atlantic has taken the integration of sustainability a step further, eliminating all departments and offering undergraduate and graduate students only one degree, in human ecology. According to President David Hales, the focus of human ecology is straightforward: "Individual humans exist in a natural and cultural environment, and human ecology is the study of how we relate to those environments."[22] All undergraduates design their own interdisciplinary majors, although there are a number of degree requirements, including the core course in human ecology. In addition, each student must perform 40 hours of community service and carry out an internship before they graduate. By the middle of senior year, all students must complete an essay on a relevant subject in human ecology of their own choosing, separate from their course work. The final semester is devoted to a capstone project that gives seniors the opportunity to reflect on and use the skills and knowledge acquired in an advanced-level project.

Perhaps better than any other institution of higher education, College of the Atlantic captures the spirit of Stephen Sterling's "third order": education as sustainability. "There is a tendency, especially in the academic world, to carve life into ever smaller pieces in order to make sense of it," observes Rich Borden, a longtime faculty member. "The aim of human ecology is to remind us that we are part of a complex and interactive living world. Its broad mandate calls us to cross the boundaries of traditional disciplines and seek fresh combinations of ideas."[23]

Ithaca College

Neither a large research university nor a small liberal arts institution, Ithaca College in upstate New York is a hybrid: a mid-sized, comprehensive institution with an 11-to-1 student-faculty ratio that offers more than 100 degree programs. It deserves a closer look because of the distinctive way it occupies this middle ground and because doing so shapes its approach to sustainability education and research. As a founding member of Associated New American Colleges, a national consortium of about 20 small and mid-sized institutions, Ithaca is committed to the vision of higher education leader Ernest Boyer, which combines the liberal arts and professional studies with a strong emphasis on experiential learning and civic engagement. This marriage of pragmatism and idealism equips Ithaca students with the ability to solve real-world problems in ways that advance the college's core values: intellect, character, creativity, community, and global citizenship.[24]

Ithaca's approach to sustainability education has three distinctive facets:

- A unique collaboration with EcoVillage at Ithaca (EVI) that gives students a wealth of opportunities to engage in innovative approaches to environmental, economic, and social sustainability;

- A broad-based effort to integrate the study of campus operations into student learning about sustainability; and

- An ongoing program of participation in the larger community around issues of climate change and sustainability.

The environmental studies faculty forged a partnership in 2002 with EcoVillage of Ithaca, an intentional community and nonprofit organization dedicated to modeling innovative approaches to ecological, economic, and social sustainability. A member of the EcoVillage Network of the Americas, EVI is one of many such communities around the world that, as Jonathan Dawson puts it, are committed to "ecological restoration, strengthening community, nurturing the local economy and/ or deepening spiritual insight."[25]

Supported in the beginning by a National Science Foundation grant, the partnership between Ithaca and EVI is designed to encourage students to carry out science-based community ecological projects. The collaboration is now part of the college's operating budget and a core component of its environmental studies program. Working in conjunction with EcoVillage educators, Ithaca has added six sustainability courses to this program, all project based on and involving extensive field work.

In the capstone course, students developed Earth Café 2050, an interactive project modeled after a lunch cafeteria where customers "order" using a self-administered questionnaire about their lifestyle. The "chefs" then give them wooden blocks representing the ecological footprint that their particular lifestyle requires. This effective technique has been presented at regional and national sustainability conferences, local Earth Day events, and orientation sessions at Ithaca College and Cornell University as well as at other universities and colleges.

Independent study projects, often pairing Ithaca faculty and EcoVillage resident experts as team teachers, have focused on the use of solar photovoltaics, GPS technology, green building, and wind power. In one undertaking students designed and constructed two mobile solar units on trailers that can be towed behind a vehicle. The purpose of these trailers is twofold: they provide opportunities for hands-on teaching for environmental studies, physics, and chemistry, and they function as an outreach tool. Similar to the Earth Café project, the solar trailers have been used for a variety of events, including powering the audiovisual and food service systems for dinner during the local Relay for Life to support the American Cancer Society.

In addition, Ithaca students and faculty have been working with local schools to offer children an early exposure to sustainability thinking and practices. In partnership with an EcoVillage resident who teaches at the elementary level, for example, Ithaca science professors offered a weeklong course for a local Montessori school using Ithaca College students as assistants. Activities included taking the Montessori students to a state park, a modern neighborhood development, and EcoVillage to compare the different ways in which nature manifested itself in these settings. The boys and girls built model photovoltaic panels and, taking on the role of land use planners, laid out what they considered an ideal community. They also made strawberry jam, which the faculty used as an opportunity to explain the hidden environmental costs of food production and transportation.[26]

A homegrown variant of the Ponderosa and Piedmont projects called the Finger Lakes Project has emerged at Ithaca. As with these other efforts, the key component of Ithaca's drive to integrate sustainability across the curriculum is a summer mini-grant program that encourages faculty to produce new courses or revise existing ones. So far, more than 40 faculty from 16 disciplines have received $1,000 grants to devise course content dealing with sustainability.[27] This program has inspired extensive activity on campus, even among nonrecipients. Using the United Nations Educational, Scientific, and Cultural Organization guidelines for sustainability education, a 2005 survey of faculty disclosed that more than 100 courses offer an in-depth examination of sustainability themes.

Sustainability education at Ithaca has led to the development of closer ties between the offices of academic and student affairs, helping to promote a more holistic approach to student learning. In response to student interest, for example, the Office of Residential Life created an affinity housing option called the Sustainably Conscious Living Community (SCLC). For the first two years, the community was located on the first floor of a traditional residence hall, housing two dozen students. Because of steadily increasing demand, the SCLC relocated in fall 2007 to a newly refurbished residence hall. Trained resident assistants and two faculty fellows support the 60 students who have opted to live more sustainably. Students take sustainability-related field trips, gather for communal meals, and participate in "town meetings" to discuss community issues.

In the fall semester, first-year students who participate in the SCLC are also required to take the first-year seminar, "Sustaining Our Worlds: Connecting People, Prosperity, and Our Planet." Taught by an interdisciplinary team of faculty from business, sociology, and the natural sciences, this course introduces first-year students to sustainability concepts and practices. Team projects explore sustainability challenges such as how to make more green products available on campus. The National Wildlife Federation's Campus Ecology Program recognized "Sustaining Our Worlds" in 2006 as a national model for innovative curriculum development in the area of environmental literacy.[28]

The increasing attention paid to reducing the campus' ecological footprint has provided many opportunities for student involvement and learning. A hallmark of an Ithaca undergraduate education is the chance to conduct applied research with faculty. Many of these research projects have examined solutions for the college's sustainability challenges. One student, for example, analyzed campus energy use and made recommendations that resulted in upgraded lighting for the library. In another ongoing project, two students have collected the data necessary to complete the college's assessment of its greenhouse gas emissions for the years 2001–2006, using the Clean Air-Cool Planet inventory.

A third student project was supported in part by an Environmental Protection Agency P3 (People, Prosperity, Planet) grant to assess the ecosystem services and alternate uses of the college's undeveloped property. Among the outcomes was the identification of an appropriate site for a commercial-scale 1.6-megawatt turbine, which would meet 3 to 5 percent of the college's energy needs. The board of trustees has approved the funding for a full feasibility study, including erecting a meteorological tower to gather wind resource data.

Perhaps the most dramatic symbol of Ithaca's commitment to sustainable education is the decision to build a new high-performance School of Business facility. The 38,000-square-foot building, completed in 2008 at a cost of about $19 million, houses not just a school, but a way of thinking and being that exemplifies ethical business practices, an understanding of organizations as citizens in their communities, and the responsible use of natural resources. The new facility, designed by Robert A. M. Stern Architects, incorporates radiant flooring heat, fritted glass to control daylight, natural ventilation, and a vegetated roof. It is the first LEED Platinum-certified business school building in the world.[29]

As the faculty and students settle into the new facility, they are exploring how to integrate sustainability into the school's curriculum. In the words of Dean Susan West Engelkemeyer, the building "will be a living teaching tool, bringing to life the lessons of sustainable practices delivered by our curriculum.... Sustainability touches every aspect of business management; it incorporates the 'triple bottom line' of people, planet, and prosperity," she notes. "Good managers need to know how to balance all the pieces."[30]

Opportunities involving the larger community outreach efforts are also an important part of the student learning experience regarding sustainability. The college's Finger Lakes Environmental Film Festival (FLEFF), for example, has gained international recognition, attracting more than 10,000 filmgoers in Spring 2008. Students play an integral role in organizing FLEFF and faculty design special one-week courses tied to the festival. The FLEFF fellows program brings outstanding graduate students of color from across the country and all disciplines to campus during the festival to immerse them in screenings, lectures, workshops, master classes, concerts, and events. The fellows engage with faculty and students from across campus, as well as with festival guests, to explore linkages among sustainable development, different media platforms, globalization, race, ethnicity, gender, and music.[31]

Ithaca College's long history of innovation and pragmatism has furnished a fertile seedbed for the sustainability initiative, which in turn has helped to facilitate the integration of a liberal education and professional studies, with a strong commitment to civic engagement. As a result, Ithaca is helping to forge a unique approach to undergraduate learning that represents the cutting edge of U.S. higher education in the 21st century.

THREE STEPS TOWARD SUSTAINABILITY EDUCATION

What practical lessons can we draw from these experiences? First, faculty should have a solid understanding of the all-encompassing nature of sustainability, the importance of and value in studying it across disciplines and from multiple perspectives, and the interconnectedness and significance of the economic, environmental, and social aspects of sustainability. To foster a greater comprehension of sustainability, bring in outside speakers, provide support for attending conferences, offer ongoing opportunities for faculty to share their research with each other, and set up listservs for discussions about related issues.

Second, a thorough and realistic assessment of the existing resources makes it possible to effectively deploy them. Identify campus academic leaders who support sustainability education and campus and community experts. Use communication tools such as electronic newsletters, campus and local newspapers, and radio and television outlets. In addition, carry out an inventory of existing courses with sustainability content and financial resources such as special funding programs, external funding sources, and department budget lines that could be reallocated. Be sure to use an agreed-upon standard for determining the extent of sustainability content in each course; otherwise, confusion and misunderstanding may lead to disappointment and disillusionment. Follow up with student assessments of the quality of the learning experience and the extent to which the course delivered on its promise regarding sustainability content.

Third, institutions should promote the available resources by highlighting special programs and courses on their Web site and in brochures and the course catalog. Be sure to employ both intrinsic and extrinsic rewards. Institutional recognition for campus work is especially critical. Publicize and attend faculty seminars, organize academic symposia on campus for students to present their work, provide faculty release time to participate in sustainability programs, and offer stipends for curriculum development workshops.

Practical Lessons from Sustainability Education

By emphasizing interactive, holistic learning, these seven institutions have moved toward the adoption of an ecological approach to sustainability education that respects and resembles the natural system in its capacity for synergy, adaptation, and evolution. By no means do these colleges and universities represent the only efforts to move in this direction. Stony Brook University on Long Island, for example, has taken a page out of Arizona State's playbook, creating an interdisciplinary college on its Southampton campus that focuses exclusively on sustainability studies. Rochester Institute of Technology, with funding from the Henry Luce Foundation, is developing an interdisciplinary PhD program in sustainability that brings together business management, public policy, engineering, and architectural design, among other disciplines.[32]

Another significant development is the growth of MBA programs in sustainable business. Stressing the interdependence of business, society, and the environment, these programs apply the concepts of the "triple bottom line," life-cycle analysis, full-cost accounting, and sustainability reporting and demonstrate how to make the business case for sustainability. The establishment of such a curriculum is largely student driven. "Business school students today are much more interested in social and environmental issues—and in business solving those issues," remarks Liz Maw, executive director of Net Impact, a networking group for leaders interested in business and social change.[33]

Leading universities such as University of North Carolina at Chapel Hill, George Washington University, Stanford University, Cornell University, Case Western Reserve University, University of California at Berkeley, and Northwestern University offer MBA concentrations in sustainable development. In addition, several business schools and colleges have MBA programs devoted to sustainability, including the Bainbridge Graduate Institute, Dominican University of California, and the Presidio School of Management. Green Mountain College and Marlboro College have online MBA programs, an innovation that other business schools and colleges are sure to adopt.[34]

Recent research on learning and adaptive change emphasizes the extent to which most people resist change even when it is in their best interest. Merely providing information about why change is necessary, attempting to persuade, or offering incentives are not sufficient to overcome this resistance. But inviting people to solve a problem or generate insights in a collaborative process produces dramatically better results.[35]

What do these findings suggest about moving toward a more effective model of sustainability education? Faculty as well as students should have a chance to operate in an environment where they can work together to define the crucial issues, pose solutions, and explore their ramifications. Doing so will transform them into cocreators of learner-centered, cross-disciplinary education and encourage them to preach what they practice.

Advancing Sustainability in a Digital World

Given the inherent conservatism of higher education, it may not be surprising that the implications of the digital revolution for promoting sustainability education have been largely overlooked. Admittedly, at first glance, the notion that digital technology can be a vital tool in the advancement of sustainability seems counterintuitive. How can microprocessors, hard drives, servers, and routers bring us to a new and more effective understanding of our relationship with each other and with nature? Doesn't this run counter to a movement committed to local food, renewable energy, green roofs, and humane communities?

The ability to tell richer, more compelling stories about the challenges we encounter and the progress we make, as well as to engage in collaborative problem solving, is essential to building a sustainable future. Digital communications undoubtedly will be at the heart of these efforts. The new media environment, as Richard Kahn and Douglas Kellner point out, is "a living, historical force and one of the keys to understanding and shaping the political and cultural life of the present age." Activists of all kinds are "using the new media to become informed, to inform others, and to construct new social and political relations." Barack Obama's successful campaign for the White House has underscored the power of the Web to build a political movement, and Al Gore has pointed to this historic election as an example of how the latest Web tools should be used to strengthen the movement to fight climate change.[36]

What is known as "Web 2.0" is becoming an especially powerful vehicle for storytelling and sharing ideas and dreams about a more sustainable world, as well as solutions for helping to make this happen. In contrast to the original use of the Internet as a groundbreaking way to distribute information to individuals, Web 2.0 offers the same individuals the capacity to build social networks from the bottom up through blogs, social bookmarking, wikis, and other tools that facilitate the cocreation of knowledge. These "communities of practice," as John Seeley Brown calls them, have formed the basis of an immersive learning environment that embraces synergy and synthesis, where we are producers as well as consumers of information.[37]

We are just beginning to grasp the potential for the digital revolution to transform education, especially how it can bring faculty and students together in ways that break down the boundaries among learning, teaching, and research. Doing so holds out the possibility of disrupting the traditional model of colleges and universities as communities of the learned and developing an alternative, less hierarchical community of learners.

Two sets of questions come to mind. First, the rise of new media has initiated a shift in authority from established elites with traditional credentials to emergent groups and individuals who have used the Web to acquire credibility and influence. What are the implications, in particular, for liberal education? What is its role in the brave new world of blogs, podcasting, instant messaging, and MySpace? Second, the Web has equipped us with powerful new tools for communicating and learning, as well as tremendous new sources of social and intellectual capital. How can we use these resources to repair the frayed fabric of the global community and facilitate sustainable development?

A growing number of ingenious uses of Web 2.0 to promote sustainability are beginning to appear. The online community Wiser Earth, for example, "maps and connects organizations and individuals addressing the central issues of our day: climate change, poverty, the environment, peace, water, hunger, social justice, conservation, human rights, and more." A combination of Wikipedia, FaceBook, and Google maps, Wiser Earth provides a directory searchable by area of focus or geographic location of more than 100,000 non-governmental organizations, seeking to link like-minded people for practical world-saving activities. Paul Hawken's Natural Capital Institute launched this project in 2007 and it has become an invaluable resource connecting to organizations committed to social justice and environmental sustainability.[38]

Wikipedia's rapid growth clearly illustrates how digital technology has opened up the floodgates, giving anyone with an online connection the ability to create content and share it with a worldwide audience. The enduring principles of liberal education—learning how to think for oneself, using evidence to forge a persuasive argument, educating the whole person, finding one's place in the world and making a difference—become even more important in a world where information bombards us from all directions all the time. In just over a decade, more than 3,000 billion pages have been put up on the Web, and recent estimates indicate that it is growing by 25,000 pages an hour.[39] Liberal education makes it possible for us to convert this information into knowledge and knowledge into wisdom. Without it, we lack the historical and cultural context, critical perspective, philosophical underpinnings, and ethical values that help us to sift through the mounting piles of data and determine what is significant and how to act on it.

The new learning ecology, then, has furnished a formidable incubator for thinking about sustainability. To paraphrase Zora Neale Hurston, the present is an egg laid by the past that contains the future inside its shell.[40] Higher education must adapt to the new learning environment sparked by the digital revolution, using it to make visible the invisible interrelationships among people, the biosphere, science, communications, arts, technology, public policy, and politics, as well as to help not only imagine but also collectively give birth to new futures. These new futures must protect rather than destroy, enhance rather than deplete, conserve rather than consume, bring hope rather than despair. There is a tremendous opportunity for colleges and universities to make a difference in the fight to create a more sustainable world, but only if they act now, boldly and imaginatively.

Notes

1. Scott Carlson, "Colleges Get Greener in Operations, but Not in Teaching," *Chronicle of Higher Education*, August 21, 2008. http://chronicle.com/daily/2008/08/4307n.htm (accessed August 24, 2008).
2. Ibid.
3. Stephen Sterling, *Sustainable Education: Re-Visioning Learning and Change* (Dartington, Devon, UK: Green Books Ltd., 2001), pp. 50, 15.
4. Ibid., pp. 60–61.
5. Mary Catherine Bateson, *Composing a Life* (New York: Grove Press, 2001), pp. 115–17.
6. Jerome Bruner, *On Knowing: Essays for the Left Hand* (Cambridge, MA: Belknap Press, 1979), pp. 20, 18.
7. Mary Taylor Huber and Pat Hutchings, *Integrative Learning: Mapping the Terrain.* (Washington, DC: Association of American Colleges and Universities, 2004), pp. 3, 4. www.carnegiefoundation. org/dynamic/publications/mapping-terrain.pdf (accessed August 23, 2008).
8. Peggy F. Barlett and Geoffrey W. Chase, eds., *Sustainability on Campus: Stories and Strategies for Change.* (Cambridge, MA: MIT Press, 2004), pp. 92–93.
9. Ibid., pp. 96–97; Northern Arizona University, "Directory of NAU Environmental Courses & Programs," *Merriam-Powell Center for Environmental Research.* www.mpcer.nau.edu/Environmental-Courses (accessed August 23, 2008).
10. Barlett and Chase, *Sustainability on Campus*, pp. 94–95.
11. Ibid., pp. 69, 80, 81–82.

12. Quoted in American Association of Colleges and Universities, "Sustainability Initiative Transforms Emory's Curriculum, One Course at a Time," *AAC&U News*. https://www.aacu.org/aacu_news/AACUNews05/August05/feature.cfm (accessed August 23, 2008); Emory University, "Syllabi and Course Modules," *The Piedmont Project*. www.scienceandsociety.emory.edu/piedmont/curriculum.htm (accessed August 23, 2008).

13. Association of American Colleges and Universities, "At Arizona State, Degree Programs Mark New Commitment to Sustainability," *AAC&U News*, October 2006. www.aacu.org/aacu_news/aacu-news06/october06/feature.cfm (accessed August 24, 2008); Stefan Theil, "The Campus of the Future," *Newsweek*, August 9, 2008. www.newsweek.com/id/151686 (accessed August 24, 2008).

14. http://schoolofsustainability.asu.edu/degrees/index.php#outcomes (accessed August 24, 2008).

15. "Conservation Drives Wrigley's Investment in ASU," June 1, 2007. http://asunews.asu.edu/stories/200706/20070601_Wrigley.htm (accessed August 24, 2008); Ron Scherer, "Sustainability Gains Status on US Campuses," *Christian Science Monitor*, December 9, 2006. www.csmonitor.com/2006/1219/p01s03-ussc.html (accessed August 24, 2008).

16. Berea College, "Green Steps: Berea College's Movement toward Sustainability," *Sustainability and Environmental Studies*. www.berea.edu/sens/greensteps (accessed August 23, 2008).

17. Juliet Eilperen, "Colleges Compete to Shrink their Mark on the Environment," *Washington Post*, June 26, 2005. http://www.washingtonpost.com/wp-dyn/content/article/2005/06/25/AR2005062501273.html (accessed August 23, 2008).

18. Berea College, "About the Department," Sustainability and Environmental Studies. www.berea.edu/sens; www.berea.edu/sens/ecovillage (accessed August 23, 2008).

19. Malcolm G. Scully, "Berea College's 'Ecological About-Face,'" *Chronicle of Higher Education*, February 11, 2005. add URLok http://chronicle.com/weekly/v51/i23/23b01101.htm (accessed August 24, 2008).

20. John Otrompke, "Teaching Green," *University Business*, June 2007. www2.universitybusiness.com/viewarticle.aspx?articleid=809 (accessed August 24, 2008).

21. John F. Brennan, "Achieving Campus Sustainability in the Curriculum and Culture," *Presidential Perspectives: A Higher Education*

Presidential Essay Series, Aramark Higher Education, 2007. www. presidentialperspectives.com/pdf/2007/Chapter%205.pdf (accessed August 24, 2008).

22. Tamar Lewin, "Eco-Education," *New York Times*, November 4, 2007. www.nytimes.com/2007/11/04/education/edlife/lewin-atlantic.html (accessed August 24, 2008).

23. College of the Atlantic, "Why We Offer One Degree." www.coa. edu/html/whyonedegree.htm (accessed August 24, 2008).

24. Peter W. Bardaglio, "Sustainability Thinking and Entrepreneurship: A Case Study," *Peer Review* 7, no. 3 (Spring 2005): pp.18–20.

25. Liz Walker, *EcoVillage at Ithaca: Pioneering a Sustainable Culture* (Gabriola Island, BC, Canada: New Society Publishers, 2005); Jonathan Dawson, Ecovillages: New Frontiers for Sustainability (White River Junction, VT: Chelsea Green Publishing Company, 2006), p. 21.

26. Susan Allen-Gil, Peter W. Bardaglio, and Liz Walker, "Educating for Sustainability: Ithaca College and EcoVillage at Ithaca," *Proceedings of the Greening of the Campus VI: Extending Connections* (Muncie, IN: Ball State University, 2005), pp. 5–17.

27. Ithaca College, *Exploring Positive Growth: The Sustainability Initiative at Ithaca College* (January–August 2006), p. 2. www.ithaca. edu/sustainability/files/PositiveGrowthReportJanuaryAugust2006. pdf (accessed August 23, 2008).

28. Erin McKigney, "College Receives National Sustainability Recognition," *Ithacan Online*, November 30, 2006. www.ithaca.edu/ithacan/articles/0611/30/news/4college_r.htm (accessed August 24, 2008).

29. Peter W. Bardaglio and Marian Brown, "Sustainability, Campus Operations, and Academic Entrepreneurship at Ithaca College," in *The Green Campus: Meeting the Challenge of Environmental Sustainability*, ed. Walter Simpson (Alexandria, VA: APPA, 2008), pp. 319–329.

30. "Building A New Business Vision," *Ithaca College Quarterly* 2 (2006). www.ithaca.edu/icq/2006v2/features/businessschool.htm (accessed August 24, 2008).

31. *Finger Lakes Environmental Film Festival*, March 31–April 6, 2008. http://www.ithaca.edu/fleff (accessed August 24, 2008).

32. Anthony DePalma, "The Sustainable Hampton," *New York Times*, July 27, 2008. www.nytimes.com/2008/07/27/education/edlife/27southampton-depalma.html (accessed August 25, 2008);

Sonja Steptoe, "Sustainable Programs," *Time*, August 10, 2007. www.time.com/time/nation/article/0,8599,1652068,00.html (accessed August 25, 2008).

33. Martha Brant and Miyoko Ohtake, "A Growth Industry," *Newsweek*, April 5, 2008. www.newsweek.com/id/130591 (accessed August 25, 2008).

34. Katherine Mangan, "People, Profit, and Planet," *Chronicle of Higher Education*, September 7, 2007. http://chronicle.com/weekly/v54/i02/02a01401.htm (accessed August 25, 2006); Maha Atal, "Designing Sustainable Leadership," *Business Week*, October 4, 2007. www.businessweek.com/innovate/content/oct2007/id2007104_718797.htm?chan=innovation_special+report+---+d-schools_special+report+---+d-schools (accessed August 25, 2008).

35. David Rock and Jeffrey Schwartz, "The Neuroscience of Leadership," *Strategy + Business* 43 (2006). www.strategy-business.com/media/file/sb43_06207.pdf (accessed August 23, 2008).

36. Richard Kahn & Douglas Kellner, "New Media and Internet Activism: From the 'Battle of Seattle' to Blogging," *New Media & Society* 6, no.1 (2004):88–89; Katie Fehrenbacher, "Al Gore Calls for Web 2.0 to Fight Climate Change," Earth2Tech.com, November 7, 2008. http://earth2tech.com/2008/11/07/al-gore-calls-for-web-20-to-fight-climate-change (accessed November 8, 2008).

37. Bryan Alexander, "Web 2.0: A New Wave of Innovation for Teaching and Learning?" *Educause Review* 41, no. 2 (2006). www.educause.edu/ir/library/pdf/ERM0621.pdf (accessed August 23, 2008); John Seeley Brown, "Growing Up Digital: How the Web Changes Work, Education, and the Ways People Learn," *Change: The Magazine of Higher Learning* 32, no. 2 (2000):10–20. www.johnseelybrown.com/Growing_up_digital.pdf (accessed August 23, 2008).

38. "About Wiser Earth." http://www.wiserearth.org/article/About (accessed February 21, 2009). For other examples, see Inês Sousa, "Leveraging the Power of Web 2.0 to Drive Sustainability," *Sustainable Minds*. www.sustainableminds.com/blog/leveraging-power-web-20-drive-sustainability (accessed February 21, 2009).

39. John Naughton, "The Age of the Permanent Net Revolution," *The Observer* (UK), March 5, 2006. http://media.guardian.co.uk/site/story/0,,1723622,00.html (accessed August 23, 2008).

40. Zora Neale Hurston, *Moses, Man of the Mountain* (1939; repr. New York: Harper Perennial, 1991), p. 194.

5

TRANSFORMING CAMPUS LIFE

A student arriving on campus as a freshman today grew up in a world where environmental issues consistently cropped up in the media and in the classroom. She may have sorted cans and bottles for recycling since she was in elementary school. She also may have implored her parents to buy organic foods at the local farmers' market and chided them when they inadvertently threw a soda bottle in the trash. In science class, she learned about the dangers of pesticides in the food supply, water pollution in her local river, and the accelerating mass extinction of species. As a high school student, she may have organized a "green team" to set up a recycling program at school.

Let's imagine one such student, "Lisa." Lisa dreams about being an environmental lawyer, writer, or activist. In deciding where to apply to college, she pores over college ratings with an eye for both academic excellence and commitment to campus sustainability. When she and her parents scout potential colleges, she is impressed on one particular campus tour with the green roof and solar panels on the science building, the native plantings throughout the campus, and the Energy Star residential hall. Lisa requests a meeting with the head of Students for a Sustainable Future, knowing that she wants to become an organizer on campus and that she has her own ideas about environmental activism. Motivated to become a successful professional yet unwilling to compromise her core values in the pursuit of a high-paying salary, she is aware that a career in clean energy offers her the opportunity for a rewarding job with potential for advancement. Lisa recognizes that the emerging carbon-constrained economy presents immense professional opportunities.

For many students, of course, sustainability may not be their chosen profession, but still they recognize its importance in their future. Some students will be drawn to academic programs that focus on sustainability, and others will pursue other fields. For both, however, the college years provide an opportunity to explore different values and ways of living. These experiences will shape their norms and expectations as they graduate, enter the workforce, and bring up their families.

By its very nature, sustainability on campus lowers the walls between academic disciplines and between academic and student affairs. It offers a rich array of possibilities for a more holistic approach to learning that more closely resembles the process students will engage in after they leave college. "It's not about telling people, 'You have to do this, you have to do that,'" notes Oberlin College undergraduate Lucas Brown. "It's about fitting sustainability into our own lives."[1]

Students who want to create a campus that is in closer alignment with their values often spark the move toward sustainability. "Students challenged us to think more green," says Chancellor Henry T. Yang of the University of California, Santa Barbara, echoing the opinion of many administrators.[2] In the process, students' passion transforms them into leaders who energize the larger community. For example, a handful of students might work diligently for two years to build a solar-power home for the Solar Decathlon. Other students visit and tour the home, inspired by a new vision of the future. What impact does this encounter have on their expectations for the house they'll want to buy in the future? Some students organize light bulb swaps where they hand out compact fluorescents to replace incandescents. How does this activity affect their consumer choices beyond light bulbs? Some students will see Leonardo DiCaprio's films and simply recall that he was on the cover of *Vanity Fair's* Green Issue, but others may be inspired to dedicate their lives to fighting global climate change. Regardless of their level of awareness and commitment, all of these students are citizens and consumers, and their time in college will have a profound impact on how they live their lives.

Greening the Dorms

The most concrete manifestation of sustainability in student life is the rapid rise of green residence halls. A dramatic example of these new facilities is the Home Depot Smart Home at Duke University, a 10-person residence hall for green living and learning that achieved LEED Platinum certification in June 2008. Designed by students and advisers, the 6,000-square-foot building is the first residence hall on any campus to achieve the top-level standard for design from the U. S. Green Building Council.

The $2 million residence hall and research laboratory is a key component of a larger program in which more than 100 students are conducting research on smart living. The primarily undergraduate program draws students from different academic disciplines to form teams and explore ways to use technology in the home. Flexible, environmentally sustainable, and technologically integrated, the Smart Home incorporates a green roof, solar cells, rainwater cisterns, and sophisticated digital electronics. Its fiber-optic network is the fastest Internet access on the campus, about 40 gigabytes per second. Workshops adjacent to the living areas enable students to experiment with and deploy new technology, while wall panels in every room open easily so that students can add features.[3]

Pitzer College, in a much bigger project, received LEED Gold certification in May 2008 for three new residence halls completed in 2007. Constructed of materials consisting of recycled content such as structural steel, concrete, gypsum board, carpeting, and insulation, the residence halls feature water-efficient landscaping, light pollution reduction, and photovoltaic roof panels. "It's really opened up a whole new part of the campus, and the students just love living there," says President Laura Trombley. It's not hard to understand why. The complex provides space for both formal and informal learning, including art studios, study rooms, a music practice room, a computer lab, wireless Internet access, apartments for faculty members, a shared community kitchen, and outdoor gardens that serve as a living laboratory for learning.[4]

Other colleges and universities have developed programs in their residence halls that involve students in sustainability activities. Giving out compact fluorescents in exchange for incandescents is just one example of how students share ideas and information about how to green their daily lives. At the University of California, Irvine, students took a standard-issue dorm room built in 1965 and set it up to demonstrate the latest in green products. Hemp towels, organic cotton sheets, and a reusable shopping basket were among the items on display, along with price tags and information about where to purchase the products. No source was more than a 10-minute bike ride from the residence hall. Student residents at Oberlin College's new sustainability house have installed a plastic hourglass timer inside the shower and keep track of their individual times. Besides water use, they studied energy use, insulation, heating and cooling, and financing in preparation for renovating the building, described as "an aging, drafty two-story house."[5]

Tulane University students organized the first Energy Star showcase dorm room in 2001, unveiling it during Homecoming and Parent/Family Weekend. The room features Energy Star lighting, office equipment, and home electronics, demonstrating the impact you can have on energy consumption by switching to more efficient products and appliances. Three sophomores lived in the two-bedroom suite; two of them coordinated the demonstration project as work-study positions and gave tours of the space. Tulane students estimated in a 2003 study that if all students living on campus chose Energy Star–labeled electronics, the university could reduce greenhouse gas emissions by almost 2 million pounds and save more than $100,000 in utility bills each academic year. When Tulane reopened in January 2006 after the devastation of Hurricane Katrina, students re-created the Energy Star dorm room with the help of donations from a number of manufacturers.[6]

Students at other campuses, including University of California, Berkeley, Humboldt State University, and California State University, San Bernardino, have also worked with their administrations to create dorm rooms that showcase Energy Star equipment. The rooms are shown to prospective students and parents on campus tours, and they illustrate students' enthusiasm and dedication and the institution's commitment to energy efficiency. All incoming student residents receive mailings of Energy Star product information and are provided with compact fluorescent lightbulbs.[7]

One of the most popular green campus activities involves competition among residence halls to reduce energy use. In February 2007, students from 15 campuses in Minnesota organized and held a Campus Energy War to determine which one could cut energy consumption the most over one month. Powered by long-distance friendships, the students organized the competition again in 2008 in conjunction with the Campus Climate Challenge. It was expanded to a national competition and renamed the National Campus Energy Challenge. The competition compared the energy and heating consumption in February 2008 to the

college or university's average from February 2005, 2006, and 2007.[8]
Initial results indicate that most successful institutions managed to reduce
their demand by about 10 percent during this period.[9]

Another popular program is RecycleMania, an annual competition
that pits colleges and universities against each other in an effort to collect
the largest amount of recyclables per capita, the largest amount of total
recyclables, the least amount of trash per capita, and the highest recycling
rate over a 10-week period. The RecycleMania Competition is a project
of the College and University Recycling Council (CURC); the Coca Cola
Company provides financial and logistical support. RecycleMania began
in February 2001 when Miami University and Ohio University went
head-to-head to see which institution could recycle the most during a
10-week competition. In 2008, 400 colleges and universities participated,
with an impressive total of 58.6 million pounds recycled.[10]

In the Solar Decathlon, sponsored by the U. S. Department of Energy's Office of Energy Efficiency and Renewable Energy, 20 college and
university teams compete to design, build, and operate the most attractive,
effective, and energy-efficient solar-powered house. More than 100,000
people visited the National Mall in Washington, D. C. during the third
Solar Decathlon in October 2007. Engineering, architectural, and other
students worked with their professors for two years, planning and building their homes and preparing for the event. University of Colorado at
Boulder won the decathlons in 2002 and 2005. In 2007, Technische
Universität Darmstadt of Germany won first place, and the University
of Maryland ranked second. Students competed in 10 areas, including
architecture, livability, uniformity of temperature and relative humidity,
hot water, lighting, and appliances. The Solar Decathlon's homes are
net-zero-energy, yield zero carbon, and feature high-tech solutions and
cost-saving benefits that don't sacrifice comfort, convenience, and aes-
thetics. Each house must also produce enough extra energy to power an
electric vehicle. When the homes are returned to their campuses, some
have been opened for tours.[11]

In a similar effort, students from Florida International University's
College of Engineering and Computing participated in the Future House
Community Project during the 2008 Summer Olympics in Beijing. As the
sole U.S. representative, the FIU team—led by Dr. Yong Tao, associate
dean for business and entrepreneurship development at the College of Engineering and Computing—designed and built a house that demonstrated
"the most unique and environmentally sustainable housing construction
practices and technologies available." Inspired by Frank Lloyd Wright's

work and the principles of feng shui, the house includes features such as geothermal heat pumps, passive and active solar systems, permeable paving, a water recycling system, and nontoxic building materials.[12]

In perhaps the most impressive statement about sustainability, students at a growing number of colleges and universities are voting to raise student fees to finance environmental sustainability funds. According to the Association for the Advancement of Sustainability in Higher Education (AASHE), at least 14 campuses in the United States and four in Canada have passed "green fees" proposals. Most initiatives seek an additional $10 to $25 a year from each student, which goes into a fund that supports the purchase of renewable energy or efforts to reduce

GREEN HOUSE FOR THE PRESIDENT

Unity College, which bills itself as "America's environmental college," has gone beyond greening its dorms to provide its president with a net-zero-energy house. President Mitchell S. Thomashow, an environmental scholar, and his wife Cindy Thomashow, executive director of the college's Center for Environmental Education, moved into the new 1,900 square-foot residence in fall 2008.

The house has solar panels on its roof and sits on a concrete pad that retains heat in the winter and helps keep the well-insulated house cool in the warmer months. South-facing windows, all triple-glazed and argon-filled, provide lots of natural light. Low-flow water fixtures, compact fluorescents, and high-efficiency appliances and mechanical systems further minimize the house's carbon footprint.

Having earned LEED Platinum certification from the U.S. Green Building Council, Unity House is designed to be flexible enough to accommodate college events and classes. The architect, Hilary B. Harris of Bensonwood Homes, stuck to a budget of $200 per square foot, according to Mitchell Thomashow, to demonstrate that a sustainable home could be built at an affordable price. The house was largely manufactured at Bensonwood, which is working with the college and the Open Prototype Initiative, started by an architecture-research group at the Massachusetts Institute of Technology.[13]

The Thomashows are writing a blog called Living Green in Unity House to share their thoughts about sustainability and their new home. "Unity House is more than just a sustainable solution," says the president. "It's a wonderful educational opportunity. We are hoping that the countless visitors to the house will be impressed, inspired, and motivated to live similarly."[14]

carbon emissions. In some cases, colleges and universities are matching some of the funds raised by students. "People have seen that it's a pretty effective way for students to make a huge difference in the reduction of a college's environmental impact," says Julian Dautremont-Smith, associate director of AASHE. "It's easy in some ways, but not an insignificant pledge. Every school we've seen hold the vote, it passes, usually by a significant amount."[15]

Dining and Healthy Eating

More students, faculty, and staff are expecting that campus dining services and events will be operated and held in an environmentally responsible manner. Aware that the produce on American plates has traveled an average of 1,500 miles, people are framing food choices in terms of carbon intensity. As concerns about fossil fuel consumption have grown, so has the number of people involved in the local food movement. As a result, locally grown and produced foods have gained in prominence and appeal. In addition, there has been a clear trend toward organically grown food.[16]

Campus dining services are responding to these shifts in preferences and offering healthier local options. More than two-thirds of colleges and universities reportedly dedicate part of their budgets to the purchase of local foods.[17] A complete shift to local foods, however, would not appeal to most people. Depending on the institution's location, it would mean eliminating popular items such as bananas, chocolate, spices, seafood, and coffee.

The issue of food supply and greenhouse gas emissions is not always clear-cut. Tom Tomich, director of the University of California Sustainable Agriculture Research and Education Programs, points out that purchasing local food is not always better environmentally. The distance that food travels is important, he says, but taking into account how it is packaged, grown, processed, and transported to market is also crucial in making decisions about its environmental impact. Are canned tomatoes a better environmental choice in the off-season, for example, than fresh tomatoes from abroad?[18]

Despite good intentions, other practices widely perceived to be more environmentally responsible are not necessarily the smart choice in terms of carbon emissions. For example, some people look askance at disposable cutlery for campus events and request biodegradable or compostable products. Compostable cutlery, however, is currently produced from corn, potatoes, and bamboo. Materials produced from corn and potatoes take food out of the supply chain, presenting a substantial ethical concern in light of global food shortages. Furthermore, the production facilities for biodegradable cutlery are located in China, so it has to be transported thousands of miles, certainly not a sustainable choice. The infrastructure for composting these materials is not always available in the United States, and they often end up in the landfill.

A less debatable trend involves dining without trays. Campuses adopting this practice have reported up to a 50 percent decline in food waste. Grand Valley State University in Grand Rapids, Michigan averages about 960 pounds in savings each week. "Not having a tray forces you to decide whether you want something enough to carry it," says Aynsley Ferguson, a junior accounting major.[19] This simple measure reduces energy and water consumption used in food preparation and washing trays. Since students do not consume as much food and soft drinks, it encourages healthier habits. Colleges and universities that had used disposable trays have also experienced dramatic declines in the amount of waste going to landfills.

Other measures include using smaller plates, which encourages smaller portions, less food waste, and less water for washing. By having recycling receptacles readily available, not using individually wrapped condiments, serving water from pitchers, and using washable dishes and cutlery, colleges and universities have made impressive progress in reducing their environmental impact. In addition, institutions are beginning to provide reusable containers for takeout food, charging students a small fee for them, and many campuses are collecting frying oil to convert to fuel for vehicles.

Food service companies, moreover, are turning to low-water dishwashers and green cleaners as well as new operational protocols that lead to substantial energy and water savings. In many kitchens, for example, the workers turn on all the ovens long before they begin food preparation, and often water runs for no purpose. These practices are changing as awareness about sustainability grows. Sodexo, for instance, made adjustments to improve the efficiency of dishwashing equipment, saving almost 1.4 million gallons of water in 2007.

Colby College Dining Services, managed by Sodexo, is an excellent example of green dining on campus. Colby purchases a substantial amount of local and organic foods, and it has implemented a fish and seafood purchasing policy that adheres to or exceeds the "Fish List," a national guideline, therefore helping to protect species with dwindling populations. All fryer oil is collected and used for biodiesel tractors on a local farm. When possible, Dining Services uses foods packaged in bulk, china and flatware, and unbleached napkins from recycled paper. Paper products have been removed from all dining halls and replaced with linen or vinyl reusable tablecloths. Dining Services also recycles cardboard and composts both pre- and post-consumer food waste in all dining halls.[20]

Emory University, another institution that contracts with Sodexo, has also made a strong commitment to purchasing local or sustainable foods. It currently purchases approximately 30 percent of all its food locally; 43 percent of produce is from the Southeast, and the university has set an ambitious goal of purchasing 75 percent local or sustainable by 2015. Emory also adheres to sustainability purchasing guidelines for several food categories, working with Food Alliance, a nonprofit organization dedicated to increasing sustainable agricultural and business practices.

Viewing mealtime as a teachable moment for students, Emory seeks to make them more aware of healthy choices beginning in their freshman year. The dining service team connects students and the community to farmers. Farmers, including some alumni, visit the campus to educate students about local and sustainable foods issues.

As part of its commitment to purchasing local food, Emory has adopted a two-tier approach. Its top priority is to buy from Georgia farmers, and its second priority is to buy within the eight-state region of the Southeast. Chaz Holt, Emory's farmer liaison, works with farmers who are interested in the university's local food program and provides guidance to those interested in becoming certified as sustainable producers with Food Alliance. "I rarely [have] to go out and rally," he comments. "The farmers are coming to me." In addition, Emory has contracted with a food distributor, Destiny Produce, to ensure that it can meet the demand on campus for local and organic food.[21]

Not many institutions have set their sights as high as Emory's goal of 75 percent local or sustainable by 2015. Nearly 250 colleges and universities, however, have committed to the Real Food Challenge, which Tim Galarneau, a food systems education and research specialist at the University of California Center for Agroecology and Sustainable Food Systems, founded in 2007. The Real Food Challenge requires that by 2020, 20 percent or more of the signatories' food purchases will meet the criteria for the program's definition of "real food," which takes into account such factors as organic ingredients, fair trade practices, local sources, and humane animal treatment. "The Real Food Challenge takes multiple issues relating to sustainable food and sets an achievable goal for the national food market," says Galarneau.[22]

What about the institution's bottom line? Howard Sacks, director of the Rural Life Center at Kenyon College, notes that the question of whether it is more economical to buy locally or nationally depends on the product. Meat, for example, is often more expensive to buy locally, while tomatoes are often cheaper. It makes a difference, too, when colleges begin to buy in bulk from local producers rather than just making occasional purchases. Larry Shinn, president of Berea College, contends that in the end buying locally is a sound fiscal policy. "Look at the rising cost of fuel," he observes. "Do you pay a little more now or wait until transportation costs get worse?"[23]

Local food purchases tend to make more financial sense for institutions in the countryside than for those in cities. In either case, doing business with local farmers can bolster rural economies in important ways. Middlebury College, a longtime leader in the local foods movement, gets about 25 percent of its food from Vermont. The college's dining services spends close to $1 million per year on local food products from more than 40 nearby farms, orchards, and food service providers. Cornell University gets 30 to 50 percent of its food from New York, according to Dean Koyanagi, the university's sustainability coordinator. In the depressed economy of upstate New York, this kind of spending has a significant impact. "Every dollar we spend [changes] hands three times," points out Koyanagi.[24]

Wellness

A commitment to sustainability on campus has also led to an increased focus on wellness. The recent explosion of recreation and wellness facilities underscores the extent to which they are seen as an essential component in the education of the whole person. Wellness centers provide the space and resources to help all members of a campus community improve their mental, physical, emotional, and spiritual well-being. In a stress-filled, complex, and competitive environment, they help the college community be healthy.

Many examples of the trend toward connecting wellness and sustainability can be found in recent campus initiatives. To help students "develop a well-rounded and balanced life," the Center for Wellness and Lifelong Learning at Northland College includes a co-curriculum involving workshops and learning experiences in ecological, spiritual, physical, emotional, intellectual, and social wellness. Notable is the inclusion of "ecological wellness," which the center defines as an "awareness of the complex relationships of humans to the built and natural environments around them, emphasizing natural systems that enable environmentally sustainable choices."[25] The Riverpoint Campus Wellness Collaborative, launched by Washington State University Spokane, offers a series of programs and events for the campus and surrounding community. One of the most popular is the Annual Healthy Fare, which provides opportunities to explore healthy lifestyle choices and features local vendors who represent recreational activities, healthy living, nutrition, health care organizations, and fitness.[26]

Campus planners are paying increased attention to how landscape design can influence the physical, social, and mental health of the community. In particular, they are encouraging more walking and greater use of bicycles. The University of Buffalo's new comprehensive physical plan seeks to improve what it calls the campus's "walkability factor" by consolidating parking space and incorporating more natural elements into the landscape. One possibility is the development of an all-season trail system linking one of the campus's most attractive features, Lake LaSalle, with the surrounding woods, and transforming the lake into a living ecosystem with year-round recreation.[27] At a time when many students have developed a stronger connection to their electronic devices than to their roommates, creating such opportunities enables them to get exercise, get acquainted with their neighbors, and become healthier and more social.[28]

Conference and Event Planning

A small but growing number of colleges, universities, and higher education associations are holding events such as convocations, commencements, and conferences that are carbon neutral and/or zero waste. This approach gives students excellent models for incorporating sustainability practices into their lives. For carbon-neutral events, organizers calculate the emissions that result from the event and then purchase carbon offsets. In some cases, the organizers offer individuals the choice to opt-in and pay a fee. At times, the costs of the carbon offsets are included in the overall budget as part of the event's overhead. Occasionally, the institution pays for the offsets for all participants. At the 2008 meeting of Smart and Sustainable Campuses at the University of Maryland, for example, one of the cosponsors, NACUBO, provided offsets for the entire conference. Each participant also received a seedling tree instead of a more conventional takeaway such as a vinyl bag. Virtual conferences are also on the rise, as videoconferencing, podcasts, and Webcasts become increasingly popular as a way to maximize participants' valuable time and minimize travel costs and greenhouse gas emissions.

Even athletic programs are starting to think about sustainability. The first climate-neutral football game took place in Gainesville, Florida, in November 2007 when the University of Florida (UF) played archrival Florida State University (FSU). UF scientists worked with the International Carbon Bank and Exchange to calculate the emissions associated with travel and lodging for the FSU team and the estimated 88,000 spectators and with operating the stadium. In partnership with the Florida Forestry Association and the Environmental Defense Fund, UF arranged for approximately 18 acres to be set aside and managed as a pine plantation forest for a decade to offset the emissions from the game. "Florida's 1,300 miles of coastline mean we're the state that is most vulnerable to climate change, so it's especially fitting that this is the first NCAA game to help tackle the problem," said Jerry Karnas, Florida Climate Project director for Environmental Defense.[29]

Inspired by the success of this event, in 2008 the University of Florida became the first university to host a carbon-neutral football season. The initiative, called Neutral Gator, partnered with a local utility company to provide compact fluorescent light bulbs to low-income neighborhoods and is working to install solar panels on campus. "Neutralize the games and get people thinking," says Dedee DeLongpre Johnston, director of UF's Office of Sustainability. "We're hoping it captures the imagination of politicians." UF hopes to purchase or create carbon offsets within 100 miles of Gainesville rather than buy them on the commodities market. Other initiatives include local reforestation projects and the purchase of methane recovery credits from Gainesville Regional Utilities.[30]

In a similar move, the University of Colorado at Boulder (CU) became the first major collegiate or professional sports program in the nation to commit to zero-waste football games. About 60 tons of game-day garbage ended up in landfills during the 2007 season—about 10 tons of trash from each home event. During the 2008 season, CU officials expected to recycle or compost 90 percent of the waste from home football games. Nearly all the food and drinks sold at the games is packaged in recyclable or compostable containers. Student volunteers staff 50 recycling stations at the stadium, making sure fans toss their trash into the right bins. Finished compost will be returned to CU for campus landscaping.[31]

Changing Behavior and Cultural Shift

Underlying all these efforts, both inside and outside the classroom, is the goal of moving from a culture of consumption to one of conservation. Simply greening campus operations is not enough. Moving toward sustainability hinges on our ability to inspire and maintain changes in behavior, expectations, and norms. We will accomplish little until people remember to turn off their computers, hop on the bus, or put their soda bottles in the recycling bin.

How one frames the message has a clear impact on how effectively it is communicated. Inundating people with facts and figures can lead to paralysis. Anthony Leiserowitz, director of the Yale University Project on Climate Change, contends that "you have to have an emotional response—bad or good—to put a high priority on doing something." But just scaring people with apocalyptic messages about the future won't work either. Instead, people have to be presented with concrete, positive actions; otherwise they can feel overwhelmed and powerless.[32]

Environmental psychologist Doug McKenzie-Mohr suggests that the most effective way to promote sustainable behavior is to adopt community-based social marketing in place of the usual information-based campaigns. In his words, community-based social marketing focuses on "initiatives delivered at the community level which focus on removing barriers to an activity while simultaneously enhancing the activities' benefits." Community-based social marketing involves four steps: (1) identifying the barriers to a particular activity; (2) developing a strategy based on these data; (3) piloting the strategy; and (4) assessing the strategy's success once it has been implemented across a community.

According to McKenzie-Mohr, among the most effective tools in community-based social marketing is commitment. Securing a small commitment at the outset leads to a successful larger request. Thus, asking someone to put a bumper sticker on his or her car about buying green products increases the possibility that the person will actually purchase these products. Another important tool is the use of eye-catching prompts that remind people to turn off the lights, turn down the thermostat, or check the air pressure in their tires. In addition, norm-based messaging can be very persuasive. Instead of asking people to conserve water, for example, publicizing the amount of water saved through conservation measures can have a powerful impact on behavior. Communicating messages that are easy to remember, clear and specific, and establish personal and community goals is also key to successful social marketing. Finally,

GRADUATION PLEDGE OF SOCIAL AND ENVIRONMENTAL RESPONSIBILITY

Students graduating at nearly 150 colleges and universities are taking the Graduation Pledge of Social and Environmental Responsibility, which originated at Humboldt State University in 1987. Typically, 50 percent of students make the commitment, which is incorporated into graduation ceremonies and symbolized with green ribbons, reflecting the students' commitment and vision for the future.

The Graduation Pledge of Social and Environmental Responsibility states:
> "I pledge to explore and take into account the social and environmental consequences of any job I consider and will try to improve these aspects of any organizations for which I work."

the careful use of incentives that reward positive action rather than penalize negative behavior is a critical tool in moving people toward more sustainable behavior.[33]

Clearly, attempts to change behavior and values raise a number of thorny issues. "Campuses will become sustainable only when they have universal buy-in and enthusiastic participation from all stakeholders," observes Derek Larson, director of the Environmental Studies Program at the College of St. Benedict/St. John's University. "This requires a cultural shift that leads people to ask themselves 'what is the most sustainable way to do this?' before making a decision, rather than asking 'what is the cheapest way to do this?' or 'how have we done this in the past?' as is common practice at most institutions."[34]

Middlebury College has been using a process of deep learning to foster a stronger culture of sustainability among students, faculty, staff, and trustees. This dynamic process is one by which an important issue such as climate change moves from hallway conversations into classrooms for problem clarification and solutions, then on to administrative decision making teams, and finally to the boardroom for policy adoption and operational changes. "This learning and leading process is now characteristic of how the college harnesses the hearts and minds of the entire community to help solve sustainability challenges," says Middlebury's Dean of Environmental Affairs, Nan Jenks-Jay. "Along the way it informs and engages every level of the college community and keeps sustainability at the forefront of thought."

Middlebury has used this process over the past 6 years to develop carbon reduction targets and strategies for meeting them, assess progress, and develop new strategies as goals are met. This process led to a 2004 commitment to reduce campus carbon emissions to 8 percent below 1990 levels by 2012. This goal will be met in 2009 after the first year of operation of a $12 million biomass gasification system. The college subsequently commited to becoming carbon neutral by 2016.

Evidence of this culture shift to sustainability can also be found in various guiding documents and plans, including Middlebury's mission statement, strategic plan, and its new campus master plan, all of which have prominently woven sustainability throughout. It can also be seen in how the president's executive staff council operates. Different senior staff members report on progress toward carbon neutrality at each trustees meeting to keep the importance of this goal broadly shared and pursued.[35]

Overshadowing such efforts is not only the transformation of a culture fueled by millions of advertising dollars and powered by decades of cheap oil and energy, but also the pace at which this change can be carried out. Just as smoking habits have been altered significantly over the last 20 years, more sustainable behaviors will probably take hold. But will they do so in time to make a difference? Although no one knows the answer to this question, the participation of colleges and universities in this effort can certainly improve our chances. For the sake of our young people, let's hope that society doesn't wait too long to acknowledge the truth of Yogi Berra's insight about the future. It may not live up to our original expectations, but it's still not too late for the future to be one that holds out a promise of well being.

Notes

1. Sara Rimer, "How Green Is the College? Time the "Showers," *New York Times*, May 26, 2008. www.nytimes.com/2008/05/26/education/26green.html (accessed September 23, 2008).

2. Janet Eastman, "Green Goes to School," *Los Angeles Times*, August 23, 2007. http://articles.latimes.com/2007/aug/23/home/hm-green23 (accessed September 23, 2008).

3. "Smart Home Gets Top Environmental Building Score," Duke University press release, June 19, 2008. www.dukenews.duke.edu/2008/06/smartleed.html (accessed September 30, 2008).

4. "Residence Halls at Pitzer College Receive Gold LEED® Certification by the U.S. Green Building Council," Pitzer College press release, May 27, 2008. www.pitzer.edu/news_center/campus_news/07-08-academic_year/2008_05_27-leed-gold.asp (accessed September 30, 2008); Landus Rigsby, "Pitzer College Dorms Become Award-Winners," *Claremont Courier*, July 9, 2008. www.claremont-courier.com/pages/Topstory070908.2.html (accessed September 30, 2008).

5. Ibid.; Rimer, "How Green Is the College?"

6. "Creating an Energy Star Showcase Dorm Room," *Energy Star*. www.energystar.gov/index.cfm?c=higher_ed.bus_dormroom (accessed September 26, 2008); K. C. Jones, "Technology Helps Tulane Dorm Go Green After Katrina Flooding." *InformationWeek*, August 10, 2007. www.informationweek.com/news/software/showArticle.jhtml?articleID=201400130 (accessed September 26, 2008).

7. "Energy-Efficient Dorm Rooms at Three California Universities," *Energy Star*. www.energystar.gov/index.cfm?c=higher_ed.bus_highered_calif_dorms (accessed September 26, 2008).

8. "FAQs," National Campus Energy Challenge 2008. http://climatechallenge.org/ncec/FAQs (accessed September 26, 2008).

9. Derek Larson, personal correspondence, August 11, 2008.

10. "General Overview," RecycleMania. www.recyclemaniacs.org/overview.htm (accessed September 26, 2008); "Final Results—RecycleMania 2008," RecycleMania. www.recyclemaniacs.org/results.aspx (accessed September 26, 2008).

11. "About the Solar Decathlon." www.solardecathlon.org/about.html (accessed September 26, 2008); "German Technische Universitat Darmstadt Wins DOE's 2007 Solar Decathlon." www.energy.gov/news/5647.htm (accessed September 26, 2008).

12. "FIU Students Building Green Home to Display at Olympics," *Diverse Issues in Higher Education*, August 13, 2007. www.diverseeducation.com/artman/publish/article_9047.shtml (accessed September 26, 2008); "FIU Future House to be Showcased during 2008 Olympics in Beijing," *Academic Affairs Update*, May 2008. http://academic.fiu.edu/newsletter/may08.htm#2 (accessed September 26, 2008).

13. Lawrence Biemiller, "Unity President Gets a Sustainable House, and a One-Shower Limit," *Chronicle of Higher Education*, July 16, 2008. http://chronicle.com/blogs/architecture/2256/unity-president-gets-a-sustainable-house-and-a-one-shower-limit (accessed November 25, 2008).

14. Mitchell Thomashow, "Unity House. More Than a Sustainable Solution, It's an Educational Opportunity," Living Green in Unity House, November 5, 2008. http://theunityhouse.blogspot.com/2008/11/unity-house-more-than-sustainable.html (accessed November 16, 2008); Unity College, "Bensenwood's Unity House Achieves LEED Platinum Status," press release, February 17, 2009. http://www.unity.edu/NewsEvents/News/UHBuildingSystems09.aspx (accessed February 20, 2009).

15. Elia Powers, "Cents and Sustainability," *Inside Higher Ed*, May 18, 2008. www.insidehighered.com/news/2007/05/18/fees (accessed September 26, 2008).

16. Andrew Martin, "If It's Fresh and Local, Is It Always Greener?" *New York Times*, December 9, 2007. www.nytimes.com/2007/12/09/business/yourmoney/09feed.html (accessed September 28, 2008).

17. Elia Powers, "Campus Food from Around the Corner," *Inside Higher Ed*, November 1, 2007. www.insidehighered.com/news/2007/11/01/local (accessed September 28, 2008).

18. Martin, "If It's Fresh and Local."

19. Bruce Horoviz, "More College Cafeterias Dump Food Trays," *USA Today*, July 22, 2008. www.usatoday.com/money/industries/food/2008-07-22-trays-college-cafeterias_N.htm (accessed September 28, 2008); Kym Reinstadler, "Grand Valley State University, Other Area Colleges Go Trayless in Cafeterias to Cut Food Waste," *Grand Rapids Press*, September 23. 2008. http://www.mlive.com/grpress/news/index.ssf/2008/09/grand_valley_state_university_1.html (accessed September 28, 2008).

20. "Green Dining," Colby College. www.colby.edu/green/dining.htm (accessed September 28, 2008).

21. "Sustainable Food," *Emory University*. http://sustainability.emory.edu/page/1008/Sustainable-Food (accessed September 28, 2008); Scott Carlson, "Colleges Chew on Local-Food Phenomenon," *Chronicle of Higher Education*, September 26, 2008. http://chronicle.com/weekly/v55/i05/05a01401.htm (accessed September 28, 2008).

22. "Participating Schools," Real Food Challenge. http://db.realfoodchallenge.org (accessed September 28, 2008); Talia Berman, "Schools Go Sustainable: Greening College Food Services," *WireTap Magazine*, May 5, 2008. www.wiretapmag.org/stories/43530 (accessed September 28, 2008).

23. Powers, "Campus Food from Around the Corner."

24. "Middlebury College," *2008 Campus Sustainability Report Card.* www.greenreportcard.org/report-card-2008/schools/middlebury-college (accessed September 28, 2008); Carlson, "Colleges Chew on Local-Food Phenomenon."

25. "Center for Wellness and Lifelong Learning," Northland College. www.northland.edu/Northland/CurrentStudents/WellnessAndLIfelongLearning (accessed September 26, 2008).

26. "Riverpoint Campus Wellness Collaborative," Washington State University Spokane Campus Resources. www.spokane.wsu.edu/campusresources/HR/wellness.asp (accessed September 26, 2008); "Riverpoint Campus Events," *Riverpoint Online.* www.spokane.wsu.edu/Communications/riverpointcampus/events.asp (accessed September 26, 2008).

27. Peter Koch, "Imagine If," *UB Today*, Spring/Summer 2008. www.buffalo.edu/UBT/UBT-archives/volume26number3/features/imagine.html (accessed September 26, 2008).

28. Todd Diacon, "I Hate Bucky Dent," *Inside Higher Ed*, September 30, 2008. www.insidehighered.com/views/2008/09/30/diacon (accessed September 30, 2008).

29. "'Swamp' Goes Green with Help of Carbon Neutral Plan," University of Florida press release, November 20, 2007. http://news.ufl.edu/2007/11/20/green-swamp/ (accessed September 25, 2008).

30. Christine Stapleton, "Gators to Even Score on Carbon," *Palm Beach Post*, August 29, 2008. www.palmbeachpost.com/localnews/content/local_news/epaper/2008/08/29/m1a_neutral_gator_0830.html (accessed September 26, 2008).

31. Brittany Anas, "CU Football Games This Season Are Going "Zero 'Waste' Green," *Rocky Mountain News*, August 6, 2008. www.rockymountainnews.com/news/2008/aug/06/cu-football-games-this-season-are-going-zero (accessed September 25, 2008).

32. Marilyn Elias, "'Green Bandwagon Is Getting a Big Push," *USA Today*, March 24, 2008. www.usatoday.com/life/lifestyle/2008-03-23-green-behavior_N.htm (accessed September 26, 2008).

33. Doug McKenzie-Mohr, "Community-Based Social Marketing," *USAID*. http://rmportal.net/tools/biodiversity-conservation-tools/putting-conservation-in-context-cd/communication-and-education-approaches-resourses/Quick-Reference-Community-based-Social-Marketing/view (accessed September 26, 2008).

34. Derek Larson, The College of St. Benedict/St. John's University, personal communication, August 11, 2008.

35. Nan Jenks-Jay, Middlebury College, personal correspondence, February 17, 2009.

"Let us envision meeting our economic and ecological challenges with our heads held high—not buried in our hands."
—Van Jones, *The Green Collar Economy*, 2008

SUSTAINABILITY, ECONOMIC DEVELOPMENT, AND COMMUNITY PARTNERSHIPS

As engines of creativity, colleges and universities have the capacity to generate solutions to such fundamental issues as climate change, clean energy, and sustainable development while preparing a skilled workforce to compete in the new global knowledge economy.[1] To meet new workforce needs, from green architects to solar energy engineers, they are integrating sustainability throughout the curriculum and giving students opportunities for hands-on learning. But if these institutions are to fulfill their potential to improve peoples' lives, then they must find even better ways to carry out the transfer of knowledge and bring innovations to the marketplace.

Higher education and the market, in Larry Penley's words, "have had a long, sometimes uneasy relationship."[2] There are many examples of how the market has distorted an institution's mission, undermined basic research, and made it difficult for faculty to pursue the truth.[3] But devising practical solutions that facilitate social advancement and economic growth and staying faithful to the distinctive mission of higher education are not always mutually exclusive. Indeed, the most important contributions of land-grant universities have combined the two.[4]

Colleges and universities now have a crucial opportunity to demonstrate that they have the agility, vision, and entrepreneurial capacity to be effective partners in generating the innovation necessary to promote both environmental stewardship and sustainable social and economic development. To do so, however, requires them to engage in a delicate and complex balancing act. They must, as Penley says, ensure that researchers are not subject to "undue influence from market forces" at the same time they enhance "the ability of the institution to take research ideas more rapidly to the marketplace."[5]

Phoenix and the New American University

Research universities are the central dynamos of modern society. They play a critical role in ensuring that the United States will remain a leader in innovation, maintain its competitive advantage, and foster a healthy economy. Arizona State University (ASU) has undertaken perhaps the highest-profile effort among research universities to redefine themselves as engines of sustainable social and economic development.

As a self-proclaimed "New American University," ASU has emphasized solving "complex, real-life problems" and making the Phoenix metropolitan area a focus of its research and teaching. Under the leadership of President Michael Crow, the university has consistently highlighted its initiatives to "bring critical issues facing the community and the region to light" and find "sustainable, environmentally conscious solutions to local problems."[6] "Universities are transformational catalysts for societal change and perform functions essential to our collective survival," Crow asserts, "but we must confront the fact that we do not fully understand the implications of human impact on the environment and are not adequately prepared to advance policies regarding the optimal intersection of human and natural systems."[7]

Explicitly proclaiming that it is "not an ivory tower," ASU insists that it "wants to make sure it has the right kind of impact: sustainable, empowering, and helping to effect positive change." What does this statement mean in practice? Among other things, it means working with local governments to build healthy, vibrant communities, partnering with school districts to improve the quality of education and high school graduation rates, and collaborating with businesses to promote technological innovation. At the heart of this commitment is a deep awareness that the success of any higher education institution depends on the success of the larger community.[8]

By focusing on such issues as renewable energy, biodesign, water, urban ecology, and community policy making, ASU not only seeks to move the metropolitan area and the state toward a more sustainable future, but also to educate and train a new generation of sustainability professionals. "Long rooted in the culture of ASU is the idea of working in interdisciplinary teams to make the world a better place," says Jonathan Fink, the Julie Ann Wrigley Director of ASU's Global Institute of Sustainability. "Through our research, education, and outreach to the community our goal is to improve the lives of future generations."

Renewable Energy

For many years, ASU has been a vigorous center of solar energy research, development, and education programs, attracting professors and researchers who have won major research grants, developed innovative solar energy systems, and built cutting-edge solar buildings and devices. In the early 1990s, the university established the Photovoltaic Testing Laboratory at its Polytechnic campus, which at the time was the only such facility in the country and one of only three in the world. More recently, ASU launched the Solar Power Laboratory, a collaboration involving the university's Global Institute of Sustainability and Ira A. Fulton School of Engineering. "The Solar Power Laboratory will further build up the university's already formidable solar energy research and develop collaborations with the energy industry to accelerate expansion of the state's economy," notes Crow. Besides stimulating economic growth, of course, the development of solar power systems will help Arizona protect its environment by increasing the use of this clean energy source.[9]

Taking his cue from ASU's long involvement with solar power development, Crow underscores the importance of working "in concert with the natural systems as opposed to in conflict with the natural systems." Nature offers "the pathway to everything we need," he contends, pointing out that it "has adapted to all kinds of problems: hot climate, cold climate, high carbon dioxide, low carbon dioxide."

In an effort to build on this vision, ASU has established a $400 million Biodesign Institute, which it claims is "the largest single investment in research infrastructure in Arizona." There researchers integrate the biosciences with engineering and computing to address such problems as cancer, infectious diseases, poor water quality, bioterrorism, and renewable energy. One interdisciplinary team, for example, is exploring photosynthesis to develop a cost-effective way to commercially produce hydrogen as a source of renewable energy.[10]

Water Management

Not surprisingly, given its location in the desert, ASU has placed a high priority on research involving water issues. In the early 1970s, researchers and their students at ASU's Center for Environmental Studies, the forerunner to the Global Institute of Sustainability, undertook long-term studies of the Colorado River in Arizona, its tributaries, and associated wildlife. Researchers and students also founded the Arizona Riparian Council in 1986 "to facilitate the exchange of information about riparian management among scientists and public agencies in the state."

Urban Ecology

The Central Arizona-Phoenix Long-Term Ecological Research project has produced a significant body of research on how humans affect and interact with their environments. It has also trained hundreds of students in interdisciplinary research methods related to urban ecology, involving 11 schools and departments at ASU. The project's outreach arm, Ecology Explorers, has collaborated with more than 140 educators in 25 school districts, four charter schools, and two private schools, most of which serve large percentages of low-income and minority children.

One of the most distinctive tools developed by ASU to facilitate policymaking and create a more sustainable future in Arizona is the Decision Theater. Tackling complex issues such as urban growth, education, and the environment, the Decision Theater's approach "involves a collaborative process, the best science available, and interactive visualization through modeling and simulation." As part of an initiative for the East Valley Water Forum, for example, Decision Theater constructed a three-dimensional water modeling tool that helps public and private agencies develop and manage limited water resources by exploring different scenarios and depicting the consequences of various decisions in virtual reality. The tool made it possible for policymakers to select actions that best lead to a sustainable water supply.[11]

From Rust Belt to Green Collar in Grand Rapids, Michigan

It's one thing for higher education to promote sustainable economic development in a Sun Belt city like Phoenix, but it's another challenge to do so in the Rust Belt. In Grand Rapids, Michigan, Grand Valley State University (GVSU) and Aquinas College have teamed up with local government and business leaders to establish the Community Sustainability Partnership (CSP) and launch a green renaissance. CSP is a coalition of more than 140 businesses, institutions, and organizations throughout west

Michigan that are committed "to work together to restore environmental integrity, improve economic prosperity, and promote social equity." By collaborating, sharing experiences, and mobilizing local resources, the partnership has helped transform the Grand Rapids area.[12]

The evidence in support of this coalition's success is not hard to find. The United Nations University recently designated the city and Community Sustainability Partnership as the first U.S. Regional Center of Expertise (RCE) in Education for Sustainable Development. Grand Rapids leads the nation in the number of LEED-certified buildings per capita, and there are plans for 50 more, in part because all new city-owned buildings are built to LEED standards. "Architects say that in the past, they had to convince owners to build green," says Mayor George Heartwell. "Now, owners are demanding it."

What about energy use? In 2005, Mayor Heartwell committed the city to deriving 20 percent of its power from renewable sources by 2008; it met that goal a year early. Not one to sit on his laurels, Heartwell increased the target to 100 percent by 2020. In the meantime, the municipal government has reduced its energy use by more than 10 percent, traffic lights have energy-saving LED bulbs, and city buses are hybrids.

Joining Heartwell in his visionary leadership have been manufacturing firms such as Herman Miller and Steelcase, well known for their green product lines and their LEED-certified buildings. "These companies have decided to make money by turning eco-friendly," reports Evan West, "in the belief that reducing the environmental cost of commerce will raise their profits, boost the regional economy, and burnish Grand Rapids' increasingly credible claim to the title of greenest city in America."[13]

Few corporate executives have done more to promote sustainability in their communities than Peter Wege, philanthropist and Steelcase's retired chairman. His many green projects include a gift of $20 million for the construction of the Grand Rapids Art Museum, the world's first LEED Gold-certified art museum. His successors at Steelcase have continued to push ahead on the sustainability front. "Environmental drivers may be the reason companies try sustainable business practices, but eventually business drivers take over," points out Dave Rinard, Steelcase's director of global environmental performance. To give just one example of how the company's sustainability strategy plays out on the ground, its LEED-certified wood-fabrication facility cost roughly 5 percent more to build than a traditional manufacturing facility, but it uses about 30 percent less energy. It took only 18 months for Steelcase to recoup the additional cost.[14]

In the 21st-century knowledge economy, quality of life is a major driver of economic development, and sustainability is a crucial component of quality of life. Even more directly, the business of sustainability establishes a foundation for revived economic growth.

Herman Miller also takes sustainability seriously. Its GreenHouse factory and offices have a distinctive look. Native plantings, including prairie grasses and wildflowers, surround the steel and brick building, and a curved glass roof provides ample natural light on the factory floor, cutting down on expenses both inside and out. A coffee bar with bamboo floors, basketball court under the glass roof, and dining room with a floor covering made of recycled tires all make it clear that this is no ordinary factory. Built in 1995, GreenHouse was one of three cutting-edge buildings the U.S. Green Building Council used to create the national LEED standards.

Like Peter Wege, Herman Miller's founder D. J. DePree insisted that his company would be a responsible steward of the environment, and this principle has remained central to the company. "People choose us for our green story," says Paul Murray, director of environmental health and safety. "We think it boosts sales." The firm has committed to an ambitious set of environmental targets for 2020: 100 percent renewable electricity (currently, it's at 63 percent), zero hazardous waste, zero landfill waste, and zero air emissions from its manufacturing operations.[15]

In becoming a national example of sustainable development, Grand Rapids has transformed itself into a living laboratory with the help of Aquinas College and Grand Valley State University. Aquinas established the nation's first undergraduate degree program in sustainable business in 2003, underwritten by a $1 million contribution from Wege. "Sustainability is not just putting out recycling bins and turning down the thermostat," observes Matt Tueth, chair of Aquinas's sustainable business program. "It's a core change." Students from the program serve as interns at businesses throughout the area. "There is a big need for companies to embrace sustainable business practices," says Fred Miller, chairman and CEO of Cascade Engineering, underscoring his interest in hiring these interns.[16]

The Center for Sustainability at Aquinas is a student-run and faculty-directed organization providing a Web-based information clearinghouse on sustainable practices for consumers, business people, nonprofit organizations, students, and government agencies. The center also conducts conferences and workshops, maintains an extensive list of publications, and organizes the Campus Sustainability Initiative. As a part of the center's outreach activities, for example, senior sustainable business student Liz Ivkovich developed an environmental management system for Pilgrim Manor, a Grand Rapids retirement community. Plans include providing teams of faculty-directed Aquinas students as a "mini-consulting firm" to address specific sustainability issues within organizations.[17]

Grand Valley State University has also developed a strong network of community ties. "Our interdisciplinary approach encompasses faculty, staff, students, and the community and is part of a comprehensive strategy," says Wendy Wenner, dean of the College of Interdisciplinary Studies. "Our commitment to economic, social and environmental sustainability empowers our students to positively affect the global community now and in the future."[18] Like their counterparts at Aquinas, Grand Valley students do community sustainability internship projects. Norman Christopher, executive director of the university's Sustainability Initiative, is a governor-appointed member of Michigan Climate Action Council and was a leader in creating the Community Sustainability Partnership. Christopher and other faculty help develop and monitor city and regional sustainability indicator reports and provide support for the development of sustainable neighborhoods and communities.[19]

The Grand Rapids experience shows how a collaboration of higher education institutions, local government, and business leaders focused on sustainability can generate an important competitive advantage for a community, even in the Rust Belt. In the 21st-century knowledge economy, quality of life is a major driver of economic development, and sustainability is a crucial component of quality of life. Even more directly, the business of sustainability establishes a foundation for revived economic growth. As the old industrial economy disappears, Grand Rapids has shown how clean technology can provide the basis for a new prosperity.[20]

Town-Gown Collaboration in Ithaca, New York

Higher education's focus on innovation extends beyond technology and economic development. Colleges and universities are also leading participants in regional collaborations involving climate change. The community of Ithaca in upstate New York has gained national visibility as a center of the climate protection movement. In 2003 the Tompkins County Legislature committed to a 20 percent reduction by 2008 of emissions generated by its operations compared to 1998. Mayor Carolyn Peterson was an original signatory of the 2005 U.S. Mayors Climate Protection Agreement, and the Ithaca Common Council in 2006 adopted a goal to lower greenhouse gas emissions to 20 percent below 2001 levels by 2016.[21] Cornell University, Ithaca College, and Tompkins Cortland Community College are all signatories of the American College and University Presidents Climate Commitment (ACUPCC), and they have devoted significant time, energy, and money to this issue. In the words of Cornell President David Skorton, "We're saying that sustainability is no longer an elective."[22]

Regional Coalition Building

The groundwork for cooperation on the issue of climate change was established in 2004 with the creation of Sustainable Tompkins, a broad-based coalition of citizens, community organizations, elected officials, educators, and professionals working to promote a more sustainable community. Funded at first by Ithaca College, the Park Foundation, Cornell University, and several area businesses, Sustainable Tompkins has become a model for regional sustainability efforts. Faculty, students, and staff from all three colleges have participated in its activities and provided leadership for the organization.

Current Sustainable Tompkins projects include the development of a green building resource hub, an online interactive map of sustainable businesses and groups, and an energy-conserving home improvement training program in underserved communities. Sustainable Tompkins has also been a partner in two conferences. The Sustainable Technology Showcase was a regional health and sustainability conference planned with the Tompkins County Chamber of Commerce and carried out in conjunction with the School of Health Sciences and Human Performance at Ithaca College. Sustainable Tompkins also organized a renewable energy conference in collaboration with the Tompkins Renewable Energy Education Alliance (TREEA), a renewable technology advocacy group convened by Ithaca College faculty and staff that includes membership from Cornell.[23]

The creation in February 2008 of the Finger Lakes Environmentally Preferred Procurement Consortium built on the work of Sustainable Tompkins and strengthened the culture of collaboration in Ithaca. It is the first consortium in New York to help negotiate pricing for environmentally friendly products. Its members are major players in the community: the three higher education institutions, Tompkins County, the City of Ithaca, the Tompkins County Chamber of Commerce, and the Tompkins-Seneca-Tioga Board of Cooperative Educational Services. "This purchasing consortium is a great example of local governments working collectively with the educational institutions and local municipalities," says Cheryl Nelson, chair of the Tompkins County sustainability team. "It is a perfect match for the county as it coincides with our own team's goals of promoting sustainability within the county."[24]

Widening the Circle of Sustainability Commitment

In light of this history of collaboration and public commitment to reduce carbon emissions, the launching of the Tompkins County Climate Protection Initiative (TCCPI) in June 2008 was a logical next step. By bringing together many of the same players from earlier sustainability initiatives and widening the circle, TCCPI has established an impressive coalition of community leaders who are committed to the reduction of greenhouse gas emissions and greater energy efficiency. It has four goals:

1. Implement a common strategy, target, and timetable for achieving significant decreases in greenhouse gas emissions

2. Create a peer-to-peer mentoring network with monthly meetings to discuss the problems and challenges involved in reducing the county's carbon footprint

3. Establish a consortium to explore financing mechanisms and purchase at a significant discount goods and services necessary to achieve greenhouse gas reduction targets

4. Develop a data collection process and benchmarking tool that will allow the coalition to carry out energy audits, establish baseline data points, identify priorities for energy efficiency retrofits that will generate the biggest returns on investment, and measure progress regarding the county's carbon footprint

With support from the Park Foundation, TCCPI has brought together higher education institutions, local government agencies, nonprofits such as the Cayuga Medical Center, Museum of the Earth, Tompkins County Cooperative Extension, and Ithaca Carshare; and key business organizations and leaders. TCCPI will undertake major energy efficiency projects to decrease electricity consumption dramatically and produce critical economic and environmental benefits associated with the climate protection effort.

Central to the efforts of TCCPI is the addition of an energy and greenhouse gas emissions component to the Tompkins County Comprehensive Plan, which was adopted by the County Legislature in December 2004. The current draft calls for an 80 percent reduction of greenhouse gas emissions by 2050, with an annual goal of 2 percent of 2006 base-year emissions over the next 40 years to achieve that reduction.[25] The county planning department has held town hall meetings to discuss this proposal, and TCCPI has taken it up as well.

Performance Systems Development (PSD), a local firm specializing in energy-efficiency software development, training, and consulting, is working with the coalition to develop a customized energy performance benchmarking and assessment toolkit and train TCCPI members in its use. Similar software tools developed by PSD have been adopted across the country; their benchmarking system is being used in an ongoing study of more than 61 million square feet of commercial space in New York City.

In addition, representatives from the Clinton Climate Initiative (CCI) met with the TCCPI coalition and individual members. Follow-up discussions have led Cornell to explore bulk purchasing of solar thermal systems that TCCPI members could purchase at a substantial discount. CCI is also supporting the development of an RFP by Cayuga Medical Center for an extensive energy efficiency retrofit.

Other noteworthy coalition activities include:

- Working with the Tompkins County Legislature to pass a bill that would repeal the sales tax (currently 8 percent) on the purchase of energy efficiency and renewable energy products and services

- Partnering with a local credit union to develop a competitively priced 18-month bridge loan program for customers who want to purchase energy-efficient and renewable-energy products and services but do not have the financial means to wait for reimbursement through the state's incentive program

- Discussing the establishment of a revolving loan fund to buy down the interest rate on these bridge loans for low-income households as well as a local carbon fund

- Creating an education committee that includes the Cornell Cooperative Extension, Museum of the Earth, and the New York State Energy Research and Development Authority's Southern Tier EnergySmart Communities program to develop a social marketing plan that will disseminate information about state energy-efficiency programs and low-cost steps homeowners, tenants, and landlords can take to reduce energy consumption

Community Livability

Besides energy efficiency and conservation, ensuring access to affordable, conveniently located housing and alternative transportation in the city of Ithaca is central to the successful reduction of greenhouse gas in the region. Cornell has taken important steps to work actively with local partners, unveiling in October 2007 a 10-year, $20 million commitment in support of the housing and transportation initiative. Working with community leaders, Cornell aims to strengthen the county's sustainable economy while promoting a cultural and social life that makes it an appealing, affordable place for faculty, staff, and students to live.[26]

Cornell officials consulted with such stakeholders as the Ithaca-Tompkins County Transportation Council and the Affordable Housing Action Group to learn how the university and the community could coordinate their plans for the best impact. For example, by working with county planners, Cornell determined that if it aligned its transportation and housing initiatives with the county's proposed nodal development strategy, it would strengthen efforts to increase the housing stock. The university also decided to roll out a range of homebuyer assistance programs for university employees that include affordable financing, a savings match, and counseling.

Following discussions with local housing representatives and other public officials, Cornell agreed in June 2008 to contribute $1.2 million over six years to a program that matches public and private funds to promote the development of additional housing. Cornell also identified local transportation projects in which it would invest $1 million annually to improve pedestrian and bicycle safety, reduce traffic and parking in and around campus, and expand alternative transportation, gaining the endorsement of the Ithaca-Tompkins County Transportation Council.

By working closely with community leaders, suggests President Skorton, Cornell's housing and transportation initiative "will have a positive ripple effect throughout the local economy." He observes that it will improve the quality of life, reduce sprawl, enhance sustainability, and make it easier for the university to recruit and retain faculty, staff, and students. In short, Cornell's collaboration with the larger community is a classic win-win situation.[27]

Greening the Economy

Many are calling for a green jobs revolution to lead us out of our current economic impasse and fuel a revitalization that will restore prosperity in

America. In *Hot, Flat, and Crowded*, Thomas Friedman issues an impassioned plea for what he calls "Code Green," a strategy for clean energy, energy efficiency, and conservation that would address global climate change and sustainability while renewing the spirit of innovation and idealism in the United States. Friedman believes that the coming green economy will create millions of new jobs, help stave off climate change, and decrease American reliance on overseas energy supplies.[28]

Such a profound economic transformation, however, will not occur quickly. It will take time, money, and energy to bring about the clean technology revolution. Paul Hannam sees four main barriers: the current economic downturn, shortage of talent, greenwashing, and the need for new energy policies.

In a tough economic time, going green can seem like a luxury. "Back to basics" becomes the default position. Yet, as Hannam contends, sustainability can "lead to greater organizational efficiency and long-term cost savings." Green innovation can provide the necessary edge for firms to survive the wrenching changes that accompany a recession and better position them to take advantage of the new economic order that emerges with recovery. Nonetheless, in Hannam's words, such companies must "demonstrate to skeptics that green business practices truly do deliver a measurable return on investment."[29]

The second critical challenge, in some ways more daunting, is the lack of qualified workers, a situation that is holding back the growth of many green industries. The nation will need to invest millions of dollars in training programs so that workers can move into green-collar jobs. MBA programs will need to retool so that they can prepare students for leadership in the new green economy. Fortunately, as the Aspen Institute reported this year, the proportion of MBA programs requiring their students to take courses focused on sustainability and corporate social responsibility leapt from 34 percent in 2006 to 63 percent in 2007.[30]

The third challenge is greenwashing, which threatens to undermine the credibility of the corporate world. Many companies view going green as a short-term branding opportunity rather than a long-term commitment to doing business differently. Transparency, accountability, and authenticity all need to be part of the drive toward more sustainable business practices if this situation is to be avoided. "The recent influx of 'green' products in all categories makes it difficult for consumers to sort out who's green and who's not," notes Hannam, adding that "Prospective employees also want to be reassured by the organization's green credentials."[31]

Finally, the need for revised government policies is clear. Without these changes it will be difficult if not impossible for sectors like renewable energy to thrive. Fossil fuels receive enormous subsidies at the cost of effective state and federal incentives necessary to promote solar, wind, and other clean technologies. The good news is that the likelihood of enacting a more progressive energy agenda is stronger than it has been in years. In addition, the need to replace the Kyoto Protocol creates new opportunities for the proper pricing of carbon emissions and other destructive environmental practices.

Despite these challenges, the United States has made important progress in greening its economy. Some of the best opportunities can be found in energy efficiency programs. Upgrading inefficient lighting, heating, ventilation, and air conditioning, electrical motors, roofing, windows, and insulation have all proven to provide significant returns on investments in the form of energy cost savings. Beyond cost savings, energy efficiency investments create jobs in the local community. Retrofitting, as Van Jones notes, provides "good jobs... that cannot be outsourced." People are employed to design, install, and sell the required technology; their spending creates jobs, and lower utility bills free up money that can be spent locally, most of which otherwise would have left the community to pay for electricity.[32]

Energy experts Jonathan Kevles and Michael Kinsley use the metaphor of a water bucket in their analysis of energy efficiency and the local economy. If we think of the local economy as a water bucket that is full when healthy, then most economic development initiatives concentrate on finding more hoses to fill the bucket. This makes sense, but less obvious and often underappreciated is the fact that the bucket is full of holes, a condition known as "economic leakage." In the case of electricity use, energy *inefficiency* is the chief factor allowing this leakage. Sealing the leaks, from this perspective, is a powerful tool for promoting economic development.[33]

Jobs created directly by energy efficiency investments range from blue-collar jobs to more technical positions, from installing high-performance windows and insulation to more efficient technology and manufacturing processes in a factory. Indirect jobs result from what economists refer to as the "economic multiplier." When electric bills decline, many of the dollars that would have left the community to pay for electricity instead recirculate in the community and create jobs, which in turn increases local spending.

Kevles and Kinsley cite a 2002 study by the RAND Corporation for the State of Minnesota, which found that energy efficiency measures generated statewide per capita energy expenditure savings of $242 between 1982 and 1992—roughly a 33 percent decline in energy expenditures that led to a statewide savings of $1.1 billion in 1998 dollars. Another 2002 study, carried out by the Southwest Energy Efficiency Project, estimated that similar investments in Arizona, Colorado, Nevada, New Mexico, Utah, and Wyoming would generate a net savings to consumers of $28 billion from 2003 to 2020, create 58,400 net new jobs in the region, and increase income in the region by $1.34 billion per year by 2020.[34]

Energy efficiency is an especially attractive proposition for communities in times of economic difficulty because these measures create jobs and savings where such opportunities are in decline. In particular, energy efficiency benefits do not depend on an upturn in the economy. Lower utility bills make a community more attractive to business, a fact obvious to those looking to start, expand, or relocate a company. In addition, because energy efficiency investments depend less on decisions made by distant governments or companies, they give communities an opportunity to regain some control over their economic destinies.

"We have to get back to a cheap energy economy, we can't drill and burn our way out of our present economic and environmental problems," Van Jones points out. "We have to invent and invest a way out of our problems, by moving into clean energy and energy conservation."[35] The task that lies ahead is clear. The only uncertainty is what role colleges and universities will play in carrying it out.

Notes

1. Michael Crow, "American Research Universities During the Long Twilight of the Stone Age," elaboration on remarks delivered at the Rocky Mountain Sustainability Summit, University of Colorado, Boulder, February 21, 2007, pp. 1–2. http://president.asu.edu/files/2007_0212StoneAge.pdf (accessed October 24, 2008).

2. Larry Edward Penley, "Beyond Pledges and Light Bulbs," *Inside Higher Ed*, March 28, 2008. www.insidehighered.com/layout/set/print/views/2008/03/28/penley (accessed October 24, 2008).

3. See David L. Kirp, *Shakespeare, Einstein, and the Bottom Line: The Marketing of Higher Education* (Cambridge, MA: Harvard University Press, 2003) for a sharp critique of current trends in higher education regarding its market orientation.

4. Graham B. Spanier and Mary Beth Crowe, "Marshalling the Forces of the Land-Grant University to Promote Human Development," in Richard M. Lerner and Lou Anna Kimsey Simon, eds., *University-Community Collaborations for the Twenty-First Century* (New York: Garland Publishing, 1998), p. 74.

5. Penley, "Beyond Pledges and Light Bulbs."

6. Stefan Theil, "The Campus of the Future," *Newsweek*, August 9, 2008. www.newsweek.com/id/151686 (accessed October 8, 2008); Arizona State University, "Leveraging Place," *Our Design Aspirations*. http://mynew.asu.edu/leveraging-place (accessed October 12, 2008).

7. Michael Crow, "New Challenges, New Solutions," *University Business*, June 2007. www.universitybusiness.com/viewarticle.aspx?articleid=1028&p=6 (accessed October 12, 2008).

8. Arizona State University, "Social Embeddedness," *Our Design Aspirations*. http://mynew.asu.edu/social-embeddedness (accessed October 12, 2008).

9. Rick Heffernon, "ASU Research Sets Stage for 'Green' Growth in Arizona," September 29, 2008. http://asunews.asu.edu/20080929_ss_sustainability (accessed October 14, 2008); "Arizona State University Creates Solar Power Laboratory," *Fox Business*, July 11, 2008. www.foxbusiness.com/story/markets/industries/industrials/ariona-state-university-creates-solar-power-laboratory (accessed October 14, 2008).

10. Ron Scherer, "'Sustainability' Gains Status on US Campuses," *Christian Science Monitor*, December 19, 2006. www.csmonitor.com/2006/1219/p01s03-ussc.html (accessed October 14, 2008); Arizona State University, "The Biodesign Institute: A Bold New Approach." www.biodesign.asu.edu/about (accessed October 14, 2008).

11. Heffernon, "ASU Research Sets Stage for 'Green' Growth."

12. "Community Sustainability Partnership." www.grpartners.org/csp.php (accessed October 21, 2008).

13. Evan West, "America's Greenest City," *Fast Company* 129 (October 2008). www.fastcompany.com/magazine/129/new-urban-eco-nomics.html (accessed October 21, 2008); Tina Lam, *Detroit Free Press*, "Grand Rapids Is Ahead of the Game in Eco-Friendly Living," October 19, 2008. www.freep.com/article/20081019/NEWS05/810190390/1001/NLETTER09?source=nletter-news (accessed October 21, 2008).

14. West, "America's Greenest City."

15. Lam, "Grand Rapids Is Ahead."

16. West, "America's Greenest City"; Lam, "Grand Rapids Is Ahead"; Aquinas College, "Sustainable Business." www.aquinas.edu/sb (accessed October 21, 2008).

17. Aquinas College, "Center for Sustainability." www.centerforsustainability.org/programs.php (accessed October 21, 2008).

18. Grand Valley State University, "GVSU Noted as 'Cutting-Edge Green' University," August 6, 2008. www.gvsu.edu/gvnow/index.cfm?fuseaction=home.read_news&id=99A4EF08-9941-539F-DB92E997E5E6C148 (accessed October 21, 2008).

19. Grand Valley State University, "Sustainability Initiative." www.gvsu.edu/sustainability/index.cfm?id=A534FE42-FB4F-0895-30C954463C8EEA43 (accessed October 21, 2008); "Making It Happen: Applied Sustainability at GVSU." http://main.gvsu.edu/cms3/assets/1ACDDEF0-A15A-67B1-F268BE06B2416593/ConfbrochureProof.pdf (accessed October 21, 2008).

20. Doug Thompson, "Sustainability: Grand Rapid's Competitive Advantage," *RevitalizationOnline*, January 4, 2007. www.revitalizationonline.com/article.asp?id=1511 (October 21, 2008).

21. "Local Action Plan to Reduce Greenhouse Gas Emissions for County Government Operations" (Tompkins County, NY), June 2003. www.co.tompkins.ny.us/emc/docs/4_ccp_local_action_plan.pdf (accessed October 18, 2008); Common Council Proceedings City of Ithaca, New York, July 5, 2006. www.ci.ithaca.ny.us/vertical/Sites/%7B5DCEB23D-5BF8-4AFF-806D-68E7C14DEB0D%7D/uploads/%7BA75C5ACA-1863-4412-8775-01E2A929B283%7D.PDF (accessed October 18, 2008).

22. Aaron Munzer, "Tompkins Colleges' 'Carbon Neutral Challenge," *Ithaca Journal*, August 2, 2008. www.theithacajournal.com/apps/pbcs.dll/article?AID=/20080802/NEWS01/808020303 (accessed October 18, 2008); Claudia H. Deutsch, "College Leaders Push for Carbon Neutrality," *New York Times*, June 13, 2007. www.nytimes.com/2007/06/13/education/13green.html (accessed October 18, 2008).

23. Peter W. Bardaglio and Marian Brown, "Sustainability, Campus Operations, and Academic Entrepreneurship at Ithaca College," *The Green Campus: Meeting the Challenge of Environmental Sustainability,* ed. Walter Simpson (Alexandria, VA: APPA, 2008), p. 328.

24. Tim Ashmore, "State's First 'Green' Consortium Aims to Save Money, Trees," *Ithaca Journal*, February 12, 2008. http://sustainithaca.org/2008/02/14/states-first-green-consortium-aims-to-save-money-trees (accessed October 20, 2008).

25. "Energy and Greenhouse Gas Emissions," www.co.tompkins.ny.us/planning/compplan/documents/9-2-08DraftEnergyElement_001.pdf (accessed October 20, 2008).

26. Willimina Bromer, "C.U. to Invest $20 Million in Ithaca," *Cornell Daily Sun*, October 19, 2007. http://cornellsun.com/node/25171 (accessed October 20, 2008).

27. David J. Skorton, "Cornell University's $20 Million Initiative Designed With the Community in Mind," *Cornell Chronicle*, June 26, 2008. www.news.cornell.edu/stories/June08/CU.local.invest.html (accessed October 20, 2008).

28. Thomas L. Friedman, *Hot, Flat, and Crowded: Why We Need a Green Revolution—and How It Can Renew America* (New York: Farrar, Straus, and Giroux, 2008).

29. Paul Hannam, "The Challenges Facing Green Job Growth," *GreenBiz.com*, September 22, 2008. www.greenbiz.com/feature/2008/09/22/the-challenges-facing-green-job-growth (accessed October 24, 2008).

30. "Aspen Institute Survey," CSRwire, April 21, 2008. http://www.csrwire.com/News/11725.html (accessed November 5, 2008).

31. Hannam, "Challenges Facing Green Job Growth."

32. Van Jones, *The Green Collar Economy: How One Solution Can Fix Our Two Biggest Problems* (New York: HarperCollins, 2008), p. 119.

33. Jonathan Kevles and Michael Kinsley, "Energy-Efficiency Managers and Economic-Development Directors—An Under-Explored Political Alliance," *RMI Solution* 22, no. 3 (Fall 2006): 6–7.

34. Ibid.

35. Maria José Viñas, "An Interview with Van Jones," *Mongabay.com*, June 23, 2008. http://news.mongabay.com/2008/0623-van_jones_interview_mj_ucsc.html (accessed October 24, 2008).

"Energy and persistence conquer all things."

—Benjamin Franklin

7

BLUEPRINT FOR CLIMATE NEUTRALITY: A ROADMAP TO SUCCESS

" C arbon neutral" was *New Oxford American Dictionary's* 2006 word of the year, defined as "calculating your total climate-damaging carbon emissions (your 'carbon footprint'), reducing them where possible, and then balancing your remaining emissions, often by purchasing a carbon offset: paying to plant new trees or investing in 'green' technologies such as solar and wind power."[1] The goal of carbon neutrality, also called climate neutrality, is gaining widespread support in higher education, as students, faculty, alumni, and other stakeholders put increasing pressure on colleges and universities to track and reduce greenhouse gas emissions.

Energy efficiency and renewable energy technologies are improving, energy markets and policies are maturing, and demand is increasing. Moving to a more efficient and self-reliant campus as a long-term strategy is the smart decision in this time of profound transformation. Whether a college or university is an early, average, or late adopter of the energy and management practices that lead to sustainability, the imperative is to translate leadership, desire, and commitment into tangible actions that dramatically reduce the carbon footprint as efficiently and quickly as possible.

Effective energy management is the most important step in the implementation of any environmental sustainability program. Because energy efficiency is significantly more affordable than purchasing additional electricity generated from coal, gas, nuclear, and renewable sources, it is not surprising that it is sometimes referred to as the "fifth fuel."

Achieving sustainability requires a range of technical, financial, and organizational expertise. If the institution doesn't have adequate internal expertise, it is prudent to engage consultants, engineers, and businesses that specialize in energy efficiency and green campus operations. These firms will analyze the individual situation and offer competitive proposals for improvements.

The first step to minimize a campus' greenhouse gas emissions is to establish an emissions baseline. The Clean-Air Cool Planet (CA-CP) Campus Carbon Calculator was developed specifically for higher education.[2] The American College and University Presidents Climate Commitment (ACUPCC) recommends this calculator or any methodology that is consistent with standards set by the Greenhouse Gas Protocol Initiative, such as the Chicago Climate Exchange and the California Climate Action Registry. The ACUPCC expects signatories to track and report emissions of the six greenhouse gases covered under the Kyoto Protocol: carbon dioxide (CO_2), methane (CH_4), nitrous oxide (N_2O), hydrofluorocarbons (HFCs), perfluorocarbons (PFCs), and sulphur hexafluoride (SF_6). The focus should be on CO_2, according to the ACUPCC, "since emissions of PFCs or SF_6 are unlikely to originate on campus, and emissions of CH_4, N_2O, and HFCs are likely to represent only a small percentage of an institution's total emissions."[3]

The Greenhouse Gas Protocol defines three scopes of emissions that should be accounted for and reported in the inventory:

1.   Direct greenhouse gas emissions occurring from sources that are owned or controlled by the institution

2.   Indirect emissions generated in the production of electricity consumed by the institution

3.   All other indirect emissions, "those that are a consequence of the activities of the institution, but occur from sources not owned or controlled by the institution"[4]

Energy Management in Existing Buildings

Effective energy management is the most important step in the implementation of any environmental sustainability program. Because energy efficiency is significantly more affordable than purchasing additional electricity generated from coal, gas, nuclear, and renewable sources, it is not surprising that it is sometimes referred to as the "fifth fuel." In most cases, by far the biggest chunk of greenhouse gas emissions on campuses results from building operations. Buildings often do not receive adequate preventive maintenance or desirable efficiency upgrades, so they are a logical place to start in any climate neutrality plan. Not only are energy efficiency improvements of existing installations generally the least expensive way to reduce the cost of operations, they may also contribute disproportionately to sustainability because they require relatively small modifications of existing infrastructure and thus avoid consuming the resources required for wholesale replacement of infrastructure.

Energy Star Portfolio Manager

Energy Star's Portfolio Manager is a free online tool to track, analyze, and manage the energy performance of buildings.[5] It allows the institution to monitor energy use in all campus buildings, including any combination of sub-metered and master metered buildings, and it may be used to augment the Clean Air-Cool Planet Campus Carbon Calculator. Portfolio Manager will provide a rating of 1 to 100 that quantifies a building's energy performance compared to similar buildings across the country. For campuses, Portfolio Manager ratings exist for residence halls, office buildings, and hospitals. Currently, other types of buildings can be tracked but not rated on the 1-to-100 scale.

The *Energy Star Building Upgrade Manual* provides comprehensive information to help guide the upgrade process. According to Energy Star, the process to improve facilities' energy performance involves five technical stages: retrocommissioning; lighting; supplemental load reductions; air distribution systems; and heating and cooling upgrades. For technical information that is beyond the scope of this book, see the *Building Upgrade Manual.* [6]

Submetering

Tracking building energy consumption is a key requirement for improving energy performance. One of the biggest challenges for colleges and universities is that many campuses are master-metered and have a few meters that serve a multitude of buildings. In these cases, it is difficult to assess where the "energy hogs" are hiding. Submetering individual buildings is generally a prudent investment because it reveals what the building's energy consumption is and where the challenges and opportunities exist. With this valuable information, the institution can prioritize energy efficiency investments. Beyond submetering buildings, enhanced metering for various systems (lighting, boilers, chillers, and constant and variable-speed drives) can provide useful data to improve energy performance.[7]

Peak Demand Management

Managing peak demand is another key element of energy management. In some utility service areas, depending on the tariff schedules, a customer's highest peak demand for a 15- or 30-minute period determines the price of electricity not just for that day or week but for future months. For example, a college or university's peak demand during the hottest afternoon in August will significantly increase its rate for several months or even a year. The utility's rationale for what it calls a ratchet charge is that it needs to have the capacity to provide electricity to its customers at peak load, so sometimes the end-user is required to pay at peak rates for several months based on its highest demand, even if that demand is only for a short period. Although ratchet charges have been imposed less frequently in recent years, they are making a comeback due to increased overall demand.

Accurate, useful energy performance data helps in the management of peak demand. Among the tools available for collecting and analyzing such information is a sophisticated information system platform from Johnson Controls that enables data-rich, smart decisions regarding maintenance management, energy management, and capital planning issues. The state of Missouri has saved approximately 32 percent on its energy costs and significantly reduced its greenhouse emissions using this platform, which collects information from about 1,000 buildings.

Submetering each building is an important component of the project. Energy usage is tracked every 15 minutes, which helps identify periods of peak demand. The data also help determine the useful life of equipment and inform decisions on whether to extend or replace it by accelerating the capital plan. Submetering also enables the allocation of energy costs to specific departments. In addition, the platform helps with supply-side rate negotiations with utilities. The system takes automatic meter readings every night and compares them to the utility's readings to pick up mistakes, ensuring that the building is utilizing the optimal rate schedule and is billed properly.[8]

THE HUMAN DIMENSION

Oberlin College has taken a different approach to energy management, emphasizing nontechnical feedback to building occupants. Wall-mounted "energy orbs" that glow different colors depending on the building's current energy use provide a quick reading for those who might walk by a quantitative readout without paying any attention to its implications. This ambient feedback, notes John Peterson, chair of Oberlin's environmental studies program and director of research at Lucid Design Group, is part of a larger effort to study the link between real-time data and consumer response. A large plasma display and kiosk in the atrium of the college's Adam Joseph Lewis Center for Environmental Studies offers viewers images of energy and water flows in real time transmitted by more than 150 sensors located throughout the building and surrounding landscape. Such approaches engage building users, educate them about ways to conserve energy by changing their behaviors, and inculcate a stronger sense of environmental stewardship.[9]

Commissioning, Recommissioning, and Retrocommissioning

After the completion of a construction project, commissioning should be carried out to verify that the HVAC, controls, and electrical systems and all building systems are working optimally and as designed. Recommissioning should be done every few years thereafter to ensure that the systems continue to work properly. Retrocommissioning is essentially the same as commissioning, but for buildings that have not previously gone through this process. Too often, commissioning, recommissioning, and retrocommissioning are overlooked, and the systems operate below par. Funds for these projects are thus well spent. Ongoing training of maintenance staff is also important to ensure that buildings run efficiently.

Comprehensive Projects

Depending on how aggressive a campus's energy management program has been through the years, some projects—such as lighting—provide quick paybacks. Instead of addressing these fast payback projects individually, it is wiser to bundle a variety of efficiency measures into a single, comprehensive project, including upgrades that may not be financially viable as stand-alone projects. As the energy savings free up funds, the college or university may take the opportunity to install renewable energy projects. Building equipment upgrades—including high-efficiency chillers, boilers, and variable-speed drives (VSDs)—can yield significant savings. Skilled energy service companies can provide analysis and recommendations.

One of the most ambitious energy management programs in higher education involves four University of Wisconsin (UW) campuses: Green Bay, Oshkosh, River Falls, and Stevens Point. As part of a state pilot project, they are required by a 2006 directive from Governor James Doyle to be energy independent and off the fossil fuel grid by 2012. Using energy performance contracts, UW Oshkosh is working with Johnson Controls to accomplish this goal using a combination of technologies. Through aggressive energy management in its buildings, the university has reduced its load and is already saving more than $167,000 annually. Additional measures will include upgrades to mechanical systems and equipment, electrical power, lighting and control systems, domestic water system controls, temperature controls systems, and the heating plant. Renewable technologies may include solar thermal and photovoltaics, wind power, biomass, cogeneration, and use of digester gas.[10]

Lighting Efficiency

One of the quickest "wins" involves upgrading inefficient lighting. Since 90 percent of the electricity consumed by incandescent bulbs is wasted in the form of heat, replacing them with compact fluorescents significantly reduces both energy consumption and heat load. The good news is that incandescents are being phased out. Federal law mandates the phasing out of incandescents beginning in 2012 and ending in 2014. Compact fluorescents use approximately 75 percent less energy than standard incandescent bulbs and last up to 10 times longer for a comparable amount of light.[11] Upgrading florescent fixtures with T5 or T8 technologies also produces substantial savings.

Heating and Cooling Systems

An effective heating, ventilation, and air conditioning (HVAC) system has a critical impact on energy performance and comfort. An engineering team can analyze and make recommendations on chillers, boilers, motors, controls, energy management systems, building envelopes, and co-generation plants. A whole-building approach makes more sense than looking at the systems individually and helps ensure that efficiency opportunities are not overlooked.

Plug Load

Decades ago, students may have arrived on campus with a stereo, alarm clock, curling iron, and electric typewriter. Now, freshmen come fully equipped with an average of 18 electronic devices ready to plug in. Laptops, printers, mobile phones with chargers, MP3 players, speakers, video game consoles, TVs, DVD players, mini-refrigerators, and microwaves have all become part of the ritual of leaving home. Students may be concerned with global warming, but most are unaware that turning off a power strip on their way out for the day can help reduce energy consumption. Phantom load or plug load—the load when a device is turned off but plugged in—accounts for 6 percent of the nation's energy consumption.[12] Educating students about the concept of plug load and encouraging them to turn off their power strips can yield significant results. An alternative is to encourage students to buy "smart strips" that automatically turn off computer peripherals and other devices when not in use.

Power Management

Power management provides a way to activate a "sleep" feature and power down monitors and computers when they are not in use for a designated amount of time. Energy Star computers and monitors are shipped from the manufacturers with the power-down feature enabled, but many people disable the feature. Energy Star provides no-cost, downloadable software to enable power management from a central location. This practice saves $25 to $75 annually per computer, simply and quickly.[13] UW Oshkosh, for example, saves $9,000 a year with Energy Star power management. University at Buffalo's "Do it in the Dark" campaign encourages students to use power management features and turn off their computers when not in use.[14]

LEED Standards for New and Existing Buildings

Many colleges and universities now require that their buildings achieve the U.S. Green Building Council's Leadership in Energy and Environmental Design (LEED) standards for new construction (LEED-NC). This green building rating system addresses five areas: sustainable site development, water savings, energy efficiency, materials and resources selection, and indoor environmental quality. LEED provides ratings—certified, silver, gold, and platinum—to encourage building owners to construct, renovate, and operate facilities in an environmentally sensitive manner.[15]

In too many cases, existing buildings are neglected as money is poured into new construction. From an energy-intensity perspective, existing buildings represent a much more significant share of energy costs and consumption and provide much more potential for lowering a campus's carbon footprint.

Fewer colleges and universities have adopted LEED for Existing Buildings Operations and Maintenance (EB O&M), although existing buildings typically represent 95 percent of the building stock on campuses. In too many cases, existing buildings are neglected as money is poured into new construction. From an energy-intensity perspective, existing buildings represent a much more significant share of energy costs and consumption and provide much more potential for lowering a campus's carbon footprint. LEED EB O&M is a performance-based system with strong energy and water components that emphasizes operational best practices.

LEED has a pilot program for institutions that want to implement the system campus-wide rather than on a case-by-case basis. For example, a policy requiring green cleaning products can be put in place for the entire campus, not just building by building. In this way, the policy will provide baseline LEED points for the whole campus.

Some institutions have decided to forego LEED certification in favor of being LEED "certifiable," which means that a particular project incorporates the elements of LEED but does not go through the process and expense of becoming certified. By avoiding the administrative fees associated with certifying the buildings, the institutions make it possible to invest more money in the building itself. On the other hand, the same level of rigor may not be achieved if the project team knows that it does not have to document its work.

In either case, the team may want to use Energy Star's Target Finder, an online tool that helps establish energy targets for new construction and rate a building design's estimated energy use on a scale of 1 to 100.[16] In this way, a building's future energy consumption is considered early in the design process and not relegated to an afterthought.

Laboratories

Laboratories are substantially more energy intensive than other campus spaces because of their safety requirements that affect ventilation and exhaust rates. In fact, labs use an average of four to six times more energy than the average office building. These facilities move 100 percent of air and exhaust in the building after just one pass through the lab, after it has been conditioned (filtered, preheated, cooled, dehumidified, reheated, humidified), typically on a 24/7 schedule. Many laboratories exhaust the entire internal volume of the building more than 10 times per hour. In contrast, classroom and office buildings recirculate air, exhaust a small amount of conditioned air, and operate 50 to 80 fewer hours per week than the typical lab building. In large research universities, energy use in labs can account for as much as two-thirds of the electricity consumed.[17]

Laboratories for the 21st Century (Labs 21), a voluntary partnership cosponsored by the U.S. Environmental Protection Agency (EPA) and U.S. Department of Energy (DOE), offers a best practices guide, design process tools, training and education, a performance rating system, and other resources. Labs 21 encourages a whole-building approach that maximizes efficiency opportunities in the design, construction, and operations of high-performance labs.[18] One of the newest energy-efficient research facilities is Joan and Sanford I. Weill Hall at Cornell University, which opened in October 2008. The $162 million, 263,000 square-foot life sciences building has a green roof that absorbs rainwater, incorporates natural lighting into its design, and uses 30 percent less energy than comparable buildings. It is one of only six university laboratory buildings to have achieved LEED Gold certification.[19]

Smart Laboratories

Making labs more efficient requires changing design practices while not compromising user safety. Laboratory ventilation standards have been generalized across many types of labs. Safety criteria—as stand-alone standards or embodied in building codes—represent the consensus of experts for a diversity of facility types and usage patterns. Therefore, safety codes necessarily and understandably represent generalized, conservative, one-size-fits-all minimum standards rather than performance-based criteria based on measurements and data pertinent to specific facilities and usage patterns. "Smarter" safety systems require more technical management and professional discernment than simply relying on a fixed standard. The challenge is to identify minimally to moderately hazardous lab environments where ventilation and exhaust rates can be reduced without compromising safety and then to monitor conditions for problems or changes.

Fortunately, control accuracy in laboratory mechanical systems has improved with the widespread adoption of direct digital controls (DDC) as well as electronic devices that control airflow, which replace pneumatic (air pressure) valves and controls. To some extent, DDC has been underexploited. However, with the advent of precision sensors, a "smart laboratory" concept emerges that combines advanced, real-time air quality measurement with the largely untapped potential of DDC building systems.

The University of California, Irvine, is performing pilot tests of sensor technologies and smart control systems that may enable a reduction of ventilation rates (air changes per hour, or ACH) in laboratories by one-third when labs are occupied and by two-thirds when labs are unoccupied. The system would, however, respond by maximizing the exhaust rate when users, based on safety training and supervision, push a "spill" button as they evacuate a lab, or when sensors detect threshold concentrations of particulates or certain gases are sensed. The maximum exhaust rate will coincide with an instant message to safety or facilities personnel, who will manually reset the HVAC system to its reduced ventilation rate. Thus, smart building sensors and controls provide a "safety net" that backs up safety training and practices, and that provides both real-time and historical air quality data to safety personnel. Extending the smart lab concept to exhaust fan and exhaust stack airspeeds (where high discharge rates typically are employed to disperse exhaust) involves using sensors to determine whether particular sensed roof conditions, such as wind speed, can enable lower exhaust-stack discharge airspeeds safely under certain measurable conditions.

The energy savings, and thus the impact on carbon emissions, from both of these smart lab pilot tests could prove substantial. Smart labs do not simply constitute the application of new sensor technologies and control algorithms. Rather, they provide a paradigm shift in the use of real-time measurements to enhance safety management, as well as an electronic log from which safety patterns can be discerned. The "smart lab" also utilizes LED task lighting for benchtops and other fixed work surfaces in conjunction with reduced overhead illumination, thus reducing heat load to help enable lower ACH rates.

In the old paradigm, a one-size-fits-all ventilation parameter was relied upon for safety and chemical spills that occurred without the knowledge of environmental health and safety staff. The smart lab concept uses information technology to provide more and better safety information for both management and users and therefore increased user safety awareness. Assuming that the smart lab pilot testing at UC Irvine proves successful, this win-win-win result is important for three reasons:

1.   It would mean that substantial reduction of laboratories' carbon footprint could be achieved without compromising user safety.

2.   It would demonstrate a technical approach that could be extended to laboratories nationwide that are ready for smart lab upgrading, since many already have DDC and variable-air volume controls.

3.   It would suggest that broad deployment is feasible because the energy savings—even net of the ongoing expense of monitoring and maintaining more sophisticated building control and safety systems—will make the required retrofits self-financeable.

The smart lab concept, which is now under construction in UC Irvine's new Sue and Bill Gross Stem Cell Research Center, could have a dramatic impact on the carbon emissions of research universities and industrial research laboratories.

Designing a LEED-Certified Laboratory: An Example

The National Renewable Energy Laboratory's (NREL) Science and Technology Facility, completed in 2006, is a state-of-the-art research facility and the first LEED Platinum federal lab in the country. Along with NREL's forthcoming Research Support Facility, this project demonstrates that LEED buildings do not have to cost more than conventional buildings, although the common perception is that LEED facilities and especially laboratories are always the more expensive option.

These projects illustrate the importance of bringing together a team of architects, engineers, building designers, end-users, financial officers, operators, and other stakeholders at the start of the project. A design charette provides the opportunity to make clear expectations, define the project's parameters, plan for efficiency in energy use and construction, and discuss challenges, opportunities, and priorities. For example, a decision to use extensive daylighting helps define the building's structure and constructability. To keep costs down, the decision can be made to use standard-size rather than custom-made materials. A design charette enables the project team to work toward the core principles of the project, eliminate unnecessary costs, and be creative with the design.

The NREL lab saves an impressive 41 percent in energy costs compared to similar facilities designed to American Society of Heating, Refrigerating, and Air-Conditioning Engineers (ASHRAE) standards, resulting in $96,000 in annual savings. Yet the building cost $318 per square foot, substantially less that the 2006 average cost of $450 per square foot for similar labs.[20] It encompasses 71,000 square feet and includes nine laboratories. The office area has 100 percent daylighting, and the building has evaporative cooling, efficient motors, fans, windows, and lighting. *R&D Magazine* recognized this project as Lab of the Year, one of the best laboratories built in the United States in 2007, and a trendsetter in laboratory design. Key factors in the magazine's decision were the low cost and the building's environmental design.[21]

Even more ambitious is NREL's Research Support Facility (RSF), a 218,000 gross square feet facility that will house 750 personnel. This project seeks to achieve LEED Platinum, substantially exceed ASHRAE energy performance standards for commercial buildings, and become one of the greenest buildings ever developed. RSF building systems are also designed to accommodate photovoltaics in a bid to pursue net zero energy at a later date. NREL defines a net zero building as one in which there is net zero site energy, source energy, cost, and emissions.[22] Its modular design and under floor distribution systems for utilities will increase energy efficiency, provide greater design flexibility, and reduce materials cost. Incorporating these strategies and technologies will result in an attractive, high-performance commercial building that will set a new energy and productivity standard constructed at a comparable cost to current commercial buildings. In addition, it will refine and demonstrate an integrated design process in a way that the process and the resulting high performance buildings can be duplicated by others.[23]

Renewable Energy

Renewable energy almost always attracts the most attention, but it makes little sense to pursue this avenue before addressing the problem of energy-inefficient facilities. As a first step, colleges and universities should first identify and implement energy efficiency upgrades that lower the energy intensity (kBtu per square foot) of campus facilities. After lowering demand, a higher percentage of renewable energy can be purchased for the same amount of money, or less money is required to attain the desired percentage.

Although renewable energy may cost more per kilowatt-hour than conventionally produced electricity, that is not always the case. Many colleges and universities are saving money through their commitment to renewable energy. The economics depend on the type of green power, prevailing rates, available rebates and incentives, type of contract, area of the country, and other factors. Colleges and universities can purchase renewable energy certificates (RECs), install renewable energy projects on-site, or combine both approaches to reduce their carbon footprints. At least 15 institutions are procuring 100 percent of their electricity from green power, and this number continues to grow. [24]

Renewable Energy Certificates and Carbon Offsets

As the Environmental Protection Agency's Green Power Partnership observes, RECs "provide buyers flexibility to offset a percentage of their annual electricity use when green power products may not be available locally." Representing "the technology and environmental attributes of electricity generated from renewable sources," RECs are most often sold in 1 megawatt-hour blocks.[25] The ACUPCC Voluntary Carbon Offset Protocol defines an offset as follows:

> A carbon offset is a reduction or removal of carbon dioxide equivalent (CO_2e) greenhouse gas (GHG) emissions that is used to counterbalance or compensate for ("offset") emissions from other activities; offset projects reducing GHG emissions outside of an entity's boundary generate credits that can be purchased by that entity to meet its own targets for reducing GHG emissions within its boundary.

GUIDELINES FOR CARBON OFFSET PROJECTS

According to the ACUPCC Voluntary Carbon Offset Protocol, high-quality carbon offset projects should

- result in actual reductions of GHG emissions;
- be transparent to help ensure validity and further the goal of education on climate disruption and sustainability;
- take into account any increases in emissions that stem from the project activity;
- have measurable, permanent emissions reductions, verified by an independent third-party auditor;
- have credits registered with a well-regarded registry, and they should not be double-counted or claimed by any other party.[26]

These guidelines can help colleges and universities navigate a market that can be confusing and is currently unregulated, and they should be consulted before going forward with carbon offsets.

To purchase RECs and offsets, an institution should decide what type, quantity, and regional or national supplier it prefers and then proceed with the procurement process. One strategy is to invest in RECs or offsets as an interim step while lowering emissions. The campus will then need fewer RECs or offsets later to reach carbon neutrality.

On-Site Renewable Energy

More and more colleges and universities are installing on-site renewable energy systems. Such projects—including wind, photovoltaics, solar hot water, biomass, and geothermal—provide significant educational opportunities for the campus community. They also invest money locally instead of sending dollars to a utility company that likely is based elsewhere. On-site renewable energy projects can supply electricity for emergency backup of critical infrastructure in case the electric grid goes down. Furthermore, on-site generation including wind, photovoltaics (PV), solar hot water, and geothermal can help stabilize energy prices because the "fuel" price is free. Prices for biomass feedstock may vary based on the contract.

Geothermal

According to the Environmental Protection Agency, a geothermal system consumes 72 percent less energy than a comparable cooling system.[27] Yale University has developed a protocol to implement a comprehensive geothermal development initiative. Following planning studies to facilitate construction of geothermal heat exchange, Yale chose a standing-column well design. Water is drawn from the bottom of the well, about 1,500 feet deep, and circulated from the well through a closed-loop heat exchange system where heat is extracted from or added to the building system. The heat exchange from the water into the earth occurs as the water travels down the well.[28]

Photovoltaics (PV)

In June 2008, Arizona State University awarded contracts to three companies to install two megawatts of solar electric modules on approximately 135,000 square feet of building rooftop space and parking structures. This project, which will meet up to 7 percent of the university's energy needs, is expected to be the largest solar power infrastructure on any U.S. campus. Through a power purchase agreement (PPA), the university will purchase the power at a set price for 15 years, the installations will have no upfront cost, and the project will generate approximately $425,000 worth of energy each year. The PPA pricing takes advantage of federal and state tax credits and incentive payments from Arizona Public Service. The university plans a seven-megawatt installation on the Tempe campus as well as installations on other campuses.[29]

Wind

In Minnesota, the University of Minnesota at Morris, Carleton College, and St. Olaf College have all installed 1.65-megawatt turbines that provide 100 percent emission-free green power.[30] In Washington, Whitman College and FPL Energy partnered to install wind turbines on college-owned farmland in 2001. At the time, the resulting 261-megawatt wind farm was the largest of its kind in the West. The project includes 450 wind turbines, 65 of which are on Whitman property. In conjunction with this project, the college instituted a three-year lecture series on renewable energy.[31]

Biomass

Biomass has the advantage of providing a consistent energy source, in contrast to wind and solar, which vary depending on the weather and time of day. The University of South Carolina, with Johnson Controls, completed a state-of-the-art biomass gasification plant that is expected to save $2 million to $3 million per year. The high-tech facility uses pine bark waste wood for fuel and will provide approximately 80 percent of the university's heat and steam needs.[32] This project has a self-funding performance contract that ensures long-term energy and operational cost reductions. Since the facility opened, the university has been able to shut down at least two fossil fuel-fired boilers. An on-site classroom provides a close-up view of the cutting-edge facility in operation and educates students on alternative energy sources.[33]

Middlebury College's new biomass gasification system, drawing on wood purchased within a 75 mile radius, puts $750,000 annually into the local economy and has reduced the institution's carbon footprint by 40 percent. The face of the plant has a glass curtain wall and is located in a highly visible area on campus. It is hard not to notice the wood chips moving by the window as they get loaded into the gasifier. The interior is well lit and all the components are brightly colored. This solution to energy independence and carbon reduction serves as a dramatic "teachable moment" for the college.[34]

Fuel Cells

Fuel cells, although still rare on campuses, are a very efficient and clean source of energy. Similar to a battery, fuel cells use an electrochemical process rather than combustion to produce electricity and hot water. The chemical energy usually comes from the hydrogen contained in natural gas. Because fuel cells do not burn the gas, they operate with almost no pollution. In addition, unlike a battery, a fuel cell does not require recharging; it will generate electricity and heat as long as fuel is supplied.[35]

The fuel cell power plant at California State University Northridge is the largest installation at any higher education institution in the world. Boasting one-megawatt of capacity, this plant produces 18 percent of the campus's base load electricity. Using both the fuel cell's heat and power, it generates electricity at twice the efficiency of a conventional electrical grid, eliminates costs associated with in-building heating and cooling equipment, reduces maintenance costs, and lowers energy usage per campus square foot. Taking all of these factors into account, CSU Northridge projects that the fuel cell plant will generate $14.5 million in net savings over the next 25 years.[36]

Space Optimization

Instead of maximizing existing space, often the perceived solution to space constraints is to construct a new building. Some colleges and universities are holding student enrollment constant but still have plans to build more square footage. Such an approach makes little sense as we enter the age of climate change.

Middlebury's LEED Platinum certified Franklin Environmental Center provides an inspiring example of how a century old, historic building can be affordably made into a 21st century green building by adaptive reuse of the structure. The building's historic character and comfort has been greatly enhanced and it is one of the most energy efficient and environmentally friendly buildings on campus. It attracts students from all majors who come to study in the building because they find it so comfortable and pleasant. Interpretive signage throughout the facility builds awareness about what sustainability is and what it looks like when integrated into building design and construction.[37]

A space utilization study as part of a master plan helps an institution optimize its existing resources, save green space, and focus on renovations and enhancements rather than new construction. As energy costs increase, colleges and universities are becoming smarter and more creative in planning and organizing the use of space and timing of activities. Space optimization may be accomplished by switching the start times of classes to alleviate the need to construct a new facility. Depending on climate, institutions are shutting down parts of their campuses during certain times of the year or increasing the length of semester breaks. For example, shortening a summer session in the Southwest reduces the need for air conditioning, and lengthening the winter break in the Northeast saves on heating costs. Some institutions have already migrated to a four-day class schedule and are closed on Fridays to lower utility bills. SUNY Cortland in upstate New York started the fall semester a week later, eliminated the fall break, added two weeks to winter break, and consolidated classrooms, in the process saving $150,000 in heating costs.[38]

Water Conservation

During the summer and fall of 2007, the southeastern United States suffered the most severe drought in 100 years. Despite very high temperatures, the University of Georgia reduced water consumption by 9 percent. The university reduced consumption by installing low-flow showerheads and toilets, prohibiting pressure washing, and shutting down campus fountains, among other measures. To increase awareness, the university established a public relations campaign called "Every Drop Counts" and developed a Web site to provide conservation tips.[39]

Although carried out during a time of crisis, this highly effective water conservation effort demonstrated steps that colleges can take to save water. LEED guidelines recommend such steps as using native plants, installing flow-reduction aerators in faucets and automatic controls on lavatory faucets, and replacing conventional urinals, showerheads, toilets, lavatory fixtures, and kitchen sinks with high-efficiency models. Additional measures include capturing graywater from showers, sinks, and lavatories for use in water closets.[40]

Transportation

Many institutions are considering telecommuting as viable options to help reduce pressures on parking and office space and reduce their footprints. Dave Newport, director of the Environmental Center at the University of Colorado at Boulder, notes that Governor Bill Ritter has issued an executive order to enhance telecommuting options in the state. "A trip not taken is that much less carbon in the air," Newport says, "and frankly... the studies show that we have more engaged and motivated employees when you give them that sort of latitude." Syracuse University's "Flexible Work and Sustainability Initiative," announced in October 2008, encourages employees to consider a variety of options concerning work schedules and transportation, including telecommuting. Chancellor Nancy Cantor emphasized both the personal and environmental benefits in her announcement. The new work-life and commuting initiatives, in her words, "are intended to help relieve the personal burden felt by so many due to fuel and commuting costs" as well as reduce greenhouse gas emissions.[41]

Colleges and universities can encourage use of public transportation by providing free or discounted transit passes and shuttles from the campus to the public transportation system. In case of emergencies, guaranteed ride-home programs provide options for employees who use mass transit. Some institutions designate high-occupancy vehicle (HOV) parking lots or alternative-fuel vehicle spaces in preferred locations while not adding new parking. In addition, allowing occasional telecommuting reduces traffic, stress, and hours behind the wheel.[42]

Car sharing is becoming increasingly popular on campuses even in rural areas. It gives students and others access to a car for short periods when necessary, reducing the need to own a car. Middlebury College partnered with Zipcar in September 2007 to introduce a car sharing service for faculty, staff, and students. Those joining the program for an annual fee of $35 have access to two Toyota Prius hybrid cars 24 hours a day, seven days a week for $8 per hour or $60 per day. Membership includes gas, maintenance, insurance, and parking. Zipcar currently has similar programs at MIT, Columbia, Georgetown, Rutgers, American University, Harvard University, University of Minnesota, University of Toronto, University of North Carolina, and University of Chicago. "For students, faculty and staff who cannot or do not want to bring privately-owned cars to campus," assistant treasurer and director of business services Tom Corbin says, "Zipcar provides a convenient and cost-effective way to run errands or even take a weekend trip."[43]

Many campuses have adopted policies to encourage bicycle use. The University of New England and Ripon College are offering free bikes to freshmen who promise to leave their cars at home, while other institutions are partnering with bike stores to offer discounts on purchases. Ripon raised $50,000 from trustees, alumni, and other donors to pay for the bikes, far less than the cost of building a new parking facility. President David C. Joyce, noting that the original goal was to sign up 40 percent of the incoming class, says that the college has far exceeded that target. Emory University and Fuji Bikes have teamed up to provide 50 bikes that can be rented at no charge at several spots around campus. Other practices to promote the use of bikes include bike exchanges that enable students and staff to pick up a bike at one end of campus for a ride to the other end and storage facilities for bikes in convenient and secure locations.[44]

The procurement of new campus vehicles provides an opportunity to green the fleet and increase the use of hybrids and natural gas buses. Webcasts, podcasts, and videoconferencing can reduce business-related travel. Other activities to lower emissions include using waste oil from cooking to fuel campus vehicles. The University of Central Oklahoma, for example, fuels campus vehicles with biodiesel produced from vegetable oil and animal fat used in the cafeteria. The university has created templates and a Web site to help others learn about this technology.[45]

Green Roofs and Landscaping

A green roof system is an extension of the existing roof which involves a high quality water proofing and root repellent system, a drainage system, filter cloth, a lightweight growing medium, and plants.[46] Green roofs provide an attractive oasis on campus while reducing the heating and cooling load of buildings, improving stormwater management, and creating learning opportunities. At the same time, they optimize space for students, staff, faculty, and visitors. Green roofs generate points for LEED buildings and demonstrate an institutional commitment to being at the front of the pack when it comes to sustainability.

Native plants used in campus landscaping reduce the need for irrigation and lower water and energy consumption and maintenance costs. They need less fertilizer, weeding, and care from maintenance staff than nonindigenous plants. Water consumption for landscaping can also be lowered by using high-efficiency irrigation systems and rain barrels for water collection. Planting deciduous trees on the south side of buildings and coniferous trees on the north side reduces energy requirements for heating and cooling of campus facilities.

Recycling and Source Reduction

At many institutions, establishing and maintaining a recycling program was the first step in the journey toward a green campus. The earliest college recycling programs date back many years and are still active. A comprehensive program includes the collection and recycling of office and mixed paper, glass, plastics, cardboard, metal, batteries, fluorescent lamps, and ink cartridges. An effective recycling program requires that it be easy, with containers located in accessible locations. To boost recycling rates, it also helps to raise the program's profile by using signage and colorful containers.

There are simple yet effective methods for source reduction. To put a dent in paper consumption, for example, a college can institute a campus-wide policy requiring double-sided copying, charging fees for printing copies, and encouraging the use of electronic information as much as possible. As with all sustainability initiatives, publicizing the environmental impacts is a key to a successful program.

Purchasing

An institution's supply chain can have a significant impact on its carbon footprint. As supply chain issues attract increasing attention, procurement officials take on new responsibilities related to sustainability. Based on the experiences of large corporations, colleges and universities are prodding their suppliers to improve their environmental and social standards. In doing so, an institution can have a positive influence on its supply chain and encourage or require that its suppliers green their operations, services, and products.

A simple and cost-effective way to improve energy performance on campus is to institute an Energy Star purchasing policy for all equipment categories that have the rating available. The Energy Star Web site includes key product criteria, savings calculators, and sample procurement language. As an example, University at Buffalo saves approximately $21,000 per year after replacing conventional vending machines with Energy Star models.[47]

AASHE Sustainability Tracking, Assessment, and Rating System (STARS)

The Association for the Advancement of Sustainability in Higher Education (AASHE) has developed Sustainability Tracking, Assessment, and Rating System (STARS), a framework for institutions that measures their progress toward sustainability. According to AASHE, "STARS is a voluntary, self-reporting framework for gauging relative progress toward sustainability for colleges and universities."[48] AASHE facilitated an open, collaborative, and inclusive process to develop the system and tapped into a wealth of expertise. STARS focuses on three major areas: education and research, operations, and administration and finance. After being piloted at more than 90 institutions, STARS 1.0 will be released in 2009.

Planning

The ACUPCC has sparked many colleges and universities to begin crafting a sustainability plan. The ACUPCC calls for signatories to initiate development of a comprehensive plan for achieving carbon neutrality as soon as possible. ACUPCC institutions are charged with completing a greenhouse gas emissions inventory within the first year (see page 126) and an institutional climate action plan within two years. AASHE has posted a number of plans on its Web site (www.aashe.org). Colleges and universities that are in the early stages of sustainability planning can find guidance in the posted campus climate action plans, strategic, and campus master plans that address sustainability and sustainability plans.

Adaptation

With evidence mounting that climate change is already under way, the conversation is beginning to shift from mitigation to adaptation. How do master planners design for the next few decades and factor in the increasing intensity of hurricanes and changing precipitation patterns? With several large insurance companies no longer insuring coastal communities, what impact will this have on the expansion plans of institutions in these communities? Adaptation strategies can include installing more self-reliant energy systems to lower dependence on the electric grid and provide emergency electric back-up in case of increased blackouts or brownouts. Contingency plans for campus evacuations in case of weather disasters should be carefully considered. A new world is coming, and we need to be prepared.[49]

Notes

1. Sebastian Blanco, "New Oxford American's Word of the Year: Carbon Neutral," *AutoblogGreen*, November 19, 2006. www.autobloggreen.com/2006/11/19/new-oxford-american-s-word-of-the-year-carbon-neutral/ (accessed April 17, 2008).
2. Download the calculator at http://cleanair-coolplanet.org/toolkit/inv-calculator.php.

3. "Implementation Guide: Information and Resources for Participating Institutions," American College and University Presidents Climate Commitment, September 2007, p. 11. www.presidentsclimatecommitment.org/pdf/ACUPCC_IG_Final.pdf (accessed April 29, 2008).

4. Greenhouse Gas Protocol Initiative, "Calculation Tools: Frequently Asked Questions." www.ghgprotocol.org/calculation-tools/faq#directindirect (accessed November 4, 2008).

5. "Portfolio Manager Overview." www.energystar.gov/index.cfm?c=evaluate_performance.bus_portfoliomanager (accessed February 28, 2008).

6. "Building Upgrade Manual." www.energystar.gov/index.cfm?c=business.bus_upgrade_manual (accessed September 26, 2008).

7. *LEED Existing Building Reference Guide*, 2nd ed. (Washington, DC: U.S. Green Buildings Council, 2006), p. 231.

8. Richard Justis, Johnson Controls, personal communication, August 1, 2008.

9. Karla Hignite, "Seeking a Smaller Footprint," *Business Officer* (July-August 2008). http://www.nacubo.org/x10717.xml (accessed September 17, 2008).

10. "Case Study, University of Wisconsin-Oshkosh, Oshkosh, Wisconsin." www.johnsoncontrols.com/publish/us/en/products/building_efficiency/case_studies2/education.html (accessed September 26, 2008).

11. "Compact Fluorescent Light Bulbs." www.energystar.gov/index.cfm?c=cfls.pr_cfls (accessed July 5, 2008).

12. "Phantom Load." www.ocf.berkeley.edu/~recycle/ssec/download/Phantom%20Load.pdf (accessed June 25, 2008).

13. "General Technical Overview of Power Management." www.energystar.gov/index.cfm?c=power_mgt.pr_power_management (accessed June 24, 2008).

14. "Computers, On 24/7, Awaiting Updates But Wasting Energy?" www.energystar.gov/ia/products/power_mgt/UofWisc_CPM_casestudy.pdf (accessed June 24, 2008); "Do It in the Dark." http://www.buffalo.edu/inthedark/index.html (accessed November 13, 2008).

15. "LEED® for Existing Buildings: Operations & Maintenance." www.usgbc.org/ShowFile.aspx?DocumentID=3617 (accessed October 8, 2008).

16. "Target Finder." www.energystar.gov/index.cfm?c=new_bldg_design.bus_target_finder (accessed April 17, 2008).

17. Wendell Brase, vice chancellor of the University of California, Irvine, contributed this paragraph and the following section about smart labs.

18. "About Labs21." www.labs21century.gov/about/index.htm (accessed February 5, 2008).

19. Liz Lawyer, "Cornell Unveils 'Green Lab Building," *Ithaca Journal*, October 11, 2008. http://www.theithacajournal.com/article/20081011/NEWS01/810110316 (accessed November 14, 2008).

20. "Science & Technology Facility Is First LEED Platinum Federal Building" (news release), April 4, 2007. www.nrel.gov/news/press/2007/507.html (accessed July 25, 2008).

21. "DOE Research Facility Receives Lab of the Year Award" (news release), April 14, 2008. www.nrel.gov/news/press/2008/585.html (accessed July 25, 2008).

22. "Getting to Zero Energy Buildings," Center for the Built Environment, University of California, Berkeley, Summer 2008. www.cbe.berkeley.edu/research/pdf_files/CBE-CenterlineSummer2008.pdf (accessed September 27, 2008).

23. Dan Arvizu, "At NREL, the Keynote is Innovation," *Innovation: America's Journal of Technology Commercialization*, February/March 2008. www.innovation-america.org/index.php?articleID=399 (accessed July 25, 2008); "Research Support Facilities." http://www.nrel.gov/sustainable_nrel/sustainable_buildings_rsf.html (accessed February 10, 2009).

24. "100% Green Power Purchasers: as of July 8, 2008." www.epa.gov/greenpower/toplists/partner100.htm (accessed October 7, 2008).

25. "Glossary." www.epa.gov/grnpower/pubs/glossary.htm (accessed June 25, 2008).

26. "ACUPCC Voluntary Carbon Offset Protocol," November 2008. See Appendix 4. For addition details, see "Investing in Carbon Offsets: Guidelines for ACUPCC Institutions," November 2008. http://www.presidentsclimatecommitment.org/documents/CarbonOffsetsGuidelines_v1.0.pdf (accessed November 14, 2008).

27. www.cleanair-coolplanet.org/renewable_tree/geothermal.php (accessed September 27, 2008).

28. Bill Johnson, Haley and Aldrich, personal communication, August 25, 2008.

29. "ASU Leads the Nation with Largest University Solar Installa-tion" (press release), June 10, 2008. http://sustainability.asu.edu/giosmain/news/campus-sustainability/asu-leads-the-nation-with-largest-university-solar-installation (accessed July 30, 2008). For more information on Power Purchase Agreements, see Chapter 8.

30. "Wind and Hydropower Technologies Program—Wind Powering America, Wind Energy for Schools Project Locations." www.wind-poweringamerica.gov/schools_projects.asp?&print#MN (accessed October 7, 2008).

31. "Whitman Farm Harvests Wind Power," *Whitman College Magazine Online Gazette*, December 2001. www.whitman.edu/magazine/december2001/W, ind%20power.html (accessed June 19, 2008).

32. Rich Rovito, "Johnson Controls Launches Biomass Power Plant, *Business Journal of Milwaukee*, December 14, 2007. http://milwaukee.bizjournals.com/milwaukee/stories/2007/12/17/story3.html?page=1 (accessed July 25, 2008).

33. "Renewable Energy Solutions, Unlocking Stored Energy in Biomass."www.johnsoncontrols.com/publish/etc/medialib/jci/be/sustainability/renewable_energy.Par.85263.File.tmp/Bi omass%20insert%20F (accessed October 7, 2008).

34. Nan Jenks-Jay, Middlebury College, personal correspondence, February 17, 2009.

35. "Fuel Cells." http://www.fuelingthefuture.org/contents/NewTechnologies.asp (accessed February 24, 2007).

36. "CSU Northridge One MW Fuel Cell Power Plant," *Best Practices Case Studies 2007*, p. 1. blogs.calstate.edu/cpdc_sustainability/wp-content/uploads/2008/05/bp2007_northridge_2.pdf (accessed February 24, 2009).

37. Nan Jenks-Jay, Middlebury College, personal correspondence, February 17, 2009.

38. Bill Massey, Sasaki Associates, personal correspondence, August 7, 2008; Mary Murphy, Nasrin Parvizi, and Paula Warnken, "Green Is Not For Money: Innovative Endeavors Towards Campus Sustain-ability," presentation at NACUBO Annual Meeting, Chicago, July 14, 2008.

39. "University Actively Looking for Additional Ways to Conserve Water," University of Georgia, October 25, 2007. www.uga.edu/aboutUGA/water_update.html (accessed July 29, 2008).

40. *LEED Existing Building Reference Guide*, pp. 123–24.

41. Society for College and University Planning, "Climate Change and Higher Education: Leadership to Achieve Climate Neutrality; A Webcast with Michael Crow, Billy Parish and Dave Newport," moderated by James Gorman, December 12, 2007; and Tim Knauss, "Want to Drive a Zipcar? Attend or Work at SU," *Syracuse Post-Standard*, October 23, 2008. http://www.syracuse.com/business/index.ssf?/base/business-13/1224752211222530.xml&coll=1 (accessed November 25, 2008).

42. Ibid., pp. 49–59.

43. "Car-Sharing Program to Help Reduce Traffic and Pollution" (press release), September 7, 2007. http://www.middlebury.edu/about/pubaff/news_releases/2007/pubaff_633247532612529679.htm (accessed November 16, 2008).

44. Katie Zezima, "With Free Bikes, Challenging Car Culture on Campus," *New York Times*, October 20, 2008. www.nytimes.com/2008/10/20/education/20bikes.html (accessed November 14, 2008); "Ripon College Gives Freshmen Free Bikes for No-Car Pledges," *Milwaukee Journal Sentinel*, August 28, 2008. www.jsonline.com/news/education/32585109.html (accessed November 4, 2008).

45. "Welcome to the Biodiesel Fuel Project at UCO." www.ucobiodiesel.com (accessed November 8, 2008).

46. "About Green Roofs." http://www.greenroofs.org/index.php?option=com_content&task=view&id=26&Itemid=40 (accessed February 5, 2009).

47. "UB Saves $21,000 Annually with 'Green' Vending Machines" (press release), February 17, 2006. www.buffalo.edu/news/7779 (accessed June 24, 2008).

48. "Sustainability Tracking, Assessment & Rating System (STARS)." www.aashe.org/stars (accessed November 8, 2008).

49. For a detailed assessment of the need to develop climate adaptation strategies, see www.aiaccproject.org. Assessments of Impacts and Adaptations to Climate Change (AIACC) is a global initiative developed in collaboration with the Intergovernmental Panel on Climate Change (IPCC) and funded by the Global Environment Facility. Its goal is "to advance scientific understanding of climate change vulnerabilities and adaptation options in developing countries." www.aiaccproject.org/about/about.html (accessed February 21, 2009).

"The dogmas of the quiet past are inadequate to the stormy present. The occasion is piled high with difficulty, and we must rise—with the occasion. As our case is new, so we must think anew and act anew. "
—**Abraham Lincoln, Annual Message to Congress, December 1, 1862**

8

FINANCING CAMPUS SUSTAINABILITY PROJECTS

In tough financial times, it's not surprising that questions arise about whether colleges and universities can afford to take on the issue of climate change mitigation. "How can I justify spending money on things that don't make business sense?" you might ask. Our answer: you can't, and you shouldn't. Green business activities, as Joel Makower insists, should be about making organizations "more resilient and competitive." In other words, it's not just about green making sense when times are tough, but also *because* they are tough.[1]

Especially when resources are increasingly limited, institutions should focus on how to better manage their energy costs. It would be a mistake to think that the recent drops in energy costs as a result of the economic downturn will have much staying power. The International Energy Agency forecasts that by 2015 oil prices will rebound to an average of $100 a barrel and will reach more than $200 by 2030.[2]

Colleges and universities that act now will experience considerable savings in the long run and make a significant dent in their carbon footprint, thus contributing to the fight against global warming. To illustrate our point, we'll look at three key areas: energy efficiency, renewable energy, and transportation. Then we'll explore the available funding sources and provide examples of campus projects that have drawn on these options.

Energy Efficiency

Strategic, smart energy management of buildings pays for itself and keeps on paying. Major cost savings resulting from effective energy management have been well documented for many years. As a simple example, if a campus still uses incandescents, it is wasting money. Lighting upgrades tend to pay back quickly, and other equipment such as chillers, boilers, variable speed drives, and motors have a range of payback periods depending on many variables. These factors include the state of the existing equipment, operating hours and characteristics, energy prices, rebates, and utility tariff structure. Efficiency upgrades lower maintenance costs, improve occupant comfort, and strengthen buildings' infrastructures.

Energy efficiency projects can be financed in a variety of ways that avoid increases in operating expenses and the need to tap into capital budgets. By adopting one of these methods, future energy savings pay for the project and the deal can be structured so that there is a positive cash flow from the start of the project. Through energy efficiency programs, the University of Buffalo has realized more than $9 million in annual savings and $65 million in cumulative cost savings, and University of New Hampshire has annual savings of $7 million.[3]

Renewable Energy

Throughout the country, renewable energy projects are reducing costs or making money for higher education institutions. Renewable energy is often more expensive today than electricity generated from coal, natural gas, or nuclear power, but there are an increasing number of exceptions. Renewable energy may be less expensive than traditionally generated electricity, depending on existing energy prices, type of contract, rebates, grants, availability of renewable resources, area of the country, and federal, state, and local tax incentives. The University of Central Oklahoma has saved more than $50,000 since 2006 through its renewable energy contract that provides 100 percent wind energy for the campus.[4] The University of Iowa had net savings of more than $1 million per year with its circulating fluidized bed boiler that burns oat hulls in place of coal.[5] Since the fuel (for example, wind, sun, or geothermal) is free, many analysts predict that renewable energy will become more cost competitive as fossil fuel prices continue to rise, and new, more cost-efficient technologies come online. Likewise, many environmental experts expect that the cost economics of renewable energy will improve due to federal carbon legislation likely to be passed during the Obama administration, financiers' inclusion of a risk premium in interest rates for fossil generation plants, and the October 2008 extension of federal production and investment tax credits for renewable energy.

Transportation

Lester Brown notes that "as the new century advances, the world is reconsidering the urban role of automobiles in one of the most fundamental shifts in transportation thinking in a century." The challenge, he says, is to "redesign communities, making public transportation the centerpiece of urban transport and making streets pedestrian and bicycle friendly." This means "replacing parking lots with parks, playgrounds, and playing fields." In doing so, we can give people more options for exercise at the same time as we reduce carbon emissions and air pollution.[6] Campuses, many of which are like mini-cities, provide the opportunity to move this vision forward.

Facilitating and paying for more public transportation in lieu of building more parking spaces on campuses saves substantial money. Capital costs range from $15,000 to $30,000 per net new parking space. The University of Colorado at Boulder has an extensive transportation demand management program that focuses on transit users, pedestrians, and bicycles. According to the university's 2004 report *Green Investment, Green Return*, the total avoided costs are more than $4.7 million. By not building more parking lots, CU-Boulder does not have to take on bond debt and has land that can be used for other buildings or green space.[7]

Stanford University's Clean Air Cash program offers monetary incentives for using alternative transportation. A member of the Commute Club is eligible for up to $234 in Clean Air Cash every year. The program provides rides in case of emergency and enables users to purchase up to eight parking passes per month for the times that they need to drive.[8] Stanford has encouraged 900 people to switch from cars to bikes and invested $4 million in improving bike facilities. To build new parking for this number of people would have cost $18 million.[9]

Why Now?

The higher education sector in the United States spends approximately $6 billion a year on energy.[10] According to the Environmental Protection Agency's Energy Star program, an institution can lower its energy bills by 30 percent or more by adopting a strategic approach to energy management.[11] Business officers who struggle with how to pay for upgrade projects often overlook the cost of maintaining the status quo. Doing nothing or delaying a project is often a more expensive alternative than paying for a project through financing. In particular, delaying energy efficiency upgrades in campus buildings can have a significant financial impact on the operating budget. Energy Star's Cash Flow Opportunity (CFO) calculator quantifies the cost of delaying an efficiency project while waiting for a capital budget allocation to pay for efficiency upgrades.[12]

Sources of Funding

Frequently used financing methods for campus sustainability projects include cash, bonds, tax-exempt lease financing, and energy performance contracts. Each method has advantages and disadvantages (see Appendix 5 for a comparison).

Energy Performance Contracts

An energy performance contract (EPC) is a performance-based contract structured to enable an institution to pay for efficiency upgrade projects with future energy savings. EPCs have been used extensively in higher education, K–12 schools, and the federal government for more than two decades because these institutions can approach investments with a long-term perspective. The amortization period for EPC projects can stretch for 15 to 20 years. Many financing mechanisms are available, depending primarily on the structural constraints (such as legal or budgeting limitations) placed on the institution. Colleges and universities may finance EPC projects using cash, bonds, operating leases, capital leases, receivable purchase agreements, loans, certificates of participation, and tax-exempt lease-purchase agreements.

The EPC financing choice may have important implications for an organization's financial statements and fiscal strategy. For example, EPCs can be funded through operating leases, which require little or no up-front capital and let one treat the costs as annual operating expenses, keeping them off the balance sheet. Capital lease options allow the institution to present the energy upgrade as an investment on the balance sheet, but may carry challenges when seeking approval since the entire lease commitment is reported on the balance sheet. Using institutional cash to pay for the energy upgrade outright is another strategic option, in which the school avoids financing costs and immediately owns its investment. Each of the many financing options available has advantages and disadvantages. The college or university should fully explore all the options with its institution's financial leadership when it is time to make the investments.

An institution contracts with an energy services company (ESCO) to design and install EPC projects. The ESCO provides a guarantee and pays the university the difference between the projected and actual savings if the savings are not achieved. The ESCO also provides operations and maintenance (O&M) after the project is installed and has a strong vested interest in ensuring that the equipment is calibrated and performing properly so that energy and cost savings do not degrade over time due to lack of proper maintenance. O&M and maintenance and verification (M&V) are usually negotiated between the parties. O&M and M&V are critical issues for any project justified on cost avoidance grounds since the difference in pre-upgrade and post-upgrade energy costs is the source of cash to both the ESCO and the school. All EPCs will focus on M&V as the baseline for payment to the ESCO. Institutions also need to analyze whether the EPC's associated costs (for example, performance guarantee, O&M, and M&V) are worth it compared to doing the project in-house. This decision will depend in part on the complexity of the project.

By using EPCs, colleges and universities can take on more comprehensive projects. The danger in pursuing only the fast-payback projects is that other energy efficiency upgrades will only get more expensive and more difficult to finance. By bundling projects that have faster paybacks (such as lighting) with projects that have longer paybacks (such as chillers, windows, and boilers), an institution may carry out comprehensive projects by extending the contract term. Depending on the project, the term might fall into the 7- to 10-year range, but 12 to 15 years is increasingly common. After about 15 to 20 years, the issue of the equipment's useful life comes into play. EPCs also present opportunities to incorporate onsite renewable energy or deferred maintenance projects that might otherwise be unaffordable. The ACUPCC-Clinton Climate Initiative's best practices toolkit and Raise the Funds: Campus Action Toolkit, published by Campus in Power, provide useful information on EPCs.

Power Purchase Agreements

A power purchase agreement (PPA) is a long-term purchase agreement between a building owner and an investor in which the investor installs, operates, maintains, and owns an on-site renewable energy system (typically photovoltaic) at the owner's facility. PPAs reduce capital risk

ACUPCC-CLINTON CLIMATE INITIATIVE PARTNERSHIP

A partnership between the American College and University Presidents Climate Commitment (ACUPCC) and the Clinton Climate Initiative (CCI) is designed to accelerate the implementation of efficiency upgrades on college and university campuses. The program seeks to facilitate the use of EPCs to encourage the installation of large efficiency projects. It is not a grant program. As part of its work with 40 cities around the globe, CCI has developed partnerships with several major ESCOs, global financial institutions, and product suppliers. ESCOs, working in collaboration with CCI, have agreed to utilize best practices and provide guaranteed savings, guaranteed maximum price, transparent pricing, and gain sharing for large energy upgrade projects. Financial institutions have agreed to make capital available for retrofit projects at commercial rates and to work with CCI and colleges and universities to develop new mechanisms and tools for financing efficiency work. A group of product suppliers has agreed to offer discounts for a range of energy efficiency products including chillers, lighting, roofing insulation, and windows. In conjunction with CCI, its ESCO and financial institution partners have committed to developing more innovative mechanisms that will benefit more end-users.

---

by ensuring a cash flow to the investor. The investor can be an energy service company, a manufacturer, or another third party that produces power. The advantage of a PPA is that the end-user generally receives a positive cash flow, with no money down, as soon as the project is installed. The company sells the output of electricity for a fixed price, often for terms of 10 or more years. The fixed price typically is equal to or less than the price the user had been paying for electricity before the project's installation. The cost economics of the projects depend on the available rebates that help make them financially feasible. The company receives any applicable utility and state rebates for the project. Colleges and universities that enter into PPAs anticipate that the cost of electricity is likely to increase over the term of the agreement and that energy prices will not drop below the fixed price. For example, Arizona State University is using PPAs for large-scale photovoltaics installations, and Los Angeles Community College District is using PPAs to install 9 megawatts of photovoltaics at its nine campuses.

Endowments

The use of endowments to advance campus sustainability is under increasing scrutiny for various reasons, including the Sustainable Endowments Institute's *College Sustainability Report Card 2009*. The report analyzes

institutions with the 300 largest endowments in the United States and
Canada that represent more than $380 billion in endowment assets and
more than 90 percent of all university endowments.[14] Some colleges have
used endowments to fund sustainability efforts on campuses, repaying
them through the resulting savings. This approach is especially feasible
for those campuses that have never employed an energy efficiency strategy
and thus can undertake projects with a one to two year payback. Often
such projects can earn a higher rate of return than that of the endowment
portfolio.[15] Carleton College, for example, borrowed from its endowment to pay for its 1.65-megawatt utility-grade wind turbine. Having
received a production tax credit from the state of Minnesota, the college
sells the wind output to its local utility, Xcel Energy, thus generating a
positive cash flow.[16]

Gifts

Gifts from alumni, corporations, and students often support sustainability initiatives. The stories behind these gifts reflect a deep commitment and passion for both the institutions and the future. The following
examples illustrate some of the exciting sustainability projects that have
been funded:

- Furman University, in conjunction with the Cliffs Communities, Duke Energy, Bank of America, *Southern Living* magazine,
  Johnston Design Group, and other supporters, constructed a
  3,400-square-foot green home on campus named the Cliffs
  Cottage. This high-performance showcase demonstrates green
  design, energy efficiency, renewable energy, and sustainable
  products and processes, and it will be among the first residential
  homes to receive LEED certification. Completed in June 2008,
  it is available for tours for a year and then will be converted
  into Furman's Center for Sustainability in 2009.[17] For this project, the university received $1.5 million from Duke Energy, a
  $750,000 gift from the Cliffs Communities, $250,000 from the
  Bank of America Charitable Foundation, at least $100,000 in
  alumni-related goods and services, $100,000 in services from
  the Johnston Design Group, and numerous smaller gifts from
  about 100 other partners.[18]

- Rice University announced a $30 million gift to construct a new
  LEED Gold residence hall in August 2007. Duncan College,
  named after donors Charles and Anne Duncan, is expected to

be 45 to 50 percent more energy efficient and 30 to 40 percent more water efficient than comparable "baseline" facilities. The concrete includes fly ash, a waste product from the local coal power industry, as a substitute for Portland cement. The innovative 50 percent substitution results in a stronger concrete at no additional cost. The project has diverted approximately 90 percent of construction waste, which will be recycled, and employs an inventive strategy of prefabricated restroom "pod" assemblies to prevent waste from being generated. As a living-learning facility, Duncan College plans a strong environmental education component through a sustainability classroom and other enhancements.[19] According to the university, it will be one of the most sustainable buildings in Houston.[20]

- In September 2007, Williams College received a $5 million gift to establish the Zilkha Center for Environmental Initiatives. The center will lead the development and management of a strategic plan for sustainability that will encompass energy management, greenhouse gas emissions reductions, waste management, environment-friendly development and purchasing, and student involvement and education.[21]

- Gerhard Andlinger, who came to the United States from Austria as the winner of a newspaper essay contest in 1948, made a $100 million gift in 2008 to his alma mater, Princeton University. This gift enables Princeton to create the Gerhard R. Andlinger Center for Energy and the Environment in the School of Engineering and Applied Science. The center will focus on accelerating research on sustainable solutions for energy and the environment, including energy efficiency, sustainable energy sources, and carbon management. The center will feature a state-of-the-art engineering research laboratory, new faculty positions, endowed funds, outreach, and a visitors program. It will support teaching and research that intersects with public policy and natural sciences and will transfer research findings quickly into the marketplace.[22]

- An anonymous Cleveland-area family pledged $4 million to Oberlin College for environmental stewardship initiatives in November 2007. Of the $4 million, $2.5 million will be used to establish an endowed chair in environmental studies, $1 million will be for technological upgrades in the Adam Joseph

Lewis Center for Environmental Studies, and $500,000 will be for environmental planning grants for the college and the city of Oberlin.[23]

Utility Rebates and Grants and System Benefit Charges

Through their demand-side management programs, some utilities provide grants and rebates to encourage the installation of energy efficiency and renewable energy projects. These utilities have a strong interest in ensuring that they can cover their customers' increasing demand for energy and avoid rolling brownouts and blackouts. As businesses, the utilities recognize that often it is more cost-effective to reduce electric demand through rebates, incentives, and educational programs than to increase supply by building a new power plant and risk the potential for community opposition and legal challenges. The utilities most likely to offer incentives have capacity constraints and are reaching peak demand. Some realize that their pivotal role in promoting a clean energy future gives their companies a strategic advantage. The Database of State Incentives for Renewables and Efficiency (DSIRE) provides detailed information on federal, state, local, and utility incentives that fund renewable energy and energy efficiency.[24]

In some cases, utilities have awarded substantial grants to colleges and universities for clean energy research and projects. The University of Minnesota received $4.5 million from the Xcel Energy Renewable Development Fund in December 2007 for research in biomass integrated gasification at ethanol plants, biomass fuel stock, improving efficiency and lowering the cost of nanocrystal silicon photovoltaic cells, and optimizing the turbine siting design of wind energy projects.[25] Xcel also made a $1.5 million grant to St. Olaf College for its $1.9 million wind turbine, which supplies about one-third of the college's electricity.

Certain states provide funding for energy efficiency and renewable energy projects. Members of the Clean Energy States Alliance will make available nearly $3.5 billion for such projects over the next decade.[26] Some states mandate system benefit charges that are collected from a small surcharge on electric bills to provide a pool of money for efficiency and renewable projects. Using this approach, the New York State Energy Research and Development Authority (NYSERDA) will have access to $1.86 billion through 2011.[27] NYSERDA distributes funding for a range of programs and projects, including many in higher education institutions.

Revolving Loan Funds

Harvard University has a well-known $12 million Green Campus Loan Fund (GCLF) that has supported more than 150 projects. Although few institutions have anything like Harvard's wealth, the basic mechanism is a replicable model. The fund provides interest-free capital for sustainability investments that have a payback period of 5 to 10 years or less. Up-front capital comes from the fund, and applicant departments agree to repay it through savings gained by "project-related reductions in utility consumption, waste removal, or operating costs." According to the university, "this formula allows departments to upgrade the efficiency, comfort, and functionality of their facilities without incurring any capital costs."[28] The fund generated a 30 percent return on investment (ROI) in 2005, significantly higher than the Harvard endowment's ROI of 19.2 percent.[29]

Timothy Den Herder-Thomas and Asa Diebolt, students at Macalester College, created and established the Clean Energy Revolving Fund (CERF) to implement sustainability projects on the campus, demonstrating that revolving loans are a viable funding source. With AASHE, they published *Creating a Campus Sustainability Revolving Loan Fund: A Guide for Students*.[30] The fund had received commitments of more than $100,000 by 2008.[31] CERF is working on a campus-wide lighting upgrade which will save $40,000 a year.[32] Half the cost will come from CERF, and the college will provide the other half. The board of trustees voted to make the college's half a donation to CERF.[33]

Renewable Energy Hedges

A renewable energy hedge, also known as a contract for differences, is a financial forward contract that gives a college or university some insulation from price volatility over the term of the contract. It is an agreement between an end user and an electricity power producer that includes a fixed or "strike" price. The two parties pay each other based on the strike price as conventional electricity prices fluctuate; therefore, the agreement acts as a green hedge. If electricity prices fall below the strike price, the end user pays the provider. If they rise above, the provider pays the end user.[34]

Southern New Hampshire University has a renewable energy hedge agreement with the wind power supplier PPM. PPM owns the 91-megawatt Maple Ridge wind farm in upstate New York. The hedge contract for 6.2 megawatts is for 15 years, through 2022. This agreement ensures an income stream for the developer and a long-term stable price for the university. The university anticipates significant financial savings through the term of the contract, and the university receives the RECs with this agreement.[35]

Student Fees

As mentioned in chapter 5, student fees have been used increasingly to fund renewable energy purchases. Often, students develop, put forth, organize, and approve referendums to boost their student fees by a few dollars up to about $25 per semester to purchase green power. These referendums frequently pass by large margins.[36] Nearly 70 percent of voting students at the University of California, Berkeley in Spring 2006 approved the student-proposed Green Initiative Fund. The University of California president then approved the fund in July 2006. The $5 a student per semester fee will raise $2 million for sustainability initiatives at Berkeley over 10 years. The fund is overseen by a grant-making committee comprised of four students and three faculty and staff members.[37]

These student fees demonstrate students' strong commitment to greening initiatives. At times, administrations have augmented student fees in recognition of these votes. Although student fees can initiate funding and get the process rolling, they generally are not an appropriate means to fund comprehensive, ongoing sustainability projects.

Research Grants and Funding

A growing number of partnerships between higher education and other sectors are focused on developing clean energy technology and combating climate change. Partners in these collaborations include federal, state, and local governments, and corporations.

Federal Government-University Collaborations

Established in 2007, The Colorado Renewable Energy Collaboratory is a research partnership that involves the National Renewable Energy Laboratory, the nation's primary laboratory for renewable energy and energy efficiency research and development, and three higher education institutions: Colorado State University, the University of Colorado at

Boulder, and Colorado School of Mines. The Collaboratory also works with public agencies, companies, nonprofit organizations, and all of Colorado's universities and colleges to:

- increase the production and use of renewable energy;
- support the development of renewable energy industries in Colorado and the nation;
- build a renewable energy economy in rural Colorado and America;
- establish Colorado as a leading center of renewable energy research and production; and
- educate the nation's energy researchers, technicians, and work force.[38]

The Collaboratory is receiving $2 million annually for three years from the state as seed money to qualify for federal and private matching funds. Its first major project is the Colorado Center for Biorefining and Biofuels (C2B2), which is working to develop new biofuels and biorefining technologies and transfer these advances to the private sector. More than two dozen large and small businesses are participating in C2B2. The private sponsors have committed more than $500,000 toward shared research projects and research fellowships, enabling C2B2 to receive $500,000 in state matching funds.

The Center for Revolutionary Solar Photoconversion (CRSP), announced in April 2008, is a new research center of the Collaboratory. According to the Collaboratory, "CRSP is dedicated to the basic and applied research necessary to create revolutionary new solar energy technologies as well as education and training opportunities." This research will make possible the creation of new, cost-efficient solar energy technologies. Future Collaboratory research centers will focus on wind energy, carbon management, and energy efficiency.[39]

The National Renewable Energy Laboratory also collaborates with Oak Ridge National Laboratory (ORNL), Georgia Institute of Technology, University of Tennessee, Dartmouth College, University of Georgia, the Samuel Roberts Noble Foundation, and private companies. This team won the contract for Department of Energy Bioenergy Science Center, a $125 million bioenergy research center that is working to find new methods to produce biofuels from such sources as switchgrass and poplar trees.[40]

A comprehensive and enduring commitment to sustainability, in short, strengthens existing income streams and creates new ones. As in corporate America, colleges and universities that grasp this insight and act on it are the ones most likely to thrive in the age of climate change.

In June 2007, the University of Wisconsin-River Falls received a $460,000 grant from the U.S. Department of Agriculture for collaboration on sustainable agriculture with Chippewa Valley Technical College and the Midwest Organic and Sustainable Education Service. The grant enables the university to establish a sustainable agriculture major within the College of Agriculture, Food, and Environmental Sciences and infuse sustainable agriculture content and practices into the college's other agriculture science programs.[41]

Corporate-University Collaborations

Collaborations between corporations and universities on clean energy research and other sustainability programs are increasing as companies recognize this strategic imperative. For example, Wal-Mart has given the University of Arkansas $1.5 million to establish the Applied Sustainability Center, an interdisciplinary initiative of the Sam M. Walton College of Business.[42] During its first year, the center's projects included an effort to lower the embodied fossil fuel content of products and identify key sustainability factors in 21st-century agriculture in the United States. The center is also conducting a speaker series and developing pilot training modules on sustainability issues.[43]

In February 2007, the oil company BP announced its selection of the University of California, Berkeley, Lawrence Berkeley National Laboratory, and the University of Illinois at Urbana-Champaign for a $500 million ($50 million a year) research effort to establish the Energy Biosciences Institute. The institute will develop biofuels from plants for transportation fuels, improve extraction of petroleum from existing reserves, and develop clean sources of energy. This unprecedented research deal has provoked considerable controversy among faculty, students, and the community, who have voiced strong concern over its implications for academic freedom, the university's integrity, and whether BP will inappropriately obtain exclusive rights to scientific discoveries. "Simply put," John Simpson of the Foundation for Taxpayer and Consumer Rights said, "the regents must make it clear that they won't let Berkeley become UCBP." According to University of California officials, however, the agreement will not violate university procedures, and BP's right to proprietary research is appropriate in consideration of the size of the donation.[44]

Sustainability as an Investment

It should be clear, then, that sustainability projects are not purely a cost, but an investment in the future of the institution. On the operational side, there are significant opportunities for reducing financial risks and cutting or hedging energy costs while reducing greenhouse gas emissions. On the academic side, there are vast opportunities for new research centers, educational programs, and collaborations with government, corporations, and nonprofits. Sustainability-oriented programs train and equip students for future professions, and they also infuse new tuition dollars into the institutions. A comprehensive and enduring commitment to sustainability, in short, strengthens existing income streams and creates new ones. As in corporate America, colleges and universities that grasp this insight and act on it are the ones most likely to thrive in the age of climate change.

Notes

1. Joel Makower, "Thinking Green in a Blue Economy," GreenBiz.com, October 20, 2008. www.greenbiz.com/blog/2008/10/20/thinking-green-a-blue-economy (accessed November 15, 2008).
2. John Porretto and Jane Wardell, "Energy Agency Warns of Impending Supply Crunch," *San Francisco Chronicle*, November 12, 2008. www.sfgate.com/cgi-bin/article.cgi?f=/n/a/2008/11/12/financial/f023054S21.DTL&feed=rss.business (accessed November 15, 2008).
3. "Comprehensive Report on UB's Energy Conservation Program." wings.buffalo.edu/ubgreen/content/programs/energyconservation/reportenergyconsv.html (accessed May 16, 2008); "Information to Help Us Conserve Natural Resources, Save Money, and Breathe Cleaner Air." www.energy.unh.edu/ (accessed May 16, 2008).
4. Lane Perry, University of Central Oklahoma, personal communication, June 25, 2008.

5. Jeri King, University of Iowa, personal communication, August 4, 2008.

6. Lester Brown, *Mobilizing to Save Civilization* (New York: W. W. Norton, 2008), p. 212.

7. Ric O'Connell and W. Toor, "Green Investment/Green Return, Measuring Sustainability Savings at the University of Colorado, Boulder," CU Environment Center, 2004. http://ecenter.colorado.edu/files/c00531aeaf1686a6f35efeef843add43140e3532.pdf (accessed June 27, 2007).

8. "Clean Air Cash." http://transportation.stanford.edu/alt_transportation/CleanAirCash.shtml#eligible (accessed May 22, 2008).

9. Will Torr, "The Road Less Traveled: Sustainable Transportation on Campus" in *The Green Campus: Meeting the Challenge of Environmental Sustainability*, W. Simpson, ed (Alexandria, VA: APPA, 2008), p. 252.

10. "Colleges and Universities." www.epa.gov/ispd/pdf/2004/collegesbw.pdf (accessed June 30, 2008).

11. "Energy Star for Higher Education." www.energystar.gov/index.cfm?c=higher_ed.bus_highereducation (accessed October 11, 2007).

12. "Tools and Resources Library." www.energystar.gov/index.cfm?c=tools_resources.bus_energy_management_tools_resources (accessed June 20, 2008).

13. For a detailed discussion of these options, please see the ACUPCC/CCI best practices toolkit at http://www.presidentsclimatecommitment.org/html/solutions_cci.htm.

14. "The College Sustainability Report Card 2009." www.GreenReportCard.org/report-card-2009/executive-summary (accessed November 8, 2008).

15. "Raise the Funds: Campus Action Toolkit." http://aashe.org/resources/documents/Raise_the_Funds_Toolkit.pdf (accessed December 23, 2008).

16. Andrea Putman and Michael Philips, *The Business Case for Renewable Energy: A Guide for Colleges and Universities* (Washington, DC: NACUBO, 2006), p. 31.

17. "Bank of America Awards University $250,000 Grant to Support Sustainability Initiatives" (press release), February 15, 2008. www.furman.edu/press/pressarchive.cfm?ID=4139 and "Southern Living's First 'Green' Showcase Home to be Constructed on Campus." www.furman.edu/press/pressarchive.cfm?ID=4021 (accessed June 19, 2008).

18. Frank Powell, Furman University, personal communication, June 25, 2008.

19. Richard Johnson, Rice University, personal communication, July 16, 2008.

20. "Rice Announces $30M Gift, Plans for 'Greenest' Building Yet" (press release), August 21, 2007. www.media.rice.edu/media/News-Bot.asp?MODE=VIEW&ID=9881&SnID=374271474 (accessed March 5, 2008).

21. Tammy Daniels, "Gift Boosts Williams' Reach for Sustainability," *iBerkshires.com*, September 21, 2007. www.iberkshires.com/story/24526/Gift-Boosts-Williams-Reach-for-Sustainability.html (accessed March 19, 2008).

22. Steven Schultz, "International Business Leader Gerhard R. Andlinger Makes $100 Million Gift to Transform Energy and Environment Research at Princeton," July 1, 2008. www.princeton.edu/main/news/archive/S21/48/54G75/index.xml (accessed August 5, 2008).

23. "4 Plus 4 Plus 4 Equals $12 Million" (press release), November 1, 2007. www.oberlin.edu/news-info/07oct/gifts.html (accessed March 5, 2008).

24. "Database of State Incentives for Renewables & Efficiency." http://dsireusa.org/ (accessed May 23, 2008).

25. "University of Minnesota Researchers Awarded More Than $4.5 Million for Renewable Energy Research" (press release), December 10, 2007. www1.umn.edu/umnnews/news_details.php?release=07 1210_3676&page=UMNN (accessed March 5, 2008).

26. "CESA Member States & Funds." www.cleanenergystates.org/Funds/ (accessed April 18, 2008).

27. "System Benefits Charge." www.dsireusa.org/library/includes/incentive2.cfm?Incentive_Code=NY07R&state=NY&CurrentPageID=1 &RE=1&EE=1 (accessed June 20, 2008).

28. "The Green Campus Loan Fund." www.greencampus.harvard.edu/gclf/ (accessed June 20, 2008).

29. Paul Grana and R. Schaffner, "Harvard Green Loan Fund Generates Greater Returns than Endowment. Energy Efficient Investments Make Business Sense," *The Harbus*, November 5, 2007. http://media.www.harbus.org/media/storage/paper343/news/2007/11/05GreenLiving/Harvard.Green.Loan.Fund.Generates.Greater.Returns.Than.Endowment-3077151.shtml (accessed June 20, 2008).

30. Asa Diebolt and T. Den Herder-Thomas, "Creating a Campus Sustainability Revolving Loan Fund: A Guide for Students" (Lexington, KY: Association for the Advancements of Sustainability in Higher Education, 2007). www.aashe.org/resources/pdf/CERF.pdf (accessed January 18, 2007).

31. "Raise the Funds: Campus Action Toolkit." http://aashe.org/resources/documents/Raise_the_Funds_Toolkit.pdf (accessed December 23, 2008).30. "Clean Energy Revolving Fund." www.macalester.edu/cerf/ (accessed July 3, 2008).

32. "Raise the Funds: Campus Action Toolkit." http://aashe.org/resources/documents/Raise_the_Funds_Toolkit.pdf (accessed December 23, 2008).

33. Christopher Wells, Macalester College, personal correspondence, July 4, 2008.

34. Andrea Putman and Michael Philips, "A Prudent Green Purchase," *Business Officer*, June 2006. www.nacubo.org/x8149.xml (accessed July 1, 2008).

35. "SNHU Goes Carbon-Neutral" (news release), May 19, 2007. www.snhu.edu/6886.asp (accessed August 15, 2008).

36. Putman and Philips, *Business Case for Renewable Energy*, p. 58.

37. "Raise the Funds: Campus Action Toolkit." http://aashe.org/resources/documents/Raise_the_Funds_Toolkit.pdf (accessed December 23, 2008).

38. "Colorado Renewable Energy Collaboratory." www.coloradocollaboratory.org/ (accessed May 26, 2008).

39. Ibid.

40. "Georgia Tech Part Of New Biofuel Research Center" (press release), June 29, 2007. www.gatech.edu/newsroom/release.html?id=1421 (accessed May 27, 2008).

41. "UWRF Receives USDA Grant for Sustainable Ag Project" (press release), June 27, 2007. www.uwrf.edu/pa/2007/0706/0627071.htm (accessed June 20, 2008).

42. "Wal-Mart Foundation Gives $1.5 Million to Fund Applied Sustainability Center" (press release), August 29, 2007. http://sustainability.uark.edu/11263.htm (accessed May 27, 2008).

43. Andrew Jensen, "Wal-Mart Donates $1.5M to UA Sustainability Center," Arkansasbusiness.com, August 29, 2007, www.arkansasbusiness.com/article.aspx?aID=99205 (accessed May 27, 2008).

44. Robert Sanders, "BP Selects UC Berkeley to Lead $500 Million Energy Research Consortium with Partners Lawrence Berkeley National Lab, University of Illinois" (press release), February 1 2007. http://berkeley.edu/news/media/releases/2007/02/01_ebi.shtml (accessed October 8, 2008); Rick DelVecchio, "Berkeley UC Faculty Critical of BP Deal, Professors Rail on Lack of Transparency, Academic Freedom," *San Francisco Chronicle*, March 9, 2007 www.sfgate.com/cgibin/article.cgi?f=/c/a/2007/03/09/BAGREOIB201. DTL (accessed October 8, 2008); Richard Paddock, "Activists Push Safeguards to Protect UC Berkeley in Research Deal with BP," *Los Angeles Times*, April 20, 2007. http://articles.latimes.com/2007/may/17/local/me-berkeley17 (accessed October 8, 2008).

"The future is already here. It's just not very evenly distributed."
—**William Gibson, science fiction writer**

CONCLUSION: SUSTAINABILITY AS A CORE STRATEGY IN HIGHER EDUCATION

G lobal warming, water shortages, soil erosion, and expanding deserts: these are not just abstract issues looming on the distant horizon. The rate of retreat in the Arctic has accelerated to the point where scientists now predict that the Arctic will be free of summer sea ice by 2030. Thousands of people are fighting and dying in Sudan over a bitter struggle for water and arable land. The battle over the Colorado River has become one of the most explosive political issues in the American West. China is losing 3,600 square kilometers of land, an area almost the size of Rhode Island, to desertification each year. The thawing of the Siberian tundra threatens to release tons of greenhouse gas emissions, including methane, which is 25 times more potent than carbon dioxide.[1] Although the effects of these changes are not evenly distributed, the evidence is all around us that, unless we take action, humankind will face an unprecedented global crisis. Given the extent of the changes, some geologists contend that we have entered a new geological epoch, the Anthropocene, in which urban industrial society has emerged as the defining geological force.[2]

Colleges and universities have a crucial role to play in creating a more positive interaction with the biosphere. But to do so they must let go of the status quo and embrace the need to reimagine the future as something more than just an extension of the present, although perhaps more efficient. They need to move outside their comfort zone and engage in what the visionary corporate CEO Ray Anderson calls "upside down thinking."[3] Just as important as the impact that higher education can have on sustainability is the impact that sustainability can have on higher education. It can liberate colleges and universities from their old ways of doing business and spark a renewed commitment to what should be their primary mission: leading the way to a more humane and sustainable world.

Sustainability, in short, must be adopted as a core strategy in higher education. It should not be seen as marginal to the real business of colleges and universities or as an add-on. It should be seen as the central organizing principle, a core strategy in an intellectual, social, and financial sense.[4] And it should be recognized that these three strands can not be unraveled and separated without undermining the capacity of higher education to be an effective force in democratic society.

As Thomas Friedman has observed in another context, "Leadership is about 'follow me,' not 'after you.'"[5] Higher education can provide the leadership to help us across the bridge to a viable, more sustainable future by demonstrating in day-to-day teaching, learning, operations, and community engagement that sustainability is not just the right thing to do but also the smart thing. Colleges and universities must lead the way in making clear that sustainability will bring about a healthier, more innovative, more successful, and more profitable future for our children, grandchildren, and all those who come after. Our ability to grapple successfully with global climate change, as Clint Wilder insists, is less about partisan political positions than "about mindset—looking ahead vs. trying to hold onto some vision of the past, some vision destined to be encroached upon by the future as surely as slowly-rising sea levels wash over the low-lying islands of the Pacific."[6] As much as at any time in recent history, we need to be looking ahead, and colleges and universities can help us make sure we do.

Integrity, Empathy, Inclusivity, Democracy

Sustainability as a core intellectual and social strategy means acknowledging that we are at an exciting yet sobering moment in human history. We have an opportunity and an imperative to reinvent our relationship to the world, even as that world is remaking itself as a result of globalization, technological innovation, the rise of the knowledge economy, and profound demographic shifts. We can no longer think only in the short term, and we can no longer waste natural resources or take the environment for granted. We must learn to care about the needs of the global society as much as those of our local community, realizing that our families' well-being is inextricably linked to the well-being of the planet. Sustainability, as David Orr puts it, is a question of "ethical design" that acknowledges that "humans are embedded in a network of obligation and are kin to all life."[7]

One of the primary tasks of educators, in this context, is to arm students both to dream and to take action. In Orr's words, they must "present a sense of hopefulness to students, and the competence to act on that hope."[8] The key is to ensure that all undergraduates receive an education solidly rooted in the liberal arts and sciences. This does not mean that there is no room for professional education at the undergraduate level. Indeed, if students are to become leaders in the effort to build a more sustainable world, then we need to create a more pragmatic kind of liberal education. "Liberal arts majors must acquire practical skills, such as managing and leading change, while professional majors must gain a wider knowledge of cultural, global, and ethical issues," observes Elizabeth Zinser.[9] In reconnecting a fragmented curriculum, students will be equipped much more powerfully to engage in the kind of creative, collaborative problem solving that sustainability demands.

A liberal education not only honors enduring values such as democracy, stewardship, truth, and respect for the individual. It also provides the ability to think ahead, adapt, and shape the future through new ideas and perspectives. Because liberal education is less about acquiring a set of facts than a way of learning, it is crucial for survival in the dawn of a new world. It equips us with the ability to face the future confidently rather than, as Eric Hoffer says, "to deal with a world that no longer exists."[10]

Seen through this lens, a reformed liberal education—one attuned to the new age that we have entered as a species—is not just another product to be consumed, but an act of creation and exploration that aims to make a positive difference in the world. It should involve experiential, project-based learning that connects the classroom and the larger world, and it should foster whole-systems thinking that focuses on the interactions between human and natural systems. How can we live full, rich lives while preserving and enhancing the natural environment? What practical steps can we take to meet the challenge of climate change?

How can we promote economic development that acknowledges natural resource limits, increases opportunities for all individuals, and leads to a more just society? These are the essential questions that we must tackle in the 21st century.

Among the most important consequences of the new liberal education should be a high regard for integrity. Most thinking about this idea involves two components: first, integrity consists of a relation one has to oneself or between parts or aspects of oneself; and second, it is connected in an important way to acting ethically. The concepts of wholeness and connectedness are central to the meaning of integrity. It is a quality that holds all the pieces together and gives them shape and meaning.[11] As such, it lies at the heart of sustainability as a way of being in the world.

Integrity may be resilient, but it is not indestructible, as the dynamics of ecosystems clearly demonstrate. In fact, like an outstanding wine, it has both strength and fragility. It is our understanding of the wine's fragility that leads us to take proper care of it.[12] In the same way, we need to appreciate the integrity of the biosphere and the responsibility we have for effective stewardship. Such an understanding is critical to any effort to build a more sustainable world. Without it, we cannot hope to break with the status quo of treating the world around us, in Thomas Berry's words, as "a collection of objects."[13]

A commitment to this kind of integrity takes moral courage, an ability to question received wisdom, confront difficult issues, and take responsibility for one's actions. As Robert F. Kennedy asserted in a 1966 speech to students in South Africa, moral courage is "a rarer commodity than bravery in battle or great intelligence" and yet it is "the one essential, vital quality for those who seek to change the world—which yields most painfully to change."[14] How do we imbue our students with this kind of integrity if we are not willing to model for them in our everyday practice of campus leadership what moral courage means?

One of the primary goals of education, especially education aimed at creating a sustainable civilization, should be to enhance our understanding of the different ways in which people see the world and experience it, while at the same time recognizing what we have in common. The philosopher Martha Nussbaum calls this quality "compassionate imagining." Education, she says, should bring "young people together not just around a pre-professional or technical training, but around a larger cultivation of their common humanity, and a deepening of the understandings that can connect one human life to another."[15]

The most important way we can demonstrate our commitment to active, engaged citizenship is to be effective stewards of our natural, social, and economic resources not only for the current generation but for all future generations. We must acknowledge that intergenerational equity is a key component of the democratic equation.

The development of such empathy is essential because sustainability by definition is a collective enterprise that cannot be pursued successfully without common action.[16] Furthermore, empathy allows us to experience a sense of belonging to the whole web of life, fostering a deep respect for the natural environment and making it possible to build a healthier and more equitable society and economy. It cultivates a sensibility that inspires students like Michelle Gardner-Quinn, a 21-year-old University of Vermont senior, who declared just days before her tragic death in 2002, "I believe that my connection to all life forms prevents me from sitting back and watching this catastrophe [global climate change]. I believe that we should understand our place in our regional ecosystems and communities, as well as pledge our allegiance to the earth as a whole."[17]

Working with, rather than against, the interconnections and interdependencies among the environment, economy, and society is the central task of our time. "This new consciousness," Al Gore observed in his speech accepting the Nobel Peace Prize in 2007, "requires expanding the possibilities inherent in all humanity." Who is to say that the "innovators who will devise a new way to harness the sun's energy for pennies or invent an engine that's carbon negative" will not live in "Lagos or Mumbai or Montevideo?" If we are to find a way out of our current predicament, as Gore contends, we must "ensure that entrepreneurs and inventors everywhere on the globe have the chance to change the world."[18]

Besides a commitment to integrity, empathy, and inclusiveness, sustainability as a core intellectual and social strategy should seek to revitalize the culture of democracy. It means affirming that democracy is a two-way street involving responsibilities as well as privileges. The democratic ideal demands that we earn our places in our communities by demonstrating that good citizenship is not just a spectator sport but rather a dynamic, living act of will. The most important way we can demonstrate our commitment to active, engaged citizenship is to be

Colleges and universities can only thrive if society and the biosphere are healthy. Any institution that is so shortsighted as to pursue its ends without taking into account the interests of the larger community or ecosystem in which it is enmeshed will not achieve sustainable success. In the end, it will find itself forced, one way or another, to deal with the fact that its future is linked to that of the larger web of social and ecological relations.

effective stewards of our natural, social, and economic resources not only for the current generation but for all future generations. We must acknowledge that intergenerational equity is a key component of the democratic equation.[19]

Colleges and universities cannot foster the democratic arts in their students if they act in nondemocratic ways as institutions. They must practice what they preach. Yet higher education in recent years has accelerated its move toward a technocratic model of governance that undercuts the culture of democracy. Committing to a democratic process—one that involves all stakeholders in decision making and seeks to fully inform them of the tradeoffs inherent in any particular course of action—necessitates a reversal of this trend.[20] Embarking on this journey will involve great difficulties and, in all likelihood, trigger disagreements about how best to move forward, but in the end it will result in a renaissance for higher education.

Closely connected to the effort to breathe new life into democratic ideas and practices is the need to find and maintain a proper balance between the individual and community. Certainly, one of the great lessons of the 20th century is that pursuing either radical individualism or radical collectivism can lead to disaster. To carry out the work of sustainability will require finding a way to preserve personal autonomy and at the same time develop community. Building a more sustainable world will simply not be possible unless we find more creative strategies to do so.

One of our most ancient and powerful stories, Jacob's return to Canaan as recounted in Genesis 32, underscores the complexities of our identities as individual human beings who live in community as well as the critical importance of nurturing both.[21] Having accumulated great personal wealth, primarily in the form of cattle and livestock, Jacob realizes that he has paid a huge emotional cost in pursuit of this goal, and he decides to return to the land of his father Isaac. Jacob has fled Canaan after falling out with his brother Esau; he dreads the reunion with Esau, but knows that he must do so to make himself whole.

On the journey home, Jacob sends his family ahead so he can spend the night alone. Seeking an opportunity for self-reflection before carrying out his difficult mission, Jacob suddenly finds himself wrestling with a mysterious man, a brawl that goes on until dawn. Out of his struggle with what is clearly his shadow self comes a profound insight: Jacob realizes that connection, not isolation, is what animates his spirit, and it will provide him with the necessary strength and wisdom to become an effective leader.

The renaming of Jacob after he comes face to face with his fears symbolizes the transformation of his consciousness and renewed commitment to his family and community. No longer will he go forth in his name but in the name of Israel. His inward struggle has led to an outward connection, preparing him not only to forge a new relation with Esau but also to assume the mantle of leadership.

Amid the diversity of individuals, distinct and unique, living in community, recognition of our common humanity is the vision that lies at the heart of creating a sustainable society. Recognizing the intertwined nature of the relationship between the individual and community, embracing integrity, cultivating empathy, promoting inclusivity, and becoming active agents of change in the revitalization of democracy are the key components of sustainability as an effective core intellectual and social strategy.

What does it mean for higher education to adopt sustainability as a core financial strategy? As we have discussed, a commitment to sustainability can both maximize the upside benefits and minimize the downside risks. It can lead to a more efficient use of limited resources, higher productivity, the development of distributed leadership on campus, greater collaboration across organizational silos, strengthened trust with external stakeholders, and an enhanced brand value that makes it easier to recruit and retain outstanding students, faculty, and staff, all of which can produce a significant competitive advantage for the institution.

Just as important, adopting sustainability as a core financial strategy means investing for the long term. Isn't this what colleges and universities already do? When it comes to nurturing the growth of endowments, some would argue that higher education needs to focus more on the short run and the resulting impact that spending some of this wealth could have on improving the well-being of society and the environment today.[22]

The point is that investments in the community and the environment, if they are strategically targeted and implemented, are in the long-term self-interest of higher education. Colleges and universities can only thrive if society and the biosphere are healthy. Any institution that is so shortsighted as to pursue its ends without taking into account the interests of the larger community or ecosystem in which it is enmeshed will not achieve sustainable success. In the end, it will find itself forced, one way or another, to deal with the fact that its future is linked to that of the larger web of social and ecological relations. Recognition of this interdependence has driven Yale University to invest in the city of New Haven and Berea College to invest in the people and land of the Appalachian South.[23]

College and university endowments, worth hundreds of billions of dollars, could be a powerful force for social and environmental good. Yet only 35 percent of the institutions surveyed in the College Sustainability Report Card 2009 invest in renewable energy and only 10 percent in community development funds. The record on shareholder engagement is similar. Only about one in six institutions have a shareholder responsibility committee that provides guidance on sustainable endowment issues. Also unimpressive is the commitment to endowment transparency. Only 37 percent of the colleges and universities surveyed make lists of their endowment holdings open to the public, and only 30 percent make proxy voting records available.[24]

Higher education institutions must embrace a larger understanding of their mission and not confine themselves simply to growing their endowments while the communities around them come unraveled and the rapid degradation of the environment continues unabated. One of the most effective ways to have a positive effect on both the environment and the local economy is for colleges and universities to set aside a certain proportion of their endowments to use as a revolving loan fund for cities and towns to use in communitywide energy efficiency retrofits. In making such investments, colleges and universities will not only help reduce the carbon footprint of the community, but also keep dollars from flowing out of the community and into the pockets of the utility companies. These dollars will recirculate in the community, increasing spending and indirectly contributing to the creation of new jobs. Of course, investments in energy efficiency and renewable energy also directly create new green-collar jobs that can provide much-needed economic stability during even the toughest of recessions.[25]

Just as important is the commitment of higher education institutions, especially research universities, to invest their financial resources in long-term research and development and in business incubators that facilitate the transfer of innovative clean energy technologies from the laboratory to the marketplace. Clint Wilder calls this our "new 'Greatest Generation' opportunity." There is little doubt that new government regulations, cap-and-trade systems, and even a carbon tax will be part of the effort to combat climate change. Ultimately, however, any successful attempt to meet the challenge of dramatically reducing greenhouse gas emissions will depend on the degree to which the potential of technological innovation can be harnessed. What is needed, Ted Nordhaus and

WORKING TOGETHER ON ALTERNATIVE ENERGY RESEARCH

Washington University in St. Louis has developed an important model for collaboration on alternative energy research. The International Center for Advanced Renewable Energy and Sustainability (I-CARES) at the university seeks to encourage and coordinate collaborative research on biofuels and other alternative energy applications. The institution has committed more than $55 million to the center, including:

- $40 million to build a new facility for the department of energy, environmental, and chemical engineering in the School of Engineering that will house I-CARES and related research projects;

- $12.5 million for five new endowed professorships in science, engineering, architecture, social science, or medicine to attract research leaders in energy, environment, and sustainability;

- at least $2.5 million over five years to seed and develop collaborative research within the university and with its regional partners through I-CARES; and

- an additional $500,000 to support the development of collaborative projects with its international partner universities in the McDonnell International Scholars Academy.

By joining with other regional and international research universities, the center will foster collaboration on the development of biofuels from plant and microbial systems and the exploration of sustainable alternative energy and environmental systems and practices.[27] It is this kind of cooperative research that will be necessary if we are to generate solutions that effectively address climate change.

Michael Shellenberger contend, is "a new military-industrial-academic complex around clean-energy sciences" similar to the one created in the postwar period around computer technology.[26]

There is no silver bullet that will stop climate change in its tracks. This does not mean, however, that technology will not play a central role in the effort to slow global warming. Most critical, we need to scale up existing technologies even as we pursue new technological solutions. We have valuable tools already at hand and should put them to work immediately rather than sitting back and waiting for the ultimate technological solution. If we do not adopt a double-tracked approach, then we run the risk of waiting until it is too late to do anything.[28]

Among the most promising of potential breakthrough technologies is the development of an integrated concentrating photovoltaic (CPV) system that combines thin film solar cells and solar concentrators. If successful, this new approach will dramatically reduce the cost of generating solar electricity, making it significantly more competitive with electricity generated by conventional fossil fuel means.[29] New designs in wind turbines promise significant gains in efficiency and commercial-scale wave and tidal farms are in the works.[30] On the biofuel front, among the most exciting developments is the possibility of using algae and forestry and agricultural wastes rather than tapping biomass derived from foodstuffs such as corn.[31] Another area with great potential is hydrogen and fuel cell technologies. Fuel cells tap the chemical energy of hydrogen to generate electricity cleanly and efficiently with heat and water as byproducts.[32] Most audacious are the efforts to design a cost-effective system for removing carbon dioxide from the atmosphere.[33] In any event, precisely because we cannot predict where the next breakthrough innovations will emerge, it is absolutely crucial that higher education institutions focus their investments on research and development in the clean energy technology arena.

Perhaps the most important impact that a long-term commitment to investing in research and development and technology transfer could have is to shift the current dominant narrative from one that emphasizes the problems and barriers to one that underscores the vast potential of human ingenuity and technological innovation.[34] Universities and colleges, especially at commencement time, generate lots of rhetoric about such ideals. By backing the values and beliefs they espouse with these kinds of investments, higher education can provide a powerful source of new narrative energy that leads to solutions we cannot currently envision.

"The difficulty lies, not in the new ideas," John Maynard Keynes remarked, "but in escaping from the old ones."[35] By letting go of ideas that have outlived their usefulness, we clear the space for fresh perspectives to emerge. By reaching out to develop partnerships with business, nonprofit organizations, and government, higher education—more than any other institution in our society—can generate the intellectual, social, political, and financial capital to escape the gravitational pull of the old, dysfunctional ideas and behaviors that have brought us to our current impasse, launching us into a new world of hope and opportunity. In the current age of climate change, the need for such transformational leadership has never been greater.

Notes

1. Lester R. Brown, *Plan B 3.0: Mobilizing to Save Civilization*, rev. ed. (New York: W.W. Norton, 2008), pp. 3, 66, 75, 80, 96, 117; Gregory Feifer, "Climate Change Cited in Siberian Landscape Shift," NPR. org, September 18, 2006. http://www.npr.org/templates/story/story. php?storyId=6098974 (accessed February 15, 2009); Kari Lydersen, "Scientists: Pace of Climate Change Exceeds Estimates," *Washington Post*, February 15, 2009. http://www.washingtonpost.com/wp-dyn/content/article/2009/02/14/AR2009021401757.html?hpid=topnews (accessed February 16, 2009).

2. Robert C. Cowen, "Has Earth Entered a New Epoch? What Geologists Think," *Christian Science Monitor*, February 7, 2008. www.csmonitor.com/2008/0207/p17s01-stgn.html (accessed August 10, 2008); Mike Davis, "Living on the Ice Shelf: Humanity's Melt Down," *TomDispatch.com*, June 26, 2008. www.tomdispatch.com/post/174949 (accessed August 17, 2008).

3. Ray Anderson, "Education for a Secure and Sustainable Future," keynote address delivered at the American College and University Presidents Climate Commitment Leadership Summit, Grand Rapids, MI, June 5, 2008.

4. Michael Crow, "American Research Universities During the Long Twilight of the Stone Age," an elaboration on remarks delivered at the Rocky Mountain Sustainability Summit, University of Colorado, Boulder, February 21, 2007, p. 3. http://president.asu.edu/files/2007_0212StoneAge.pdf (accessed August 8, 2008).

5. Thomas L. Friedman, "Lead, Follow, or Move Aside," *New York Times*, September 26, 2007. www.nytimes.com/2007/09/26/opinion/26friedman.html (accessed August 10, 2008).

6. Clint Wilder, "Clean Tech's Future (and Present): A Battle of Mindsets," *Clean Edge*, November 5, 2007. www.cleanedge.com/views/index.php?id=5002 (accessed August 10, 2008).

7. Jay Parini, "The Greening of the Humanities," *New York Times*, October 29, 1995. http://query.nytimes.com/gst/fullpage.html?res=990CE6DC113CF93AA15753C1A963958260 (accessed August 10, 2008); David W. Orr, *The Nature of Design: Ecology, Culture, and Human Intention* (New York: Oxford University Press, 2002), p. 10.

8. Quoted in Marci Janas, "Ancestry and Influence: A Portrait of David Orr," September 17, 1998. www.oberlin.edu/news-info/98sep/orr_profile.html (accessed August 10, 2008).

9. Elisabeth Zinser, "Making the Case for Liberal Education," *Liberal Education*, Winter 2004, p. 39. www.aacu.org/liberaleducation/le-wi04/le-wi04feature3.cfm (accessed August 10, 2008).

10. Quoted in Roland Barth, *Learning by Heart* (San Francisco: Jossey-Bass, 2004), p. 28.

11. Damian Cox, Marguerite La Caze, and Michael Levine, "Integrity," *Stanford Encyclopedia of Philosophy* (Fall 2005 edition), ed. Edward N. Zalta. http://plato.stanford.edu/archives/fall2005/entries/integrity (accessed August 10, 2008).

12. George W. Harris, *Dignity and Vulnerability: Strength and Quality of Character* (Berkeley: University of California, 1997), p. 6.

13. Thomas Berry, *The Great Work: Our Way into the Future* (New York: Bell Tower Books, 2007), p. 16.

14. Robert F. Kennedy, "Day of Affirmation Address," remarks delivered at Cape Town University, June 6, 1966, Cape Town, South Africa. www.americanrhetoric.com/speeches/rfkcapetown.htm (accessed August 10, 2008).

15. Martha Nussbaum, "Liberal Education and Global Responsibility," remarks delivered at the Institute for Chief Academic Officers, Council of Independent Colleges, November 3, 2002 Santa Fe, NM. www.cic.edu/conferences_events/caos/previouscaos/nussbaum_talk.pdf (accessed August 10, 2008).

16. Lawrence Humber, "Sustainable Communities." www.helium.com/items/329838-essays-sustainable-communities (accessed August 10, 2008).

17. Michelle Gardner-Quinn, "This I Believe: A Reverence for All Life," August 5, 2007. www.npr.org/templates/story/story. php?storyId=12444698 (accessed August 10, 2008).

18. Al Gore, Nobel Peace Prize Acceptance Speech, October 10, 2007, Oslo, Norway. http://nobelprize.org/nobel_prizes/peace/laureates/2007/gore-lecture_en.html (accessed August 10, 2008).

19. David W. Orr, "Law of the Land," *Orion Magazine*, January/February 2004. www.orionmagazine.org/index.php/articles/article/133 (accessed August 10, 2008).

20. Thomas C. Longin, "Institutional Governance: A Call for Collaborative Decision-Making in American Higher Education," in *A New Academic Compact: Revisioning the Relationship between Faculty and Their Institutions*, ed. Linda A. McMillin and William G. (Jerry) Berberet (Bolton: Anker Publishing Co., 2002), pp. 211–21.

21. Gen. 32:1-30, *New Oxford Annotated Bible*, Revised Standard Version.

22. Alan Finder, "Yale to Increase Endowment Spending," *New York Times*, January 7, 2008. www.nytimes.com/2008/01/07/education/07cnd-yale.html?ex=1357448400&en=a2eaf79113fc6798&ei=5088&partner=rssnyt&emc=rss (accessed August 10, 2008).

23. David McKay Wilson, "Yale and New Haven Find Common Ground," *New York Times*, December 16, 2007. www.nytimes.com/2007/12/16/nyregion/nyregionspecial2/16yalect.html?_r=2&ref=nyregionspecial2&oref=slogin&oref=slogin (accessed August 10, 2008); Christopher Gutsche and Kathleen Smith, "Appalachian Ecovillage," *Yes!*, Summer 2005. www.yesmagazine.org/article.asp?ID=1259 (accessed August 10, 2008).

24. *College Sustainability Report Card 2009*, Sustainable Endowments Institute. www.greenreportcard.org/report-card-2009/executive-summary/trends (accessed November 9, 2008).

25. Van Jones and Ben Wyskida, "Creating Green-Collar Jobs," TomPaine.com, January 23, 2007. www.tompaine.com/articles/2007/01/23/creating_greencollar_jobs.php (accessed August 10, 2008).

26. Clint Wilder, "Our New 'Greatest Generation' Opportunity," *Clean Edge*, June 2, 2008. www.cleanedge.com/views.php?id=5382 (accessed August 10, 2008); Ted Nordhaus and Michael Shellenberger, "Second Life: A Manifesto for a New Environmentalism," *The New Republic*, September 24, 2007, p. 32.

27. International Center for Advanced Renewable Energy and Sustainability, Washington University in St. Louis. http://i-cares.wustl.edu/index.htm (accessed August 10, 2008).

28. George Craford et al., "Profits and Prophets in Clean Energy," *Innovation: America's Journal of Technology Commercialization*, February/March 2008. www.innovation-america.org/archive.php?articleID=398 (accessed August 10, 2008); Alex Nikolai Steffen, "The Next Green Revolution," *Wired* 14, no. 5 (May 2006). www.wired.com/wired/archive/14.05/green.html (accessed August 10, 2008).

29. "NREL and Optony Collaborate on Developing Cost-Competitive Approach for Solar Electricity." www.nrel.gov/solar/news/2008/615.html (accessed August 10, 2008).

30. Brian Westenhaus, "Fact Check on the New Wind Turbine Design," *New Energy and Fuel*, February 4, 2008. http://newenergyandfuel.com/ http://newenergyandfuel/com/2008/02/04/fact-check-on-the-new-wind-turbine-design/ (accessed August 10, 2008); Michael Kanellos, "Wave Power to Go Commercial in California," CNET-News.com, December 17, 2007. http://news.cnet.com/Wave-power-to-go-commercial-in-California/2100-13840_3-6223220.html?hhTest=1 (accessed August 10, 2008).

31. Ken Silverstein, "The Algae Attraction," *Renewable Energy World*, June 17, 2008. www.renewableenergyworld.com/rea/news/story?id=52777 (accessed August 10, 2008); Martin LaMonica, "Cellulosic Ethanol: A Fuel for the Future?" CNETNews.com, August 14, 2007. http://news.cnet.com/Cellulosic-ethanol-A-fuel-for-the-future/2100-11392_3-6202328.html?hhTest=1 (accessed August 10, 2008).

32. "Hydrogen and Fuel Cells Research." http://www.nrel.gov/hydrogen (accessed February 24, 2009).

33. Bryan Appleyard, "Climate Change: We Have the Power," *Times Online*, November 4, 2007. www.timesonline.co.uk/tol/news/uk/science/article2772943.ece (accessed August 10, 2008).

34. William E. Easterling III, Brian H. Hurd, and Joel B. Smith, *Coping with Global Climate Change: The Role of Adaptation in the United States*, Pew Center on Global Climate Change, June 2004. www.pewclimate.org/docUploads/Adaptation.pdf (accessed August 10, 2008).

35. John Maynard Keynes, *The General Theory of Employment, Interest, and Money* (New York: Harcourt, 1964), p. viii.

SUGGESTED READINGS

Adelson, Glenn, James Engell, Brent Ranalli, and K. P. Van Anglen, eds. *Environment: An Interdisciplinary Anthology*. New Haven: Yale University Press, 2008.

Astin, Helen and Alexander Astin. *Leadership Reconsidered: Engaging Higher Education in Social Change*. Battle Creek, MI: W. K. Kellogg Foundation, 2000.

Barlett, Peggy F., and Geoffrey W. Chase. *Sustainability on Campus: Stories and Strategies for Change*. Cambridge, MA: MIT Press, 2004.

Berry, Thomas. *The Great Work: Our Way into the Future*. New York: Bell Tower, 1999.

Brown, Lester R. *Plan B 3.0: Mobilizing to Save Civilization*. Rev. ed. New York: W.W. Norton, 2008.

Clark, Robert and Jennifer Ma. *Recruitment, Retention, and Retirement in Higher Education: Building and Managing the Faculty of the Future*. Northampton, MA: Edward Elgar Publishing, 2005.

Collins, Jim. *Good to Great: Why Some Companies Make the Leap and Others Don't*. New York: HarperCollins, 2001.

Creighton, Sarah Hammond. *Greening the Ivory Tower: Improving the Environmental Track Record of Universities, Colleges, and Other Institutions*. Cambridge, MA: MIT Press, 1998.

Davenport, Thomas H. *Thinking for a Living: How to Get Better Performance and Results from Knowledge Workers*. Cambridge, MA: Harvard Business School Press, 2005.

Dawson, Jonathan. *Ecovillages: New Frontiers for Sustainability*. White River Junction, VT: Chelsea Green Publishing Company, 2006.

Dychtwald, Ken Tamara J. Erickson, and Robert Morison. *Workforce Crisis: How to Beat the Coming Shortage of Skills and Talent.* Cambridge, MA: Harvard Business School Press, 2006.

Eagan, David, Julian Keniry, and Justin Schott. *Higher Education in a Warming World: The Business Case for Climate Leadership on Campus.* Reston, VA: National Wildlife Federation, 2008.

Edwards, Andres R. *The Sustainability Revolution: Portrait of a Paradigm Shift.* Gabriola Island, BC, Canada: New Society Press, 2005.

Esty, Daniel C., and Andrew S. Winston. *Green to Gold: How Smart Companies Use Environmental Strategy to Innovate, Create Value, and Build Competitive Advantage.* New Haven: Yale University Press, 2006.

Friedman, Thomas L. *Hot, Flat, and Crowded: Why We Need a Green Revolution—and How It Can Renew America.* New York: Farrar, Straus, and Giroux, 2008.

_____. *The World is Flat: A Brief History of the Twenty-First Century.* Rev. ed. New York: Farrar, Straus and Giroux, 2006.

Helm, Dieter, ed. *Climate-Change Policy.* Oxford, Eng.: Oxford University Press, 2005.

Huber. Mary Taylor and Pat Hutchings. *Integrative Learning: Mapping the Terrain.* Washington, DC: Association of American Colleges and Universities, 2004.

Jones, Van. *The Green Collar Economy: How One Solution Can Fix Our Two Biggest Problems.* New York: HarperCollins, 2008.

Kirp, David L. *Shakespeare, Einstein, and the Bottom Line: The Marketing of Higher Education.* Cambridge, MA: Harvard University Press, 2003.

Kutscher, Charles, ed. *Tackling Climate Change in the U.S.: Potential U.S. Carbon Emissions Reductions from Energy Efficiency and Renewable Energy by 2030.* Boulder, CO: American Solar Energy Society, 2007.

Lerner, Richard M. and Lou Anna Kimsey Simon, eds. *University-Community Collaborations for the Twenty-First Century.* New York: Garland Publishing, 1998.

Makower, Joel. *Strategies for the Green Economy: Opportunitites and Chllenges in the New World of Business.* McGraw-Hill, 2008.

McKenzie Mohr, Doug, and William Smith. *Fostering Sustainable Behavior: An Introduction to Community-Based Social Marketing.* Gabriola Island, BC, Canada: New Society Press, 1999.

McKibbin, Warren J. and Peter Wilcoxen. *Climate Change Policy After Kyoto: Blueprint for a Realistic Approach*, Washington, DC: Brookings Institute Press, 2002.

National Leadership Council for Liberal Education and America's Promise. *College Learning for the New Global Century.* Washington, DC: Association of American College and Universities, 2007.

Orr, David W. *Earth in Mind: On Education, Environment, and the Human Prospect.* 10th anniversary ed. Washington, DC: Island Press, 2004.

Pink, Daniel H. *A Whole New Mind: Why Right-Brainers Will Rule the Future.* New York: Riverhead Books, 2006.

Putman, Andrea, and Michael Philips. *The Business Case for Renewable Energy: A Guide for Colleges and Universities.* Washington, DC: NACUBO, 2006.

Rappaport, Ann, and Sarah Hammond Creighton. *Degrees that Matter: Climate Change and the University.* Cambridge, MA: MIT Press, 2007.

Senge, Peter et. al. *The Necessary Revolution: How Individuals and Organizations Are Working Together to Create a Sustainable World.* New York: Doubleday, 2008.

Sevier, Robert A. *Building a Brand That Matters: Helping Colleges Capitalize on the four Essential Elements of a Block-Buster Brand.* Hiawatha, IA: Strategy Publishing, 2002.

Simpson, Walter, ed. *The Green Campus: Meeting the Challenge of Environmental Sustainability.* Alexandria, VA: APPA, 2008.

Sterling, Stephen. *Sustainable Education: Re-visioning Learning and Change.* Dartington, Devon, UK: Green Books Ltd., 2001.

Sullivan, William M. and Matthew S. Rosin. *A New Agenda for Higher Education: Shaping a Life of the Mind for Practice*. San Francisco: Jossey-Bass, 2008.

Walker, Liz. *EcoVillage at Ithaca: Pioneering a Sustainable Culture*. Gabriola Island, BC, Canada: New Society Publishers, 2005.

ORGANIZATIONAL RESOURCES

Toward a Sustainable Future

Clean Energy and Energy Efficiency

Alliance to Save Energy—www.ase.org

American Council for an Energy Efficient Economy—www.aceee.org

American Council on Renewable Energy—www.acore.org

Apollo Alliance—www.apolloalliance.org

Database of State Incentives for Renewables & Efficiency—www.dsireusa.org/

Renewable Energy Policy Project—www.repp.org

U.S. Department of Energy Office of Energy Efficiency and Renewable Energy—www.eere.energy.gov

U.S. Department of Energy National Renewable Energy Lab—www.nrel.gov

U.S. Environmental Protection Agency Energy Star—www.energystar.gov

U.S. Environmental Protection Agency Green Power Partnership—www.epa.gov/greenpower

Climate Change

Clean Air-Cool Planet—www.cleanair-coolplanet.org

Climate-National Oceanic and Atmospheric Administration—www.noaa.gov/climate.html

Climate Challenge—www.climatechallenge.org

U.S. Environmental Protection Agency-Climate Change—www.epa.gov/climatechange

The Climate Project—www.theclimateproject.org

Clinton Climate Initiative—www.clintonfoundation.org/what-we-do/clinton-climate-initiative

Intergovernmental Panel on Climate Change—www.ipcc.ch/index.htm

OneClimate—www.oneclimate.net

1Sky—www.1sky.org/about

Pew Center on Global Climate Change—www.pewclimate.org

U.S. Climate Action Partnership—www.us-cap.org

Local Food and Sustainable Agriculture

Intervale Center—www.intervale.org

Phillies Bridge Farm Project—www.philliesbridge.org

Stratford Ecological Center—www.stratfordecologicalcenter.org

Sustainable Food Lab—www.sustainablefoodlab.org

World Wide Opportunities on Organic Farms—www.wwoof.org

Global Sustainability Policy

Earth Policy Institute—www.earth-policy.org

United Nations Division for Sustainable Development—www.un.org/esa/sustdev

World Resources Institute—www.wri.org

Worldwatch Institute—www.worldwatch.org

Sustainability and Business

GreenBiz.com—www.greenbiz.com

Institute for Market Transformation to Sustainability—http://mts.sustainableproducts.com

Network for Business Innovation and Sustainability—www.nbis.org

World Business Council for Sustainable Development—www.wbcsd.org

Sustainability in Higher Education

American College and University Presidents Climate Commitment—www.presidentsclimatecommitment.org

Association for the Advancement of Sustainability in Higher Education—www.aashe.org

Campus Consortium for Environmental Excellence—www.c2e2.org

Campus Environmental Resources Center—www.campuserc.org

College and University Recycling Council—www.nrc-recycle.org/curc.aspx

Disciplinary Associations Network for Sustainability—www.aashe.org/dans

Higher Education Associations Sustainability Consortium—www.heasc.net

National Wildlife Federation Campus Ecology—www.nwf.org/campusecology

Second Nature—www.secondnature.org

UNESCO Teaching and Learning for a Sustainable Future—www.unesco.org/education/tlsf

University Leaders for a Sustainable Future—www.ulsf.org

U.S. Partnership for Education for Sustainable Development—www.uspartnership.org

Sustainable Design

Architecture 2030—www.architecture2030.org

Biomimicry—www.biomimicry.net

BuildingGreen—www.buildinggreen.com

Center for a New American Dream—www.newdream.org

Cradle-to-Cradle Design—www.greenblue.org

Environmental Justice Network—www.ejnet.org

Global Footprint Network—www.footprintnetwork.org

Natural Capitalism—www.natcap.org

The Natural Step—www.naturalstep.org

Precautionary Principle: Science & Environmental Health Network—www.sehn.org

Rocky Mountain Institute—www.rmi.org

Sustainability Institute—www.sustainer.org

U.S. Green Building Council—www.usgbc.org

AMERICAN COLLEGE & UNIVERSITY PRESIDENTS CLIMATE COMMITMENT

We, the undersigned presidents and chancellors of colleges and universities, are deeply concerned about the unprecedented scale and speed of global warming and its potential for large-scale, adverse health, social, economic and ecological effects. We recognize the scientific consensus that global warming is real and is largely being caused by humans. We further recognize the need to reduce the global emission of greenhouse gases by 80% by mid-century at the latest, in order to avert the worst impacts of global warming and to reestablish the more stable climatic conditions that have made human progress over the last 10,000 years possible.

While we understand that there might be short-term challenges associated with this effort, we believe that there will be great short-, medium-, and long-term economic, health, social and environmental benefits, including achieving energy independence for the U.S. as quickly as possible.

We believe colleges and universities must exercise leadership in their communities and throughout society by modeling ways to minimize global warming emissions, and by providing the knowledge and the educated graduates to achieve climate neutrality. Campuses that address the climate challenge by reducing global warming emissions and by integrating sustainability into their curriculum will better serve their students and meet their social mandate to help create a thriving, ethical and civil society. These colleges and universities will be providing students with the knowledge and skills needed to address the critical, systemic challenges faced by the world in this new century and enable them to benefit from the economic opportunities that will arise as a result of solutions they develop.

We further believe that colleges and universities that exert leadership in addressing climate change will stabilize and reduce their long-term energy costs, attract excellent students and faculty, attract new sources of funding, and increase the support of alumni and local communities. Accordingly, we commit our institutions to taking the following steps in pursuit of climate neutrality:

1. Initiate the development of a comprehensive plan to achieve climate neutrality as soon as possible.

    a. Within two months of signing this document, create institutional structures to guide the development and implementation of the plan.

    b. Within one year of signing this document, complete a comprehensive inventory of all greenhouse gas emissions (including emissions from electricity, heating, commuting, and air travel) and update the inventory every other year thereafter.

    c. Within two years of signing this document, develop an institutional action plan for becoming climate neutral, which will include:

        i. A target date for achieving climate neutrality as soon as possible.

        ii. Interim targets for goals and actions that will lead to climate neutrality.

        iii. Actions to make climate neutrality and sustainability a part of the curriculum and other educational experience for all students.

        iv. Actions to expand research or other efforts necessary to achieve climate neutrality.

        v. Mechanisms for tracking progress on goals and actions.

2.   Initiate two or more of the following tangible actions to reduce greenhouse gases while the more comprehensive plan is being developed.

    a. Establish a policy that all new campus construction will be built to at least the U.S. Green Building Council's LEED Silver standard or equivalent.

    b. Adopt an energy-efficient appliance purchasing policy requiring purchase of ENERGY STAR certified products in all areas for which such ratings exist.

    c. Establish a policy of offsetting all greenhouse gas emissions generated by air travel paid for by our institution.

    d. Encourage use of and provide access to public transportation for all faculty, staff, students and visitors at our institution

e. Within one year of signing this document, begin purchasing or producing at least 15% of our institution's electricity consumption from renewable sources.

f. Establish a policy or a committee that supports climate and sustainability shareholder proposals at companies where our institution's endowment is invested.

g. Participate in the Waste Minimization component of the national RecycleMania competition, and adopt 3 or more associated measures to reduce waste.

3. Make the action plan, inventory, and periodic progress reports publicly available by providing them to the Association for the Advancement of Sustainability in Higher Education (AASHE) for posting and dissemination.

In recognition of the need to build support for this effort among college and university administrations across America, we will encourage other presidents to join this effort and become signatories to this commitment.

Signed,

The Signatories of the American College & University Presidents Climate Commitment

Source: www.presidentsclimatecommitment.org

AMERICAN COLLEGE & UNIVERSITY PRESIDENTS CLIMATE COMMITMENT

Signatories by Institution

(as of February 26, 2009)

Presidents and chancellors listed below signed the ACUPCC for their institutions, but may no longer be with that institution.

Adams State College, CO
David P. Svaldi, President

Agnes Scott College, GA
Elizabeth Kiss, President

Alamo Community Colleges System
(5 institutions), TX
Bruce Leslie, Chancellor

Alaska Pacific University, AK
Douglas M. North, President

Albion College, MI
Peter T. Mitchell, President

Alfred University, NY
Charles M. Edmondson, President

Allegheny College, PA
Richard J. Cook, President

Alliant International University, CA
Geoffrey M. Cox, President

American Public University
System, WV
Wallace E. Boston, Jr., President

American University, DC
Cornelius M. Kerwin, President

Ancilla College, IN
Ronald L. May, President

Anna Maria College, MA
Jack P. Calareso, President

Antioch University Los Angeles, CA
Neal King, President

Antioch University New England, NH
David Caruso, President

Antioch University Santa Barbara, CA
Michael Mulnix, President

Antioch University, Seattle, WA
Cassandra Manuelito-Kerkvliet,
President

Appalachian State University, NC
Kenneth E. Peacock, President

Aquinas College, MI
C. Edward Balog, President

Arizona State University, AZ
Michael Crow, President

Auburn University, AL
Jay Gouge, President

Augsburg College, MN
Paul C. Pribbenow, President

Austin College, TX
Oscar C. Page, President

Babson College, MA
Leonard Schlesinger, President

Bainbridge Graduate Institute, WA
Gifford Pinchot, President

Ball State University, IN
Jo Ann M. Gora, President

Bard College, NY
Leon Botstein, President

Bates College, ME
Elaine Tuttle Hansen, President

Bellevue Community College, WA
B. Jean Floten, President

Bemidji State University, MN
John Quistgaard, President

Benjamin Franklin Institute of
Technology, MA
Michael Taylor, President

Bentley College, MA
Gloria C. Larson, President

Berea College, KY
Larry D. Shinn, President

Bergen Community College, NJ
G. Jeremiah Ryan, President

Berkshire Community College , MA
Paul E. Raverta, President

Berry College, GA
Stephen R. Briggs, President

Binghamton University (SUNY), NY
Lois B. DeFleur, President

Birmingham-Southern College, AL
G. David Pollick, President

Black Hills State University, SD
Kay Schallenkamp, President

Boise State University, ID
Robert W. Kustra, President

Bowdoin College, ME
Barry Mills, President

Bowie State University, MD
Mickey L. Burnim, President

Brandeis University , MA
Jehuda Reinharz, President

Bridgewater State College, MA
Dana Mohler-Faria, President

Bristol Community College, MA
John J. Sbrega, President

Broome Community College, NY
Laurence D. Spraggs, President

Bryn Mawr College, PA
Nancy J. Vickers, President

Bucknell University, PA
Brian C. Mitchell, President

Bunker Hill Community College, MA
Mary L. Fifield, President

Butte College, CA
Diana VanDerPloeg, President

Cabrillo College, CA
Brian King, President

Caldwell Community College &
Technical Institute, NC
Kenneth A. Boham, President

California State Polytechnic
University, Pomona, CA
J. Michael Ortiz, President

California State University,
Bakersfield, CA
Horace Mitchell, President

California State University, Chico, CA
Paul J. Zingg, President

California State University,
Monterey Bay, CA
Dianne Harrison, President

Cape Cod Community College, MA
Kathleen Schatzberg, President

Carleton College, MN
Robert A. Oden Jr., President

Carolinas College of Health
Sciences, NC
Ellen Sheppard, President

Carteret Community College, NC
Joseph T. Barwick, President

Cascadia Community College, WA
William Christopher, President

Case Western Reserve University, OH
Barbara Snyder, President

Castleton State College, VT
David S. Wolk, President

Catawba College, NC
Robert E. Knott, President

Cedar Valley College, TX
Jennifer Wimbish, President

Central College, IA
David H. Roe, President

Central Connecticut State
University, CT
John W. Miller, President

Central New Mexico Community
College, NM
Katharine W. Winograd, President

Central Washington University, WA
Jerilyn S. McIntyre, President

Centralia College, WA
James Walton, President

Centre College, KY
John A. Roush, President

Century College, MN
Lawrence P. Litecky, President

Chabot-Las Positas Community
College District, CA (2 institutions)
Joel L. Kinnamon, Chancellor

Chaffey Community College, CA
Henry D. Shannon, President

Chandler-Gilbert Community
College, AZ
Maria Hesse, President

Charles R. Drew University of
Medicine and Science, CA
Susan Kelly, President

Chatham University, PA
Esther L. Barazzone, President

Chicago State University, IL
Elnora Daniel, President

Cincinnati State Technical &
Community College, OH
John Henderson, President

Claremont McKenna College, CA
Pamela Brooks Gann, President

Clark University, MA
John Bassett, President

Clemson University, SC
James F. Barker, President

Coast Community College District
(3 institutions), CA
Kenneth D. Yglesias, Chancellor

Coconino Community College, AZ
Leah Bornstein, President

Coe College, IA
James R. Phifer, President

Colby College, ME
William D. Adams, President

Colby-Sawyer College, NH
Thomas C. Galligan Jr., President

Colgate University, NY
Rebecca Chopp, President

College of Alameda, CA
Cecilia Cervantes, President

College of Charleston, SC
George Benson, President

College of Marin, CA
Frances L. White, President

College of Menominee Nation, WI
S. Verna Fowler, President

College of New Jersey, The, NJ
R. Barbara Gitenstein, President

College of Saint Benedict, MN
MaryAnn Baenninger, President

College of Saint Rose, NY
R. Mark Sullivan, President

College of St. Catherine, MN
Andrea Lee, President

College of the Atlantic, ME
David Hales, President

College of the Holy Cross , MA
Michael McFarland, President

College of the Sequoias, CA
William Scroggins, President

Colorado State University, CO
Larry Edward Penley, President

Columbus State Community
College, OH
Valeriana Moeller, President

Community College of Denver, CO
Christine Johnson, President

Concordia College-New York, NY
Viji George, President

Concordia University, NE
Brian L. Friedrich, President

Concordia University, OR
Charles E. Schlimpert, President

Connecticut College, CT
Leo I. Higdon, President

Coppin State University, MD
Reginald S. Avery, President

Cornell College, IA
Leslie H. Garner, Jr., President

Cornell University, NY
David J. Skorton, President

County College of Morris, NJ
Edward J. Yaw, President

Dakota County Technical College, MN
Ronald E. Thomas, President

Davidson College, NC
Thomas W. Ross, President

Delta College, MI
Jean Goodnow, President

De Pauw University, IN
Brian Casey, President

Des Moines Area Community
College, IA
Robert Denson, President

Dickinson College, PA
William G. Durden, President

Dillard University, LA
Marvalene Hughes, President

Drake University, IA
David Maxwell, President

Drew University, NJ
Robert Weisbuch, President

Drury University, MO
John Sellars, President

Duke University, NC
Richard H. Brodhead, President

Durham Technical Community
College, NC
William G. Ingram, President

Dutchess Community College, NY
D. David Conklin, President

Eastern Connecticut State
University, CT
Elsa Nuñez, President

Eastern Iowa Community College
District (3 institutions), IA
Patricia Keir, Chancellor

Eastern University, PA
David Black, President

Eastern Washington University, WA
Rodolfo Arévalo, President

Eckerd College, FL
Donald R. Eastman III, President

Edmonds Community College, WA
Jack Oharah, President

Emerson College, MA
Jacqueline W. Liebergott, President

Emory & Henry College, VA
Rosalind Reichard, President

Everett Community College, WA
David Beyer, President

Fairfield University, CT
Jeffrey von Arx, President

Ferrum College, VA
Jennifer L. Braaten, President

Finger Lakes Community College, NY
Barbara G. Risser, President

Fitchburg State College, MA
Robert V. Antonucci, President

Florida Atlantic University, FL
Frank T. Brogan, President

Florida Gulf Coast University, FL
Richard Pegnetter, Interim President

Florida International University, FL
Modesto A. Maidique, President

Foothill-De Anza Community
College District (3 institutions), CA
Martha J. Kanter, Chancellor

Fort Lewis College, CO
Brad Bartel, President

Framingham State College, MA
Timothy J. Flanagan, President

Franklin College, IN
James G. Moseley, President

Franklin & Marshall College, PA
John A. Fry, President

Franklin Pierce University, NH
George J. Hagerty, President

Frostburg State University, MD
Jonathan C. Gibralter, President

Furman University, SC
David E. Shi, President

Gainesville State College, GA
Martha T. Nesbitt, President

GateWay Community College, AZ
Eugene Giovannini, President

Gateway Technical College, WI
Bryan D. Albrecht, President

George Mason University, VA
Alan G. Merten, President

Georgia Institute of Technology, GA
G. Wayne Clough, President

Georgia Southern University, GA
Bruce Grube, President

Georgian Court University, NJ
Rosemary E. Jeffries, President

Gettysburg College, PA
Katherine Haley Will, President

Goddard College, VT
Mark Schulman, President

Goshen College, IN
James E. Brenneman, President

Goucher College, MD
Sanford J. Ungar, President

Governors State University, IL
Elaine P. Maimon, President

Grand Rapids Community
College, MI
Juan R. Olivarez, President

Grand Valley State University, MI
Thomas J. Haas, President

Granite State College, NH
Karol LaCroix, President

Green Mountain College, VT
John F. Brennan, President

Greenfield Community College, MA
Robert Pura, President

Guilford College, NC
Kent John Chabotar, President

Gustavus Adolphus College, MN
James L. Peterson, President

Hamilton College, NY
Joan Hinde Stewart, President

Hampshire College, MA
Ralph J. Hexter, President

Harford Community College, MD
James La Calle, President

Hartnell College, CA
Phoebe K. Helm, President

Harvey Mudd College, CA
Maria Klawe, President

Haverford College, PA
Thomas R. Tritton, President

Haywood Community College, NC
Rose H. Johnson, President

Heartland Community College, IL
Jonathan, M. Astroth, President

Hillsborough Community College, FL
Gwendolyn W. Stephenson, President

Hiram College, OH
Thomas Chema, President

Hiwassee College, TN
James A. Noseworthy, President

Hobart and William Smith
Colleges, NY
Mark D. Gearan, President

Hocking College, OH
John Light, President

Hollins University, VA
Nancy Oliver Gray, President

Holyoke Community College, MA
William Messner, President

Houghton College, NY
Shirley Mullen, President

Houston Community College, TX
Mary S. Spangler, President

Howard Community College, MD
Kathleen B. Hetherington, President

Huertas Junior College, PR
Edwin Ramos-Rivera, President

Huston-Tillotson University, TX
Larry L. Earvin, President

Illinois Central College, IL
John Erwin, President

Illinois College, IL
Axel D. Steuer, President

Illinois State University, IL
Al Bowman, President

Indiana State University, IN
Lloyd W. Benjamin, President

Institute of Construction
Management & Technology, AZ
Steve Cooper, President

Interdenominational Theological
Center, GA
Michael A. Battle, President

Inver Hills Community College, MN
Cheryl Frank, President

Iowa Lakes Community College, IA
Harold Prior, President

Ithaca College, NY
Peggy R. Williams, President

Jackson Community College, MI
Daniel Phelan, President

James Madison University, VA
Linwood H. Rose, President

Jamestown Community College, NY
Gregory DeCinque, President

Jewish Theological Seminary, NY
Arnold M. Eisen, Chancellor

Johnson County Community
College, KS
Terry A. Calaway, President

Juniata College, PA
Thomas R. Kepple Jr., President

Kalamazoo College, MI
Eileen B. Wilson-Oyelaran, President

Kankakee Community College, IL
Jerry W. Weber, President

Kansas Wesleyan University, KS
Philip P. Kerstetter, President

Keene State College, NH
Helen F. Giles-Gee, President

Kennesaw State University, GA
Daniel S. Papp, President

Kent State University, Stark, OH
Betsy Boze, President

Keystone College, PA
Edward G. Boehm, Jr., President

Labette Community College, KS
George C. Knox, President

Lafayette College, PA
Daniel Weiss, President

LaGrange College, GA
F. Stuart Gulley, President

Lake Michigan College, MI
Randall R. Miller, President

Lake Superior College, MN
Kathleen Nelson, President

Lake Washington Technical
College, WA
L. Michael Metke, President

Lakeshore Technical College, WI
Michael A. Lanser, President

Lane Community College, OR
Mary Spilde, President

Laney College, CA
Frank Chong, President

Lansing Community College, MI
Judith Cardenas, President

Lasell College , MA
Michael Alexander, President

Lee College, TX
Martha Ellis, President

Lesley University, MA
Margaret A. McKenna, President

Lewis & Clark College, OR
Thomas J. Hochstettler, President

Lewis & Clark Community College, IL
Dale T. Capman, President

Life University, GA
Guy Riekeman, President

Linfield College, OR
Thomas Hellie, President

Lorain County Community
College, OH
Roy A. Church, President

Loras College, IA
James Collins, President

Los Angeles Community College District (9 institutions), CA
Darroch F. Young, Chancellor

Loyola Marymount University, CA
Robert B. Lawton, President

Loyola University, LA
Kevin Wildes, President

Luther College, IA
Richard L. Torgerson, President

Lynchburg College, VA
Kenneth R. Garren, President

Macalester College, MN
Brian C. Rosenberg, President

Madison Area Technical College, WI
Bettsey L. Barhorst, President

Maharishi University of Management, IA
Bevan Morris, President

Manchester Community College, CT
Jonathan M. Daube, President

Manchester Community College, NH
Darlene Miller, President

Manhattanville College, NY
Richard Berman, President

Mary Baldwin College, VA
Pamela Fox, President

Marymount Manhattan College, NY
Judson R. Shaver, President

Massachusetts College of Art, MA
Katherine Sloan, President

Massachusetts College of Liberal Arts, MA
Mary K. Grant, President

Massachusetts Maritime Academy, MA
Richard G. Gurnon, President

Massasoit Community College, MA
Charles Wall, President

MassBay Community College, MA
Carole M. Berotte Joseph, President

McDaniel College, MD
Joan Develin Coley, President

McLennan Community College, TX
Dennis F. Michaelis, President

Medical University of South Carolina, SC
Raymond S. Greenberg, President

Mercer County Community College, NJ
Patricia C. Donohue, President

Mercyhurst College, PA
Thomas J. Gamble, President

Merritt College, CA
Robert A. Adams, President

Mesa Community College, AZ
Larry K. Christiansen, President

Messiah College, PA
Kim S. Phipps, President

Metropolitan State College of Denver, CO
Stephen M. Jordan, President

Metropolitan State University, MN
William J. Lowe, President

Middlebury College, VT
Ronald D. Liebowitz, President

Middlesex Community College, MA
Carole A. Cowan, President

Midwestern State University, TX
Jesse W. Rogers, President

Mills College, CA
Janet L. Holmgren, President

Minneapolis Community &
Technical College, MN
Phillip Davis, President

Minnesota State Community &
Technical College, MN
Ann M. Valentine, President

Mississippi Valley State University, MS
Roy C. Hudson, Interim President

Missouri University of Science &
Technology
John F. Carney III, Chancellor

Monroe Community College, NY
R. Thomas Flynn, President

Montana State University, MT
Geoffrey Gamble, President

Monterey Institute of International
Studies, CA
Clara Yu, President

Montgomery County Community
College, PA
Karen A. Stout, President

Morrisville State College, NY
Raymond W. Cross, President

Mount St. Mary's University, MD
Thomas H. Powell, President

Mount Union College, OH
Richard F. Giese, President

Mount Wachusett Community
College, MA
Daniel M. Asquino, President

Mountain View College, TX
Felix A. Zamora, President

Naropa University, CO
Thomas B. Coburn, President

Nashua Community College, NH
Lucille Jordan, President

Nassau Community College, NY
Sean A. Fanelli, President

National Graduate School of
Quality Management , MA
Robert Battryn Gee, President

New College of Florida, FL
Gordon E. Michalson, Jr., President

New England Institute of
Technology, RI
Richard I. Gouse, President

New Mexico State University
(5 institutions), NM
Mike V. Martin, President

New York University, NY
John Edward Sexton, President

Norfolk State University, VA
Carolyn Meyers, President

North Arkansas College, AR
Jeff Olson, President

North Carolina State University, NC
James L. Oblinger, President

North Central Michigan College, MI
Cameron Brunet-Koch, President

North Lake College, TX
Herlinda M. Glasscock, President

North Seattle Community College, WA
Ronald H. LaFayette, President

North Shore Community College, MA
Wayne M. Burton, President

Northeastern University, MA
Joseph E. Aoun, President

Northern Arizona University, AZ
John D. Haeger, President

Northern Essex Community
College, MA
David F. Hartleb, President

Northern Kentucky University, KY
James C. Votruba, President

Northern New Mexico College, NM
José Griego, President

Northland College, WI
Karen I. Halbersleben, President

Northland Pioneer College, AZ
Jeanne Swarthout, President

Oberlin College, OH
Nancy S. Dye, President

Ocean County College, NJ
Jon Larson, President

Ohio University, OH
Roderick J. McDavis, President

The Ohio State University, OH
E. Gordon Gee, President

Ohlone College, CA
Douglas Treadway, President

Olympic College, WA
David C. Mitchell, President

Onondaga Community College, NY
Debbie L. Sydow, President

Orange County Community College
(SUNY), NY
William Richards, President

Oregon College of Art & Craft, OR
Bonnie Laing-Malcolmson, President

Oregon Institute of Technology, OR
David M. Woodall, President

Oregon State University, OR
Edward J. Ray, President

Pacific Lutheran University, WA
Loren J. Anderson, President

Paine College, GA
George C. Bradley, President

Palo Verde College, CA
James W. Hottois, President

Park University, MO
Beverley Byers-Pevitts, President

Pasadena City College, CA
Paulette Perfumo, President

Paul Smith's College , NY
John W. Mills, President

Peninsula College, WA
Thomas Keegan, President

Penn State Berks, PA
Susan Phillips Speece, Chancellor

Pine Manor College, MA
Gloria Nemerowicz, President

Pitzer College, CA
Laura Skandera Trombley, President

Plymouth State University, NH
Sara Jayne Steen, President

Point Loma Nazarene University, CA
Bob Brower, President

Polytechnic University, NY
Jerry Hultin, President

Pomona College, CA
David W. Oxtoby, President

Portland Community College, OR
Preston Pulliams, President

Portland State University, OR
Daniel O. Bernstine, President

Pratt Institute, NY
Thomas F. Schutte, President

Prescott College, AZ
Dan Garvey, President

Presidio School of Management, CA
Steven L. Swig, President

Purchase College, NY
Thomas J. Schwarz, President

Quinsigamond Community
College, MA
Gail E. Carberry, President

Ramapo College of New Jersey, NJ
Peter Mercer, President

Randolph College, VA
Virginia Hill Worden, President

Rhodes College, TN
William E. Troutt, President

Rice University, TX
David W. Leebron, President

Richard Stockton College of New
Jersey, NJ
Herman J. Saatkamp, Jr., President

Richland College, TX
Stephen K. Mittelstet, President

Rider University, NJ
Mordechai Rozanski, President

Rio Salado College, AZ
Linda Thor, President

Rochester Community and Technical
College, MN
Donald D. Supalla, President

Rockland Community College, NY
Cliff L. Wood, President

Roger Williams University, RI
Roy Nirschel, President

Rose-Hulman Institute of
Technology, IN
Gerald S. Jakubowski, President

Rosemont College, PA
Sharon Latchaw Hirsh, President

Rowan University, NJ
Donald J. Farish, President

Roxbury Community College, MA
Terrence A. Gomes, President

Saint John's University, MN
Dietrich Reinhart, President

Saint Peter's College, NJ
Eugene J. Cornacchia, President

Saint Xavier University, IL
Judith A. Dwyer, President

Salem Community College, NJ
Peter Contini, President

Salem State College, MA
Nancy D. Harrington, President

Salisbury University, MD
Janet Dudley-Eshbach, President

San Bernardino Community College
District, (2 Institutions), CA
Donald F. Averill, Chancellor

San Francisco State University, CA
Robert A. Corrigan, President

San Joaquin Delta College, CA
Raul Rodriguez, President

Santa Clara University, CA
Paul L. Locatelli, President

Santa Fe Community College, NM
Sheila Ortego, President

Santa Monica College, CA
Chui L Tsang, President

School of the Art Institute of
Chicago, IL
Wellington Reiter, President

Scottsdale Community College, AZ
Arthur W. DeCabooter, President

Seattle Pacific University, WA
Philip W. Eaton, President

Seattle University, WA
Stephen V. Sundborg, President

Sewanee: The University of the
South, TN
Joel Cunningham, President

Shenandoah University, VA
James A. Davis, President

Shoreline Community College, WA
Lee D. Lambert, President

Simmons College, MA
Susan C. Scrimshaw, President

Simpson College, IA
John W. Byrd, President

Skagit Valley College, WA
Gary Tollefson, President

Smith College, MA
Carol T. Christ, President

South Dakota College of Mines &
Technology, SD
Charles Ruch, President

South Puget Sound Community
College, WA
Gerald Pumphrey, President

South Suburban College, IL
George Dammer, President

Southern Connecticut State
University, CT
Cheryl Joy Norton, President

Southern New Hampshire
University, NH
Paul J. LeBlanc, President

Southern Oregon University, OR
Mary Cullinan, President

Southern Polytechnic State
University, GA
Lisa A. Rossbacher, President

Southwestern College, KS
W. Richard Merriman, Jr., President

Southwestern University, TX
Jake B. Schrum, President

Springfield College, MA
Richard Flynn, President

Springfield Technical Community
College, MA
Ira Rubenzahl, President

St. Clair Community College, MI
Rose B. Bellanca, President

St. Lawrence University, NY
Daniel F. Sullivan, President

St. Louis Community College
at Florissant Valley, MO
Marcia Pfeiffer, President

St. Mary's College of Maryland, MD
Jane O'Brien, President

St. Norbert College, WI
Thomas Kunkel, President

State University of New York,
Empire State College, NY
Alan R. Davis, President

State University of New York at
Albany, NY
George M. Philip, President

State University of New York
College at Cortland, NY
Erik J. Bitterbaum, President

State University of New York at
Fredonia, NY
Dennis L. Hefner, President

State University of New York at
Geneseo, NY
Christopher C. Dahl, President

State University of New York at
New Paltz, NY
Steven G. Poskanzer, President

State University of New York at
Oswego, NY
Deborah F. Stanley, President

State University of New York at
Potsdam, NY
John E. Schwaller, President

State University of New York
College of Environmental Science
and Forestry, NY
Cornelius B. Murphy Jr., President

Stetson University, FL
H. Douglas Lee, President

Stony Brook University, NY
Shirley Strum Kenny, President

Sullivan County Community
College, NY
Mamie Howard Golladay, President

Sussex County Community
College, NJ
Constance Mierendorf, President

Sweet Briar College, VA
Elisabeth S. Muhlenfeld, President

Syracuse University, NY
Nancy Cantor, Chancellor

Temple University, PA
Ann Weaver Hart, President

Texas Christian University, TX
Victor J. Boschini, Chancellor

The City College of New York, NY
Gregory H. Williams, President

The Community College of
Baltimore County, MD
Sandra Kurtinitis, President

The Evergreen State College, WA
Thomas L. Purce, President

The George Washington
University, DC
Steven Knapp, President

The New School, NY
Bob Kerrey, President

Tiffin University, OH
Paul Marion, President

Toccoa Falls College, GA
W. Wayne Gardner, President

Tompkins Cortland Community
College, NY
Carl E. Haynes, President

Towson University, MD
Robert L. Caret, President

Transylvania University, KY
Charles L. Shearer, President

Trinity College, CT
James F. Jones, Jr., President

Trinity University, TX
John R. Brazil, President

Truckee Meadows Community
College, NV
Dolores Sanford, President

Tulane University, LA
Scott Cowen, President

Union College, NY
Stephen C. Ainlay, President

Union Theological Seminary, NY
Joseph C. Hough, Jr., President

Unity College, ME
Mitchell S. Thomashow, President

University at Buffalo, NY
John B. Simpson, President

University of Alaska, Anchorage, AK
Elaine P. Maimon, Chancellor

University of Arizona, AZ
Robert N. Shelton, President

University of Arkansas, AR
G. David Gearhart, Chancellor

University of Baltimore, MD
Robert Bogomolny, President

University of California
(10 institutions), CA
Robert C. Dynes, President

University of California, Berkeley, CA
Robert Birgeneau, Chancellor

University of California, Davis, CA
Larry Vanderhoef, Chancellor

University of California, Irvine, CA
Michael Drake, Chancellor

University of California, Los
Angeles, CA
Norman Abrams, Acting Chancellor

University of California, Merced, CA
Steve Kang, Chancellor

University of California, Riverside, CA
Robert D. Grey, Chancellor

University of California, San Diego, CA
Mary Anne Fox, Chancellor

University of California, San
Francisco, CA
J. Michael Bishop, Chancellor

University of California, Santa
Barbara, CA
Henry Yang, Chancellor

University of California, Santa
Cruz, CA
George Blumenthal, Chancellor

University of Central Florida, FL
John C. Hitt, President

University of Central Missouri, MO
Aaron Podolefsky, President

University of Central Oklahoma, OK
Roger Webb, President

University of Cincinnati, OH
Nancy L. Zimpher, President

University of Colorado at Boulder, CO
G.P. "Bud" Peterson, Chancellor

University of Colorado at Colorado
Springs, CO
Pamela Shockley-Zalabak, Chancellor

University of Colorado at Denver
and Health Sciences Center, CO
M. Roy Wilson, Chancellor

University of Connecticut, CT
Michael J. Hogan, President

University of Delaware, DE
Patrick Harker, President

University of Denver, CO
Robert D. Coombe, Chancellor

University of Florida, FL
Bernard Machen, President

University of Hawai'i at Manoa, HI
Denise Eby Konan, Interim Chancellor

University of Houston-Downtown, TX
Max Castillo, President

University of Houston-Victoria, TX
Tim Hudson, President

University of Idaho, ID
Timothy P. White, President

University of Illinois at Chicago, IL
Sylvia Manning, Chancellor

University of Illinois at Urbana-
Champaign, IL
Richard Herman, Chancellor

University of LaVerne, CA
Stephen Morgan, President

University of Louisville, KY
James R. Ramsey, President

University of Maine, ME
Robert A. Kennedy, President

University of Maine at Augusta, ME
Richard Randall, President

University of Maine at
Farmington, ME
Theodora J. Kalikow, President

University of Maine at Fort Kent, ME
Richard W. Cost, President

University of Maine at Machias, ME
Cynthia E. Huggins, President

University of Maine at
Presque Isle, ME
Don N. Zillman, President

University of Maryland,
Baltimore, MD
David J. Ramsay, President

University of Maryland, Baltimore
County, MD
Freeman A. Hrabowski, III, President

University of Maryland Biotechnology
Institute, MD
Jennie C. Hunter-Cevera, President

University of Maryland Center for
Environmental Science, MD
Donald F. Boesch, President

University of Maryland, College
Park, MD
C. D. Mote, Jr., President

University of Maryland, Eastern
Shore, MD
Thelma B. Thompson, President

University of Maryland University
College, MD
Susan C. Aldridge, President

University of Massachusetts
(5 institutions), MA
Jack M. Wilson, President

University of Massachusetts,
Amherst, MA
Thomas W. Cole Jr., Interim Chancellor

University of Massachusetts
Boston, MA
Michael F. Collins, Chancellor

University of Massachusetts
Dartmouth, MA
Jean F. MacCormack, Chancellor

University of Massachusetts
Lowell, MA
David J. MacKenzie, Chancellor

University of Massachusetts
Worcester, MA
Michael F. Collins, Interim Chancellor

University of Memphis, TN
Shirley C. Raines, President

University of Miami, FL
Donna E. Shalala, President

University of Minnesota, MN
Robert H. Bruininks, President

University of Minnesota, Morris, MN
Jacqueline Johnson, Chancellor

University of Mississippi, MS
Robert C. Khayat, President

University of Missouri, MO
Gary Forsee, President

University of Missouri, Columbia
Brady J. Deaton, Chancellor

University of Missouri, Kansas
City, MO
Leo M. Morton, Interim Chancellor

University of Missouri, St. Louis, MO
Thomas F. George, Chancellor

University of Montana
(4 institutions), MT
George M. Dennison, President

University of Nevada, Las Vegas, NV
David B. Ashley, President

University of Nevada, Reno, NV
Milton D. Glick, President

University of New England, ME
Danielle N. Ripich, President

University of New Hampshire, NH
J. Bonnie Newman, Interim President

University of New Mexico
(5 institutions), NM
David J. Schmidly, President

University of North Carolina at
Chapel Hill, NC
James Moeser, Chancellor

University of North Dakota, ND
Charles E. Kupchella, President

University of North Texas, TX
Gretchen M. Bataille, President

University of Oklahoma Norman
Campus , OK
David L. Boren, President

University of Oregon, OR
Dave Frohnmayer, President

University of Pennsylvania, PA
Amy Gutmann, President

University of Pittsburgh at
Titusville, PA
William A. Shields, President

University of Portland, OR
E. William Beauchamp, President

University of Puget Sound, WA
Ronald R. Thomas, President

University of Redlands, CA
Stuart Dorsey, President

University of Rhode Island, RI
Robert L. Carothers, President

University of Richmond, VA
Edward L. Ayers, President

University of Saint Thomas, MN
Dennis Dease, President

University of South Carolina
(8 institutions), SC
Andrew A. Sorensen, President

University of South Dakota, SD
James W. Abbott, President

University of South Florida, FL
Judy Genshaft, President

University of Southern Maine, ME
Richard L. Pattenaude, President

University of Southern Mississippi, MS
Martha Dunagin Saunders, President

University of St. Francis, IL
Michael Vinciguerra, President

University of Tennessee, Chattanooga
Campus, TN
Roger G. Brown, Chancellor

University of Tennessee, Knoxville
Campus, TN
Loren W. Crabtree, Chancellor

University of the Arts, PA
Miguel Angel Corzo, President

University of Utah, UT
Michael K. Young, President

University of Vermont, VT
Daniel Mark Fogel, President

University of Washington, WA
Mark A. Emmert, President

University of Washington Bothell, WA
Steven G. Olswang, Interim Chancellor

University of Washington Tacoma, WA
Patricia Spakes, Chancellor

University of Wisconsin-Eau Claire, WI
Brian Levin-Stankevich, Chancellor

University of Wisconsin-Green Bay, WI
Bruce Shepard, Chancellor

University of Wisconsin-Oshkosh, WI
Richard H. Wells, Chancellor

University of Wisconsin-River Falls, WI
Donald Betz, Chancellor

University of Wisconsin-Stevens
Point, WI
Linda Bunnell, Chancellor

University of Wisconsin-Stout, WI
Charles W. Sorensen, Chancellor

University of Wisconsin-Superior, WI
Julius Erlenbach, Chancellor

University of Wisconsin-Whitewater, WI
Martha Saunders, Original Signatory
Richard J. Telfer, Current Chancellor

University of Wyoming, WY
Tom Buchanan, President

Ursinus College, PA
John Strassburger, President

Utah State University, UT
Stan L. Albrecht, President

Vermilion Community College, MN
Joe Sertich, President

Victor Valley Community College, CA
Robert M. Silverman, President

Villanova University, PA
Peter M. Donohue, President

Virginia Commonwealth
University, VA
Eugene P. Trani, President

Virginia Wesleyan College, VA
William T. Greer, Jr., President

Wagner College, NY
Richard Guarasci, President

Warren Wilson College, NC
William Sanborn Pfeiffer, President

Washington & Jefferson College, PA
Tori Haring-Smith, President

Washington and Lee University, VA
Kenneth P. Ruscio, President

Washington College, MD
Baird Tipson, President

Washington State University
(4 institutions), WA
Elson S. Floyd, President

Washtenaw Community College, MI
Larry Whitworth, President

Weber State University, UT
F. Ann Millner, President

Webster University, MO
Richard S. Meyers, President

Wells College, NY
Lisa Marsh Ryerson, President

Wentworth Institute of
Technology, MA
Zorica Pantic, President

Wesley College, DE
Scott D. Miller, President

Wesleyan College, GA
Ruth A. Knox, President

Wesleyan University, CT
Michael S. Roth, President

West Valley College, CA
Philip L. Hartley, President

Westchester Community College, NY
Joseph N. Hankin, President

Western Connecticut State
University, CT
James W. Schmotter, President

Western Oregon University, OR
John P. Minahan, President

Western State College of Colorado, CO
Jay W. Helman, President

Western Technical College, WI
Lee Basch, President

Western Washington University, WA
Karen Morse, President

Westfield State College, MA
Barry M. Maloney, Interim President

Westminster College, UT
Michael S. Bassis, President

Whatcom Community College, WA
Kathi Hiyane-Brown, President

Wheelock College, MA
Jackie Jenkins-Scott, President

Whittier College, CA
Sharon D. Herzberger, President

Whitworth University, WA
William P. Robinson, President

Wilkes University, PA
Joseph E. Gilmour, President

Willamette University, OR
M. Lee Pelton, President

William Paterson University, NJ
Arnold Speert, President

Wilson College, PA
Lorna Duphiney Edmundson, President

Wilson Community College, NC
Rusty Stephens, President

Winona State University, MN
Judith A. Ramaley, President

Wofford College, SC
Benjamin B. Dunlap, President

Worcester State College, MA
Janelle Ashley, President

World Learning/SIT Graduate
Institute, VT
Carol Bellamy, President

Xavier University, OH
Michael J. Graham, President

Yeshiva University, NY
Richard M. Joel, President

Source: *www.presidentsclimatecommitment.org/html/signatories.php*

HIGHER EDUCATION ASSOCIATIONS SUSTAINABILITY CONSORTIUM

American Association of Community Colleges (AACC)—www.aacc.nche.edu
ACPA-College Student Educators International (ACPA)— www.myacpa.org
American Association of State Colleges & Universities (AASCU)—www.aascu.org
American Council on Education (ACE)—www.acenet.edu
Association of Higher Education Facilities Officers (APPA)—www.appa.org
Association for the Advancement of Sustainability in Higher Education (AASHE)—
www.aashe.org
Association of College & University Housing Officers International (ACUHO-I)—
www.acuho-i.org
Association of Governing Boards of Universities & Colleges (AGB)—www.agb.org
Council for Christian Colleges & Universities (CCCU)—www.cccu.org
National Association for Campus Activities (NACA)—www.naca.org
National Association of College & University Business Officers (NACUBO)—
www.nacubo.org
National Association of Educational Procurement (NAEP)—www.naepnet.org
National Association of Independent Colleges & Universities (NAICU)—
www.naicu.org
National Intramural-Recreational Sports Association (NIRSA)—www.nirsa.org
Society for College & University Planning (SCUP)—www.scup.org

Statement of Shared Principles and Activities:

- Open exchange of information, knowledge, and experiences regarding sustainability within higher education among HEASC member associations;
- Capacity building within each respective HEASC member association to incorporate sustainability activities into ongoing programming and practices;
- Sustainability-related training for HEASC member association staff;
- Integration of sustainability-related training into HEASC member associations' professional development programs;
- Aligning HEASC member association Annual Conferences and other professional development activities with sustainable practices;
- Connecting HEASC member associations to the best expertise, resources and information in sustainability for higher education;
- Communicating trends in sustainability in higher education, including HEASC activities, to constituents of HEASC member associations;
- Cooperating in joint projects with other associations and organizations that advance sustainability, where feasible;
- Encouraging college and university leaders to embrace sustainability as a core campus value.

Source: www2.aashe.org/heasc/index.php

ACUPCC VOLUNTARY CARBON OFFSET PROTOCOL

AMERICAN COLLEGE & UNIVERSITY
PRESIDENTS CLIMATE COMMITMENT

ACUPCC Voluntary Carbon Offset Protocol

November 2008

I. *Whereas,* a carbon offset is a reduction or removal of carbon dioxide equivalent (CO_2e) greenhouse gas (GHG) emissions that is used to counterbalance or compensate for ("offset") emissions from other activities; offset projects reducing GHG emissions outside of an entity's boundary generate credits that can be purchased by that entity to meet its own targets for reducing GHG emissions within its boundary; it is in the interest of the American College & University Presidents' Climate Commitment (ACUPCC) institutions to ensure that investments in carbon offsets result in real GHG reductions; it is in the interest of said institutions to ensure that carbon offset projects add value to their education, research, and service missions by helping to create a healthy, just, and sustainable society...*and*

1. The higher education sector has the influence, the responsibility, and the diversity of skills needed to develop capabilities for society to re-stabilize the earth's climate, making its proactive leadership vital for successfully addressing climate disruption...*and*

2. The ACUPCC is an institutional and collective commitment by presidents and chancellors to achieve GHG neutrality on their campuses and accelerate the research and educational efforts of higher education to equip society to do the same... *and*

3. Signatories of the ACUPCC have committed to creating a Climate Action Plan within two-years of their institutions implementation start date that will include a target date for GHG neutrality and interim milestone targets... *and*

4. Signatories agree that the primary responsibility is to act directly to reduce their own GHG emissions by first planning, funding, and initiating programs that avoid GHG emissions (e.g. conservation), reduce GHG emissions (e.g. efficiency), and replace GHG emissions sources (e.g. direct renewable energy programs) ... *and*

5. The ACUPCC indicates that notwithstanding the primary efforts of colleges and universities to directly reduce their GHG emissions by planning, funding, and initiating avoidance, reduction, and replacement programs, it is nevertheless important to internalize the cost of carbon emissions, and it is unlikely that colleges and universities will in the near future be able to directly achieve GHG neutrality without the supplemental investment in carbon offsets... *and*

6. Signatories may determine investing in offsets, by developing offset projects themselves, investing directly in offset projects, or purchasing credits generated from offset projects, to be an effective way of achieving interim targets and climate neutrality and/or creating a financial incentive for reducing internal emissions... *and*

7. When done correctly, investment in carbon offsets is scientifically valid and results in the absolute reduction of greenhouse gas emissions to the atmosphere.

AMERICAN COLLEGE & UNIVERSITY
PRESIDENTS CLIMATE COMMITMENT

II.   *Therefore*, the ACUPCC Institutions have developed a set of guidelines that each will voluntarily apply to any investments in carbon offsets or participation in carbon markets they may undertake as part of their efforts to achieve GHG neutrality, and that will provide guidance for making investments and reducing the risks associated with those investments. The guidelines are as follows:

   1. **Offset projects are real and emissions reductions are additional:** Projects result in actual reductions of GHG emissions and would not have otherwise occurred under a reasonable and realistic business-as-usual scenario.

   2. **Offset projects are transparent:** Project details (including project type, location, developer, duration, standard employed, etc.) are known to the institution and communicated to stakeholders in a transparent way to help ensure validity and further the goal of education on climate disruption and sustainability.

   3. **Emissions reductions are measurable:** Projects result in measurable reductions of GHG emissions.

   4. **Emissions reductions are permanent:** Projects result in permanent reductions of GHG emissions.

   5. **Emissions reductions are verified:** Projects result in reductions of GHG emissions that have been verified by an independent third-party auditor that has been evaluated using the accompanying criteria.*

   6. **Offset projects are synchronous:** Projects result in reductions of GHG emissions that take place during a distinct period of time that is reasonably close to the period of time during which the GHG emissions that are being offset took place.*

   7. **Offset projects account for leakage:** Projects take into account any increases in direct or indirect GHG emissions that result from the project activity.

   8. **Credits are registered:** Credits generated from project activities are registered with a well-regarded registry that has been evaluated using the accompanying criteria.*

   9. **Credits are not double-counted:** Credits generated from project activities are not double-counted or claimed by any other party.*

   10. **Credits are retired:** Credits are retired before they are claimed to offset an institution's annual greenhouse gas inventory, or a portion thereof.

---

* For more details and guidance on the characteristics of an "independent third-party auditor," a "reasonably close" time period, "a well-regarded registry," and strategies for ensuring against double counting, please see the accompanying document to this protocol: *Investing in Carbon Offsets: Guidelines for ACUPCC Institutions.*

Source: www.presidentsclimatecommitment.org/offsetprotocol.php

FINANCING MECHANISMS

	CASH	BONDS	TAX-EXEMPT LEASE	PERFORMANCE CONTRACTS
Interest Rates	N/A	Lowest tax-exempt rate	Low tax-exempt rate	Can be taxable or tax-exempt
Financing Term	N/A	May be 20 years or more	Up to 10 years is common and up to 12 or 15 years is possible for large projects	Typically up to 10 years but may be as long as 15 years
Other Costs	N/A	Underwriting legal opinion, insurance, etc.	None	May have to pay engineering costs if contract not executed
Approval Process	Internal	May require taxpayers' approval or public referendum. Bond counsel opinion letter required.	Internal approvals needed; simple attorney letter required	RFP usually required; internal approvals needed
Approval Time	Current budget period	May be lengthy; process may take years	Fast; generally within a week of receiving all requested documentation	Fast; similar to the Tax-Exempt Lease

	CASH	BONDS	TAX-EXEMPT LEASE	PERFORMANCE CONTRACTS
Funding Flexibility	N/A	Very difficult to go above the dollar ceiling	Can set up a Master Lease, which allows you to draw down funds as needed	Relatively flexible; an underlying Municipal Lease is often used
Budget Used	Either	Capital	Operating	Operating or Capital
Largest Benefit	Direct access if included in budget	Low interest rate because it is backed by the full faith and credit (taxing powers) of the public entity	Allows you to buy capital equipment using operating dollars	Provides performance guarantees which help approval process
Largest Hurdle	Never seems to be enough money available for projects	Very time consuming	Identifying the project to be financed	Identifying the project to be financed and selecting the ESCO

Source: www.energystar.gov/ia/business/easyaccess.pdf

INDEX